Lecture Notes in Computer Science 15270

Founding Editors

Gerhard Goos

Juris Hartmanis

The series Lecture Notes in Computer Science (LNCS), including its subseries Lecture Notes in Artificial Intelligence (LNAI) and Lecture Notes in Bioinformatics (LNBI), has established itself as a medium for the publication of new developments in computer science and information technology research, teaching, and education.

LNCS enjoys close cooperation with the computer science R & D community, the series counts many renowned academics among its volume editors and paper authors, and collaborates with prestigious societies. Its mission is to serve this international community by providing an invaluable service, mainly focused on the publication of conference and workshop proceedings and postproceedings. LNCS commenced publication in 1973.

Enrico Formenti · Jérôme Durand-Lose

Editors

Machines, Computations, and Universality

10th International Conference, MCU 2024
Nice, France, June 5–7, 2024
Revised Selected Papers

 Springer

Editors
Enrico Formenti ⓘ
Université Côte d'Azur
Nice, France

Jérôme Durand-Lose ⓘ
University of Orléans
Orléans, France

ISSN 0302-9743   ISSN 1611-3349 (electronic)
Lecture Notes in Computer Science
ISBN 978-3-031-81201-9   ISBN 978-3-031-81202-6 (eBook)
https://doi.org/10.1007/978-3-031-81202-6

This Springer imprint is published by the registered company Springer Nature Switzerland AG
The registered company address is: Gewerbestrasse 11, 6330 Cham, Switzerland

If disposing of this product, please recycle the paper.

Preface

This volume contains the papers presented at the 10th International Conference on Machines, Computations and Universality (MCU 2024), organized by the Laboratoire d'Informatique, Signaux et Systèmes de Sophia Antipolis (I3S) of the Université Côte d'Azur (France). Previous events in the series were located at the University of Debrecen, Hungary (2022); the Paris Est Créteil Val de Marne University, France (2018); Eastern Mediterranean University (Famagusta), North Cyprus (2015); University of Orléans, France (2007); University of Saint Petersburg, Russia (2004); Moldova State University, Moldova (2001); University of Metz, France (1998). The first edition was held in Paris in 1995. The 8th edition was supposed to take place in Wien in 2020 but it was canceled because of the COVID-19 pandemic.

The scope of the conference topics includes, but is not limited to, computation in the setting of various discrete models (Turing machines, register machines, cellular automata, tile assembly systems, rewriting systems, molecular computing models, neural models, …), analog and hybrid models (BSS machines, infinite-time cellular automata, real machines, quantum computing, …) and the meaning and implantation of universality in these contexts. Particular emphasis is given towards search for frontiers between decidability and undecidability in the various models, search for the simplest universal models, computational complexity of predicting the evolution of computations in the various models, and parallel computing models and their connections to decidability, complexity and universality. Topics of interest include (but are not limited to): analog computation, automata theory, cellular automata, classical computability and degree structures, computability theoretic aspects of programs, computable analysis and real computation, computable structures and models, continuous computing, decidability of theories, DNA computing, self-assembly and tiling, dynamical systems and computational models, emerging and non-standard models of computation, finite model theory, generalized recursion theory, higher type computability, hypercomputational models, infinite-time Turing machines, membrane computing, molecular computation, morphogenesis and developmental biology, multi-agent systems, natural computation and hybrid systems, neural nets and connectionist models, physics and computability, proof theory and computability, randomness and Kolmogorov complexity, relativistic computation, swarm intelligence and self-organisation, theory of Petri nets (resp., Turing, Counter, Register, Signal machines), universality of systems.

We are very grateful to our invited speakers who gave very interesting and brilliant talks: Daniela Genova, University of North Florida, USA; Maurice Margenstern, University of Lorraine, France; Antonio Enrico Porreca, Aix-Marseille University, France; Svetlana Puzynina, St. Petersburg State University, Russia; Nicolas Schabanel, École Normale Supérieure de Lyon, France.

The conference received 14 submissions (10 regular papers, 1 invited paper and 3 short talk submissions). Each submission was carefully reviewed by at least two Program Committee (PC) members. Based on these reviews, the PC decided to accept 8 regular papers and 3 short talks, in addition to the invited paper. The members of the PC and the list of external reviewers can be found at the end of this preface. We are grateful for the high-quality work produced by the PC and the external reviewers. Overall this volume contains 8 contributed papers and a paper from one of the invited speakers which covers her talk.

The conference also provided the opportunity to other young and established researchers to present work in progress or work already published elsewhere. This year in addition to regular submissions, the PC accepted 3 high-quality informal presentations (short talks) on various aspects in theoretical computer science. A list of accepted presentation-only submissions is given later in this front matter.

So overall, the conference program consisted of five invited talks, 8 presentations of contributed papers, and 3 informal short talks in the area of theoretical computer science.

It is our pleasure to thank the team behind the EasyChair system and the Lecture Notes in Computer Science team at Springer, who together made the production of this volume possible. Finally, we thank all the authors and the invited speakers for their high-quality contributions, and the participants for making MCU 2024 a success.

August 2024

Jérôme Durand-Lose
Enrico Formenti

Organization

Program Committee Chairs

Jérôme Durand-Lose	University of Orléans, France
Enrico Formenti	Université Côte d'Azur, France

Steering Committee

Erzsébet Csuhaj-Varjú	ELTE Eötvös Loránd University, Hungary
Jérôme Durand-Lose (Chair)	University of Orléans, France
Rudolf Freund	TU Wien, Austria
Daniela Genova	University of North Florida, USA
Maurice Margenstern	University of Lorraine, France
Benedek Nagy	Eastern Mediterranean University, Turkey
Alberto Ottavio Leporati	University of Milano-Bicocca, Italy
Shinnosuke Seki	University of Electro-Communications, Tokyo, Japan
Bianca Truthe	Justus-Liebig-Universität, Germany
György Vaszil	University of Debrecen, Hungary
Sergey Verlan	University of Paris Est Créteil, France

Program Committee

Battyányi Péter	University of Debrecen, Hungary
Besozzi Daniela	University of Milano-Bicocca, Italy
Bournez Olivier	École Polytechnique, France
Csuhaj-Varjú Erzsébet	Eötvös Loránd University, Hungary
Durand-Lose Jérôme	University of Orléans, France
Fernau Henning	University of Trier, Germany
Flocchini Paola	University of Ottawa, Canada
Formenti Enrico	Université Côte d'Azur, France
Freund Rudolf	University of Vienna, Austria
Hirvensalo Mika	University of Turku, Finland
Kari Jarkko	University of Turku, Finland
Martin Bruno	Université Côte d'Azur, France
Nagy Benedek	Eastern Mediterranean University, North Cyprus

Okhotin Alexander	Saint Petersburg State University, Russia
Patitz Matthew	University of Arkansas, USA
Perdrix Simon	CNRS, LORIA, France
Prodanoff Zornitza	University of North Florida, USA
Rauch Christian	University of Gießen, Germany
Riscos-Núnez Agustín	University of Seville, Spain
Vaszil György	University of Debrecen, Hungary
Verlan Serghei	Paris-East Créteil University

Additional Reviewer

Bianca Truthe

Abstracts of Short Talk Contributions

Counting Simple Rules in Semi-Conditional Grammars Is Not Simple

Henning Fernau, Lakshmanan Kuppusamy, and Indhumathi Raman

Abstract. A semi-conditional grammar is a form of regulated rewriting system. Each rule consists of a context-free core rule $A \to w$ and (possibly) two strings w_+, w_-; the rule is applicable if w_+ (the permitting string) occurs as a substring of the current sentential form, but w_- (the forbidden string) does not. The maximum lengths i, j of the permitting or forbidden strings, respectively, give a natural measure of descriptional complexity, known as the *degree* of such grammars. Such a grammar is called *simple* if for each rule, either the permitting or the forbidden string is missing. As the simplicity requirement turns out to be a severe restriction and causes other descriptional complexity parameters to grow, we refine the study by introducing, as an additional parameter, the number of non-simple rules. Employing several normal form results on phrase-structure grammars as derived by Geffert (1991) and Masopust and Meduna (2007), we prove several new computational completeness results that interpolate between what was known so far on general and simple semi-conditional grammars.

This paper has been presented at CiE 2024.

Computing Eulerian Magnitude Homology

Giuliamaria Menara and Luca Manzoni

Abstract. We develop the first diagonal algorithm, a breadth-first-search based algorithm to compute the first diagonal Eulerian magnitude homology groups of a graph G. To do this, we leverage the close relationship between the combinatorics of the homology boundary map and the substructures appearing in the graph.

On Concatenations of Regular Circular Word Languages

Bilal Abdallah and Benedek Nagy

Abstract. In this paper, we define two classes of regular languages of circular words based on finite automata. The weakly accepted circular languages REG_w, in fact, are regular languages that are same as their cyclic permutations. Closure properties of this class are investigated. We provide also regular-like expressions for these languages. The 1-wheel concatenation (of circular words and their languages), an operation that is commutative but not associative, is also studied in details. The strongly accepted circular languages, REG_s, are in fact, more complex. We leave open the question, whether all of them are regular or not.

Contents

Complexity of Infinite Words

Svetlana Puzynina$^{(\boxtimes)}$

Saint Petersburg State University, 7–9 Universitetskaya emb.,
199034 Saint Petersburg, Russia
s.puzynina@gmail.com

Abstract. Complexity of infinite words is a widely studied field in combinatorics on words. A classical notion of a complexity of an infinite word is defined as a function counting, for each n, the number of its distinct factors (or blocks of consecutive letters) of length n. In their 1938 seminal paper on symbolic dynamics, Morse and Hedlund gave a relation between factor complexity and periodicity in infinite words; namely, they proved that each aperiodic infinite word w has factor complexity at least $n + 1$ for each length n. They further showed that an infinite word w has factor complexity $n + 1$ for each length n if and only if w is binary, aperiodic and balanced, i.e., w is a Sturmian word. In this paper, we consider various modifications of the notion of a complexity of infinite words and generalizations of Morse and Hedlund theorem.

Keywords: complexity of infinite words · Sturmian words · Morse and Hedlund theorem

1 Introduction

In this paper we provide a survey of results on a problem of relations between complexity and periodicity in combinatorics on words. Combinatorics on words is a relatively new rapidly growing area of theoretical informatics and discrete mathematics. Its main object is a word, i. e., a finite or infinite sequence of symbols taken from a finite set called an alphabet. The field has many connections, not only to topics in computer science and mathematics, but also to other scientific disciplines. Inside mathematics, such areas include, for example, certain parts of algebra (e.g., combinatorial group theory and semigroups), probability theory, number theory, and symbolic dynamics. Combinatorics on words has been particularly connected to and motivated by theoretical computer science, e.g., automata theory and pattern matching algorithms.

Periodicity is one of the fundamental properties of words. An infinite word w is called ultimately periodic if there exist finite words u and v such that $w = uv^\omega$,

The study was supported by Russian Science Foundation, project 23-11-00133. Conference travel expenses have been covered by Projet 'NOW' of RISE Academy, Université Côte d'Azur.

and (purely) periodic if u is an empty word. One of important problems in periodicity theory is the study of local conditions ensuring global periodicity of an infinite word. Various local conditions and their effect to a general structure of a word have been considered in combinatorics on words. We consider such conditions defined by *factor complexity*, which is defined as a function $p(n)$ counting the number of factors of length n, and various its generalisations.

A celebrated result of Morse and Hedlund states that every aperiodic (meaning non-ultimately periodic) infinite word $w \in \Sigma^{\mathbb{N}}$, over a non empty finite alphabet Σ, contains at least $n + 1$ distinct factors of each length n (or, equivalently, is factor complexity function is at least $n + 1$ for each n). They further showed that an infinite word w has complexity $n + 1$ for each length n if and only if w is binary, aperiodic and balanced, i.e., w is a Sturmian word. Thus Sturmian words are those aperiodic words of lowest factor complexity. They arise naturally in many different areas of mathematics including combinatorics, algebra, number theory, ergodic theory, dynamical systems and differential equations. Sturmian words also have implications in theoretical physics as 1-dimensional models of quasi-crystals, and in theoretical computer science where they are used in computer graphics as digital approximation of straight lines. Despite their simplicity, Sturmian words possess some very deep and mysterious properties. For more on Sturmian words, we refer to [13] and to Chap. 2 in [27].

There have also been numerous attempts at extending the Morse-Hedlund theorem in higher dimensions. A celebrated conjecture of M. Nivat states that any 2-dimensional word having for some integers m and n at most mn distinct $m \times n$ blocks must be periodic [30]. To this day the Nivat conjecture remains open despite many efforts of different researchers. The conjecture has been verified, for example, for m or n less or equal to 3 (see [12,37]), for uniformly recurrent words [25] in a weak form for complexity bounded by $\frac{mn}{2}$ [11], an in an asymptotic form [26]. A very interesting higher dimensional analogue of the Morse-Hedlund theorem was recently obtained by Durand and Rigo in [14] in which they reinterpret the notion of periodicity in terms of Presburger arithmetic. Its abelian variant has been considered in [33]. For more on Nivat's conjecture refer to the paper indicated above and references therein, and in this survey, we focus on the one-dimensional case.

The paper is organized as follows. In Sect. 2, we give necessary definitions and notation and provide some examples. In Sect. 3, we discuss factor complexity and state Morse and Hedlund theorem. In Sect. 4, we give a brief introduction to Sturmian words. In subsequent sections we discuss various types of complexities and related generalizations of Morse and Hedlund theorem, as well as words of minimal complexity of this type. In Sect. 11 we give a summary of the results discussed in the paper and state an open question.

2 Definitions and Notation

Let Σ be a finite non-empty set called an alphabet. A *finite word* over the alphabet Σ is any finite sequence of its symbols. By an *infinite word* w we mean an element $w = w_0 w_1 w_2 \cdots \in \Sigma^{\mathbb{N}}$. Although in the one-dimensional case we usually consider one-way infinite words, most of the notions and results we discuss extend to biinfinite words, i.e., elements from $\Sigma^{\mathbb{Z}}$.

The set of finite words over an alphabet Σ is denoted by Σ^* and the set of non-empty words is denoted by Σ^+. We let $|w|$ denote the length of a word $w \in \Sigma^*$. The empty word is denoted by ε and by convention we set $|\varepsilon| = 0$. The set of words of length n over the alphabet Σ is denoted by Σ^n. A *factor* of a finite or an infinite word is any finite sequence of its consecutive letters; we let $\mathcal{L}(w)$ denote the set of factors of w. We set $\mathcal{L}_n(w) = \mathcal{L}(w) \cap \Sigma^n$.

An infinite word w is called *recurrent* if each its factor occurs in it infinitely many times. An infinite word w is called *uniformly recurrent* if for each integer n there exists an integer N such that each factor of w of length N contains all factors of w of length n. In other words, a word is uniformly recurrent if each its factor occurs in it with bounded gap. An infinite word w is called *eventually periodic* if there exist integers N and T such that $w_{n+T} = w_n$ for each $n \geq N$. An infinite word w is called *purely periodic* if $w_{n+T} = w_n$ for each $n \geq 0$. A word is *aperiodic* if it is not ultimately periodic.

A *substitution* is a map h from Σ to Σ^* such that the image of every letter is nonempty. The notion of a substitution is generalized from letters to words in a natural way by concatenation: $h(uv) = h(u)h(v)$. If for a letter $a \in \Sigma$, the word $h(a)$ has length at least 2 and begins with a, the substitution has a unique fixed point beginning with a, which is the infinite word $\lim_{n \to \infty} h^n(a)$. An infinite word is called *purely morphic* if it is a fixed point of a substitution.

Example 1. One of the most studied words is the Thue-Morse word $\boldsymbol{TM} = 0110100110010110\ldots$, which can be defined as the fixed point of the substitution $\mu : 0 \mapsto 01, 1 \mapsto 10$. The word can be defined in various ways. For example, if $[n]_2$ is the binary expansion of n, then

$$\boldsymbol{TM}_n = \begin{cases} 0, \text{ if } |[n_2]|_1 \text{ is even;} \\ 1, \text{ if } |[n_2]|_1 \text{ is odd.} \end{cases}$$

It is easy to show that the Thue-Morse word is aperiodic. The word is known to avoid overlaps, i.e., it does not have factors of the form $axaxa$ for $a \in \Sigma$ and $x \in \Sigma^*$.

Another family of words treated in this paper is the family of Toeplitz words, which is defined iteratively as follows. Consider a word $v \in \Sigma(\Sigma \cup ?)^+$, where the ? is a special symbol which does not belong to Σ, and v contains at least one ?. We then define a *Toeplitz word* with pattern v as follows: Starting from the word v^ω, we replace the occurrences of the characters ? with the word v^ω, then in the new word we again replace the remaining occurrences of ? with v^ω and so on, thus defining a word without ?.

Example 2. The most famous Toeplitz word is the *regular paperfolding word* defined by the pattern 0?1?:

$$p = 001001100011011000100 \cdots$$

which, contrarily to the Fibonacci and the Thue–Morse words, cannot be obtained as the fixed point of a substitution. More generally, one can construct an infinite (actually, uncountable) family of words, called *paperfolding words*, by alternating the replacements of the occurrences of ? with v_0^ω and v_1^ω, where $v_0 = 0?1?$ and $v_1 = 1?0?$, according to a binary directive sequence.

3   Factor Complexity and Morse and Hedlund theorem

Factor complexity is one of the most important notions in combinatorics on words. First introduced by G.A. Hedlund and M. Morse in their 1938 seminal paper on Symbolic Dynamics under the name of block growth, the factor complexity provides a useful measure of the extent of randomness of the word and more generally of the subshift it generates.

Definition 1. *Given an infinite word w over Σ, the factor complexity of w is the integer function $p_w(n) = |\mathcal{L}(x) \cap \Sigma^n|$ counting the number of distinct factors of length n of w, for each $n \geq 0$.*

Clearly, the complexity function satisfies some straightforward properties. First, it must be non-decreasing. Secondly, it is bounded from above by $|\Sigma|^n$. Third, the following inequality must hold: $p_w(n + m) \leq p_w(n)p_w(m)$.

A celebrated theorem of Morse and Hedlund gives a link between periodicity and factor complexity:

Theorem 1 (Morse and Hedlund, [28]). *Let w be an infinite word. If there exists n such that $p_w(n) \leq n$, then w is eventually periodic.*

Clearly, periodic words have bounded complexity. Moreover, there exist words satisfying $p_w(n) = n + 1$ for each $n \geq 0$, and they correspond to the family of Sturmian words [29]. Thus Sturmian words can be regarded as the simplest aperiodic words. We discuss them in more detail in the next section.

Example 3. The Thue-Morse word $\boldsymbol{TM} = 0110100110010110\ldots$ considered in Example 1 has linear complexity. Its complexity function is described precisely and it is in fact $\Theta(n)$, i.e., its complexity is fluctuating and lies between two linear functions.

As a corollary from Morse and Hedlund theorem, we immediately obtain that there are no words of complexity between constant and linear (say, growing as $\log n$ or $\sqrt{n}$). One can ask two natural questions. First, given a word w, what is its complexity function? The same question can be asked about some family of infinite words. And in the opposite direction: given a function $f(n)$, does there exist a word with complexity $f(n)$? In both cases one can work either with the exact complexity or with the asymptotic complexity, i.e., identifying complexities f and f' if they satisfy $f(n) = \Theta(f'(n))$. We remark the second question is open in the full generality.

As an example of the first problem, there exists a complete characterization of possible growth rates of complexity functions of fixed points of morphisms. This characterization has been obtained in a series of papers, finally completed by Pansiot [31], and states that there are 5 classes of possible complexity growths: $\Theta(1)$, $\Theta(n)$, $\Theta(n \log n)$, $\Theta(n \log \log n)$ and $\Theta(n^2)$. We remark that a similar question for morphic words, i.e., words of the form $g(\lim_{n \to \infty} f^n(a))$, is open.

For more on the factor complexity function, we refer to a survey [7].

4 Sturmian Words

Sturmian words can be defined as infinite words which have complexity $n + 1$ for each n. They admit various types of characterizations of geometric and combinatorial nature, e.g., they can be defined via balance, morphisms, rotations, etc. (see Chap. 2 in [27]).

An equivalent characterization of Sturmian words can be given via mechanical words as follows. Given $\alpha \in (0,1)$, $\rho \in [0,1)$, an *upper* (resp., *lower*) *mechanical word* of slope α is defined by $s_i = \lfloor \alpha(n+1) + \rho \rfloor - \lfloor \alpha n + \rho \rfloor$ (resp., $s_i' = \lceil \alpha(n+1) + \rho \rceil - \lceil \alpha n + \rho \rceil$). Geometrically, one can consider a line $y = \alpha x + \rho$ on the plane, and put $s_i = 1$ if the line intersects a horizontal integer line between i and $i + 1$, and 0 otherwise (see Fig. 1).

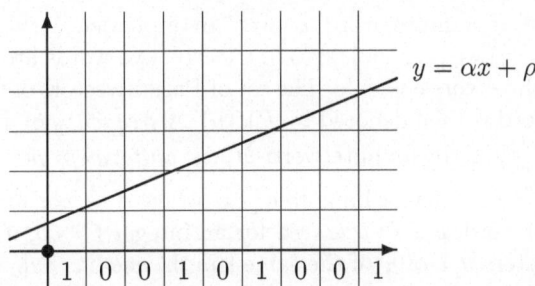

Fig. 1. Mechanical words

The family of Sturmian words is known to coincide with the family of irrational mechanical words (see, e.g., Chapter 2 in [27]). In fact, the irrational number α is the frequency of 1's in the corresponding mechanical words.

Example 4. The most studied Sturmian word the *Fibonacci word*

$$f = 010010100100101001 \cdots ,$$

which can be obtained as the fixed point of the substitution $0 \mapsto 01, 1 \mapsto 0$. The Fibonacci word is a Stumian word, so its complexity equals $n + 1$ for each n. Indeed, for instance, for $n = 3$ it has four distinct factors: 0010, 0100, 0101 and 1010. The Fibonacci word is a mechanical word with $\alpha = \rho = \varphi - 1$, where $\varphi = \frac{\sqrt{5}+1}{2}$ is the golden ratio.

The definition of Sturmian words via complexity applied for length 1 implies that Sturmian words are binary. A natural question is, what is the minimal complexity of aperiodic words over an alphabet of cardinality $d > 2$? In fact, Morse and Hedlund theorem can be easily reformulated for $d > 2$: if there exists n such that the factor complexity of an infinite word over a d-letter alphabet is at most $n + d - 2$, then the word is ultimately periodic. There also exist words over a d-letter alphabet of complexity $n - d + 1$, and they are completely characterized. In fact, if they are recurrent, then they are morphic images of Sturmian words under some specific morphisms [15].

5   Abelian Complexity

Given a finite word u over an alphabet Σ and a letter $a \in \Sigma$, we let $|u|_a$ denote the number of occurrences of a in u.

Definition 2. *Two finite words u and v are abelian equivalent, denoted by $u \sim_{ab} v$, if $|u|_a = |v|_a$ for each letter a. In other words, u and v are permutations of one another.*

It is straightforward that abelian equivalence is indeed an equivalence relation on the set of finite words. For a survey on abelian properties of words we refer to [16].

Parikh vector of a finite word v over an alphabet $\Sigma = \{a_1, \ldots, a_k\}$ is defined as $PV(v) = (|v|_{a_1}, \ldots, |v|_{a_k})$ [32]. Clearly, two words are abelian equivalent if their Parikh vectors coincide. The set of Parikh vectors of factors of length n of an infinite word is then denoted by $PV(n)$. A *frequency* of a in a finite word v is $\mathrm{freq}_v(a) = \frac{|v|_a}{|v|}$. A (bi-)infinite word w has *uniform frequency* of a letter a if the ratio $\frac{|w_k \cdots w_{k+n-1}|}{n}$ has a limit $\mathrm{freq}_w(a)$ when $n \to \infty$, uniformly in k. A (finite or infinite) word w is *C-balanced* for an integer $C > 0$, if for every letter a and any two factors u, v of w of the same length, one has $||u|_a - |v|_a| \leq C$. For $C = 2$, the constant is usually omitted and the word is called *balanced*.

Similarly to factor complexity, the *abelian complexity* $a_w(n)$ of an infinite word w is defined as a function which counts the number of distinct abelian classes of factors of length n occurring in w [8,34]. It easy to see that, similarly to factor complexity, the abelian complexity also gives a characterization of periodicity:

Lemma 1. *[9] A infinite word w is purely periodic if and only if there exists n such that $a_w(n) = 1$.*

Clearly, if an infinite word w is ultimately periodic, then its abelian complexity is bounded. On the other hand, there exist aperiodic words of bounded abelian complexity. For example, Sturmian words are aperiodic and have abelian complexity 2 for each n, and moreover this is a characterization:

Theorem 2. *[9] Let w be an aperiodic infinite word. Then w is a Sturmian word if and only if $a_w(n) = 2$ for each $n \geq 1$.*

Therefore, Sturmian words are aperiodic words of minimal abelian complexity as well. The maximal abelian complexity is realized, for example, by words with maximal factor complexity. We have:

Proposition 1. *For all infinite words w over Σ, $|\Sigma| = k$ and for all $n \geq 0$,*

$$1 \leq a_w(n) \leq \binom{n+k-1}{k-1}.$$

The following proposition relating C-balance to bounded abelian complexity is straightforward:

Proposition 2. *Let w be an infinite word. Then the abelian complexity of w is bounded if and only if w is C-balanced for some $C > 0$.*

Example 5. For the Thue-Morse word $\boldsymbol{TM} = 0110100110010110\ldots$, defined as the fixed point of the substitution $\mu : 0 \mapsto 01$, $1 \mapsto 10$, it is easy to see that its abelian complexity satisfies:

$$a_{TM}(n) = \begin{cases} 2, \text{ if } n \text{ is odd}; \\ 3, \text{ if } n \text{ is even}. \end{cases}$$

Example 6. Another example of an aperiodic word of bounded complexity is the Tribonacci word $\boldsymbol{TR}$, which can be defined as the fixed point of the morphism $0 \mapsto 01$, $1 \mapsto 02$, $2 \mapsto 0$. This is also the simplest example of Arnoux-Rauzy words. For every $n \geq 1$, the abelian complexity of the Tribonacci word satisfies $a_{TR}(n) \in \{3,4,5,6,7\}$. Moreover, each of these five values is assumed. [35]

In [34] it has been proved that there are recurrent words of abelian complexity 3, but there are no recurrent words of abelian complexity 4 [10]. However, there are recurrent words with ultimately constant complexity c for every c [36].

We will now discuss the (abelian) complexity of morphic words, which is more complicated than their factor complexity. The abelian complexity of purely morphic words is completely classified only for fixed points of binary morphisms (more precisely, complexity limsup has been classified). Note first that the balance function of primitive morphisms has been characterized by Adamczewski [1]. As an immediate corollary of this characterization, we get a classification of complexities of fixed points of primitive binary morphisms. If we write $f(x) = \Omega'(g(x))$ if $\limsup_{x \to \infty} f(x)/g(x) > 0$, then the complexity of a pure morphic word is either $\Theta(1)$, or $O \cap \Omega'(\log n)$, or $O \cap \Omega'(n \log_{\theta_1} \theta_2)$, where θ_1 and θ_2 are the first and second most significant eigenvalues of φ. A classification of abelian complexities of non-primitive binary morphisms is due to Blanchet-Sadri, Fox and Rampersad [4] completed by Whiteland [38]: it can be either $\Theta(1)$, or $\Theta(n)$, or $\Theta(n/\log n)$, or $\Theta(n^{\log_k l})$ with $1 < k < l$, or it can fluctuate between $\Theta(1)$ and $\Theta(\log(n))$.

6   Maximal Pattern Complexity and Its Abelian Version

The *pattern complexity* is yet another modification of the notion of a factor complexity, introduced by Kamae and Zamboni [21]. A *pattern S* is a k-element subset of nonegative integers: $S = \{s_1 < s_2 < \cdots < s_k\}$. For an infinite word w, we put

$$w[S] = w_{s_1} w_{s_2} \cdots w_{s_k}.$$

For each n, the word $w[n + S]$ is called an S-factor of w, where $n + S = \{n + s_1, n + s_2, \ldots, n + s_k\}$. We let $F_w(S)$ denote the set of all S-factors of w. The pattern complexity $patt_w(S)$ is then defined by

$$patt_w(S) = |F_w(S)|,$$

and the *maximal pattern complexity* $patt_w^*(k)$ by

$$patt_w^*(k) = \sup_{\substack{S \subset \mathbb{N} \\ |S|=k}} patt_w(S).$$

Theorem 3. *[21] An infinite word w over a finite alphabet Σ is eventually periodic if and only if there exists an integer k such that $patt_w^*(k) \leq 2k - 1$.*

In [21], the authors also show that Sturmian words have maximal pattern complexity equal to $2k$ for each k. Thus, they also have the smallest pattern complexity amongst non-periodic words. However, they are not the only ones: as an example, there exist some non-recurrent binary words with density of 1's equal to 0, which have the same maximal pattern complexity function. In [22], the authors show that some restricted class of Toeplitz words also has the same complexity function. In the paper, the authors call words with minimal maximal pattern complexity among non-periodic words *pattern sturmian words*.

An infinite word w over an alphabet Σ of cardinality d is called *periodic by projection* if there exists a nonempty set $B \subsetneq \Sigma$ such that $1_B(w) = 1_B(w_0)1_B(w_1)1_B(w_2)\cdots \in \{0,1\}^{\mathbb{N}}$ is ultimately periodic (where 1_B denotes the characteristic function of B). A word is *aperiodic by projection* if it is not periodic by projection. The following connection between the maximal pattern complexity and periodicity is known:

Theorem 4. *[19] Let w be an infinite aperiodic by projection word over Σ, $|\Sigma| = d \geq 2$. Then for every positive integer k, $patt_w^*(k) \geq dk$.*

We can then define an abelian analogue of the notion of the pattern complexity by

$$patt_w^{ab}(S) = |F_w(S)/ \sim_{ab}|,$$

and the *maximal pattern abelian complexity* $patt_w^{*ab}(k)$ by

$$patt_w^{*ab}(k) = \sup_{S \subset \mathbb{N}, |S|=k} patt_w^{ab}(S).$$

Then the following abelian analogue of Theorem 4 holds:

Theorem 5. *[20] Let w be a recurrent and aperiodic by projection infinite word over Σ, $|\Sigma| = d \geq 2$. Then for every positive integer k,*

$$patt_w^{*ab}(k) \geq (d-1)k + 1.$$

When $d = 2$, the equality always holds. Moreover, for $k = 2$ and general d, there exists w satisfying the equality.

In the abelian case, the condition of recurrence is necessary, since there exist non-recurrent counterexamples satisfying the inequality.

7   Cyclic Complexity

In this section we consider another measure of complexity, cyclic complexity, which consists in counting the factors of each given length of an infinite word up to conjugacy.

Definition 3. *Two words u and v are said to be* conjugate *if and only if $u = w_1 w_2$ and $v = w_2 w_1$ for some words w_1, w_2.*

In other words, two words are conjugate if they are equal when read on a circle. The conjugacy relation is an equivalence over Σ^*, whose classes are called conjugacy classes (or circular words, or necklaces). The *cyclic complexity* $c_w(n)$ of a word is then defined as the function which counts the number of conjugacy classes of factors of each given length $n \geq 0$.

Example 7. For the Thue-Morse word

$$\boldsymbol{TM} = 0110100110010110 \cdots$$

We have four conjugacy classes of length 4:
$\{0010, 0100\}$,
$\{0110, 1001, 1100, 0011\}$,
$\{0101, 1010\}$,
$\{1011, 1101\}$.

The following analogue of the Morse-Hedlund theorem holds for cyclic complexity:

Theorem 6. *[5] A word w is ultimately periodic if and only if it has bounded cyclic complexity.*

The factor complexity does not distinguish between Sturmian words of different slopes. In contrast, for cyclic complexity the situation is quite different:

Theorem 7. *[5] Let w be a Sturmian word. If w' is an infinite word whose cyclic complexity is equal to that of w, then up to renaming letters, w' and w have the same set of factors. In particular, w' is also Sturmian.*

It is easy to see that a word is (purely) periodic if and only if there exists an integer n such that all factors of length n are conjugate. Therefore, the minimum value of the cyclic complexity of a non-periodic word is 2. So, it is reasonable to consider $\liminf_{n\to\infty} c(n)$, which must be at least 2 for aperiodic words. For Sturmian words, it turns out to be exactly 2:

Proposition 3. *[5] For a Surian word w, one has $\liminf_{n\to\infty} c(n) = 2$.*

However, this is not a characterization of Sturmian words: in fact, a certain family of Toeplitz words, which includes the period-doubling word defined by pattern 010?, for which $\liminf_{n\to\infty} c(n) = 2$.

8   Group Complexity

In this chapter we consider a broad generalization of the Morse-Hedlund theorem via group actions.

Let S_n denote the symmetric group of order n and $G \subseteq S_n$ its subgroup We consider the G-action $G \times \{1, 2, \ldots, n\} \to \{1, 2, \ldots, n\}$ given by $g(i)$ and let $\epsilon(G)$ denote the number of distinct orbits, i.e.,

$$\epsilon(G) = \mathrm{Card}(\{G(i) \,|\, i \in \{1, 2, \ldots, n\}\})$$

where $G(i) = \{g(i) \,|\, g \in G\}$ denotes the G-orbit of i. For instance, if G is the trivial subgroup of S_n consisting only of the identity, then $\epsilon(G) = n$, while if G contains an n-cycle, then $\epsilon(G) = 1$. We note that $\epsilon(G)$ depends strongly on the embedding of G in S_n, and in fact is not a group isomorphism invariant, even for isomorphic subgroups of S_n. For instance, the subgroups $G_1 = \{e, (1,2), (3,4), (1,2)(3,4)\}$ and $G_2 = \{e, (1,2)(3,4), (1,3)(2,4), (1,4)(2,3)\}$ are two embeddings of the Klein four-group $\mathbb{Z}/2\mathbb{Z} \times \mathbb{Z}/2\mathbb{Z}$ in S_4, and yet $\epsilon(G_1) = 2$ while $\epsilon(G_2) = 1$. On the other hand, it is easily checked that $\epsilon(G)$ depends only on the conjugacy class of G in S_n.

Let Σ be a finite non-empty set. For each $n \geq 1$, let Σ^n denote the set of all words $u = u_1 u_2 \cdots u_n$ with $u_i \in \Sigma$. There is a natural G-action $G \times \Sigma^n \to \Sigma^n$ given by $g * u : i \mapsto u(g^{-1}(i))$ for each $i \in \{1, 2, \ldots, n\}$. In terms of the word representation we have $g * u = u_{g^{-1}(1)} u_{g^{-1}(2)} \cdots u_{g^{-1}(n)}$. In particular, we have $g * u \sim_{ab} u$ for all $g \in G$.

Let $w = w_0 w_1 w_2 \cdots \in \Sigma^{\mathbb{N}}$ be an infinite word. Then G defines an equivalence relation $\sim_G$ on $\mathrm{Fact}_w(n) = \{w_i w_{i+1} \cdots w_{i+n-1} \,|\, i \geq 0\}$, the set of factors of w of length n, given by $u \sim_G v$ if and only if $g * u = v$ for some $g \in G$, in other words if u and v are in the same G-orbit relative to the action of G on Σ^n. We can now define the group complexity of an infinite word:

Definition 4. *Let w be an infinite word and $\omega = (G_n)_{n\geq 1}$ a sequence of subgroups G_n of S_n. The associated group complexity function $p_{\omega,w} : \mathbb{N} \to \mathbb{N}$ counts, for each length n, the number of $\sim_{G_n}$ equivalence classes of factors of length n of an infinite word x.*

The cyclic complexity, considered in the previous section, is a particular case of the group complexity. Indeed, in the definition of group complexity, one can take the sequence of cyclic groups $G_n = \langle (12 \cdots n) \rangle$ and obtain the cyclic complexity.

We are interested in the number of distinct $\sim_G$ equivalence classes, i.e., $\mathrm{Card}(\mathrm{Fact}_x(n)/\sim_G)$. Unlike $\epsilon(G)$, this quantity is not a conjugacy invariant of G in S_n. For instance, consider the cyclic subgroups $G_1 = \langle \sigma_1 \rangle$ and $G_2 = \langle \sigma_2 \rangle$ of S_4 where $\sigma_1 = (1,2,3,4)$ and $\sigma_2 = (1,3,2,4)$. Let x denote the Fibonacci word fixed by the substitution $0 \mapsto 01, 1 \mapsto 0$. Then $\mathrm{Fact}_x(4) = \{0010, 0100, 0101, 1001, 1010\}$ and

$$\mathrm{Fact}_x(4)/\sim_{G_1} = \{[0100 \overset{\sigma_1}{\curvearrowright} 0010]; [0101 \overset{\sigma_1}{\curvearrowright} 1010]; [1001]\}$$

while

$$\mathrm{Fact}_x(4)/\sim_{G_2} = \{[0010 \overset{\sigma_2}{\curvearrowright} 0100]; [0101 \overset{\sigma_2}{\curvearrowright} 1001 \overset{\sigma_2}{\curvearrowright} 1010]\}.$$

Theorem 8. *Let $w \in \Sigma^{\mathbb{N}}$ be aperiodic. Then for every infinite sequence $\omega = (G_n)_{n \geq 1}$, $G_n \leq S_n$, we have $p_{\omega,w}(n) \geq \epsilon(G_n) + 1$ for each $n \geq 1$. Moreover, if $p_{\omega,w}(n) = \epsilon(G_n) + 1$ for each $n \geq 1$, then w is Sturmian.*

To obtain a converse to Theorem 8, we restrict to all infinite sequences $(G_n)_{n \geq 1}$ of abelian subgroups of S_n. The following constitutes a partial converse to Theorem 8:

Theorem 9. *Let w be a Sturmian word. Then for each infinite sequence $\omega = (G_n)_{n \geq 1}$, $G_n \leq S_n$, of abelian permutation groups there exists $\omega' = (G'_n)_{n \geq 1}$ with G_n isomorphic to G'_n such that for each $n \geq 1$ we have $p_{\omega',w}(n) = \epsilon(G'_n) + 1$.*

Remark 1. Let $\omega = (Id_n)_{n \geq 1}$, where Id_n denotes the trivial subgroup of S_n consisting only of the identity. Then $\epsilon(Id_n) = n$ for each $n \geq 1$. Moreover, for each infinite word w, we have that $p_{\omega,w}(n) = \mathrm{Card}(\mathrm{Fact}_w(n))$. Thus applying Theorem 8 to ω we deduce that every aperiodic word w contains at least $n + 1$ distinct factors of length n and that if w has exactly $n + 1$ distinct factors of each length n, then w is Sturmian. Conversely, if w is Sturmian, then Theorem 9 applied to ω implies that w contains exactly $n + 1$ distinct factors of length n. Thus we recover the full Morse-Hedlund theorem. On the opposite extreme, applying Theorem 8 to the sequence $\omega = (S_n)_{n \geq 1}$, we recover a result of Coven and Hedlund in [9].

9 k-Abelian Complexity

In this section we consider another version of a complexity function, which is an intermediate notion between the factor and the abelian complexities.

Definition 5. *Let k be a positive integer. Two words u and v are k-abelian equivalent, denoted by $u \sim_k v$, if $|u|_t = |v|_t$ for every word t of length at most k, where $|w|_t$ denotes the number of occurrences of the factor t in w.*

This defines a family of equivalence relations $\sim_k$, bridging the gap between the usual notion of abelian equivalence (when $k = 1$) and equality (when $k = \infty$).

Equivalently, u and v are k-abelian equivalent if the following two conditions hold:

– $|u|_t = |v|_t$ for every word t of length exactly k;
– $\mathrm{Pref}_{k-1}(u) = \mathrm{Pref}_{k-1}(v)$ and $\mathrm{Suff}_{k-1}(u) = \mathrm{Suff}_{k-1}(v)$ (or $u = v$, if $|u| < k-1$ or $|v| < k-1$).

For instance, $00101 \sim_2 01001$, but $00101 \not\sim_2 00011$. It is clear that k-abelian equivalence implies k'-abelian equivalence for every $k' < k$. In particular, k-abelian equivalence for any $k \geq 2$ implies abelian equivalence, that is, 1-abelian equivalence.

Given an infinite word w, we consider the associated complexity function $p_w^{(k)} = |(\mathcal{L}(w) \cap \Sigma^n)/\sim_k|$, which counts the number of k-abelian equivalence classes of factors of w of length n.

The following theorem gives a sufficient condition of aperiodicity, generalizing Morse and Hedlund theorem (Theorem 1 and its abelian analog Lemma 1:

Theorem 10. *[24] Let k be a positive integer and w an aperiodic word. If there exists an integer n such that $p_w^{(k)}(n) < f^{(k)}(n)$, where*

$$f^{(k)}(n) = \begin{cases} n+1 & \text{for } 0 \leq n \leq 2k-1, \\ 2k & \text{for } n \geq 2k, \end{cases}$$

then w is ultimately periodic.

Similarly to factor and abelian complexities, k-abelian complexity allows to characterize Sturmian words, giving a generalization of Coven and Hedlund Theorem 2:

Theorem 11. *[24] Let k be a positive integer and w an aperiodic word. The following conditions are equivalent:*

– *w is Sturmian;*
– $p_w^{(k)}(n) = \begin{cases} n+1 & \text{for } 0 \leq n \leq 2k-1, \\ 2k & \text{for } n \geq 2k. \end{cases}$

Interestingly, the 2-abelian complexity of the Thue-Morse word is unbounded [23] (unlike the abelian complexity).

The following theorem makes use of Szemeredi's theorem and gives a connection between k-abelian complexity and repetitions in words. In particular, it implies that k-Abelian repetitions are unavoidable in words having bounded k-Abelian complexity:

Theorem 12. *[24] Fix $k \geq 1$. Let w be an infinite word over a finite alphabet Σ having bounded k-abelian complexity. Let $D \subseteq \mathbb{N}$ be a set of positive upper density, that is*

$$\limsup_{n \to \infty} \frac{|D \cap \{1, 2, \ldots, n\}|}{n} > 0.$$

Then, for every positive integer N, there exist i and l such that $\{i, i+l, i+2l, \ldots, i+Nl\} \in D$ and the N consecutive blocks $(x[i+jl, i+(j+1)l-1])_{0 \leq j \leq N-1}$ of length l are pairwise k-abelian equivalent. In particular, w contains k-abelian powers for arbitrarily large k.

10   Arithmetic Complexity

The arithmetical complexity approach has been introduced by Avgustinovich, Fon-der-Flaass, Frid [3]. In the arithmetic complexity approach, instead of contiguous factors, we consider arithmetical factors, i.e., factors along arithmetic progressions. The topic of arithmetic complexity is motivated by the famous 1927 theorem by Van der Waerden, stating that for an infinite word $w = w_0 w_1 \cdots$ on a finite alphabet Σ there exist arbitrarily long arithmetical progressions $k, k+p, \ldots, k+np$ such that $w_k = w_{k+p} = \cdots = w_{k+np}$. For an infinite word w, the arithmetical closure $\mathcal{L}_A(w)$ is defined as the language consisting of all words of the form $w_k w_{k+p} \cdots w_{k+np}$ for arbitrary k, p, and n. The Wan-der-Waerden theorem can be reformulated in these terms as follows: for each infinite word w and each integer n, there exists a letter a such that $a^n \in \mathcal{L}_A(w)$. Similarly, the result of Szemeredi, 1975, is that the same holds for each letter of positive upper density. The arithmetical complexity counts the complexity of this language:

Definition 6. *For an infinite word w, its* arithmetical complexity $a_w(n)$ *is defined as a function counting for each n the number of words of $\mathcal{L}_A(w)$ of length n.*

The behaviour of the arithmetical complexity is not determined only by the factor complexity growth: if the latter grows linearly, the arithmetical complexity can increase both linearly and exponentially. An exponential growth is given for example by a certain family of morphic words including the famous Thue-Morse word, while the linear growth is attained on a family of Toeplitz words with low complexity [3]. More precisely, for the Thue-Morse words (and in fact for a family of fixed points of uniform morphisms containing the Thue-Morse word) the arithmetical closure contains all words:

Proposition 4. *[3] For the Thue-Morse word $\boldsymbol{TM}$, one has*

$$\mathcal{L}_A(\boldsymbol{TM}) = \{0, 1\}^*.$$

However, there exist words of linear arithmetical complexity. For example, for the paperfolding word, which can be defined as a Toeplitz word with pattern $0?1?$, its arithmetical complexity is equal to $8n + 4$ for sufficiently large values of n [3].

The relation between low arithmetical complexity and periodicity is a bit more complicated than for the factor complexity. In [2], the authors study uniformly recurrent non-periodic words of lowest arithmetical complexity. Contrary to the factor complexity, the results are of asymptotic nature: the authors provide a family of words with decreasing lower limits of arithmetical complexity divided by n, which tend to be minimal. This family of words has decreasing upper and lower limits of arithmetical complexity, tending to $3n$ and $2n$, respectively. More precise statement is given by the following theorem, describing the behaviour of asymptotic minimal arithmetical complexity of uniformly recurrent words:

Theorem 13. *[2] Let $\mathcal{R}$ denote the set of all non-periodic uniformly recurrent infinite words. Then the following holds:*

1. $\inf_{w \in \mathcal{R}} \overline{\lim}_{n \to \infty} \frac{a_w(n)}{n} = 3$
2. $\inf_{w \in \mathcal{R}} \underline{\lim}_{n \to \infty} \frac{a_w(n)}{n} = 2$ *and* $\underline{\lim}_{n \to \infty} \frac{a_w(n)}{n} > 2$ *for each* $w \in \mathcal{R}$
3. $\min_{w \in \mathcal{R}} a_w(n) = 2n + 2$ *for* $n \geq 2$.

Besides that, the words of asymptotically smallest arithmetical complexity in this context are characterized: it is proved that they correspond to a certain family of Toeplitz words (we refer to [2] for their description). The authors emphasize that their results only concern uniformly recurrent words, and that for non-uniformly recurrent words the minimal arithmetical complexity might be different. Remarkably, the family of words of low arithmetical complexity does not include Sturmian words and moreover, their complexity is not linear. In [17], it has been shown that words of linear arithmetical complexity also correspond to some family of Toeplitz words. As for Sturmian words, in [6] and [18] it is shown that the uniform upper and lower bounds for arithmetical complexity of Sturmian words are $O(n^3)$. The bounds are different, and the precise arithmetical complexity depends on the slope of a Sturmian word.

11   Summary

In this survey, we considered several generalizations of the notion of a complexity of an infinite word and associated variations and extensions of Morse and Hedlund theorem giving a link between periodicity and small complexity in infinite words. Together with factor complexity, we considered the following notions of a complexity: abelian and k-abelian complexities, group complexity, maximal pattern complexity and arithmetic complexity. In most cases, these alternative notions of complexity may be used to detect and characterize ultimately periodic words. Generally, amongst all aperiodic words, Sturmian words have the lowest possible complexity, although in some cases they are not the only ones (for instance, a restricted class of Toeplitz words is found to have the same maximal pattern complexity as Sturmian words). Table 1 summarizes the results discussed in the paper:

The general open question is the following:

Table 1. Minimal complexity of aperiodic words for different complexity functions.

complexity type	minimal complexity	words family
factor	n+1	Sturmian
abelian	2	Sturmian
cyclic	$\liminf = 2$	Sturmian+
group	$\varepsilon(G_n) + 1$	Sturmian
maximal pattern	2n+1	Sturmian+
k-abelian	$\min(2k, n+1)$	Sturmian
arithmetical	linear	(asymptotically) Toeplitz

Problem 1. What kind of condition on complexity makes Sturmian words to be the words of minimal complexity amongst the aperiodic words?

References

1. Adamczewski, B.: Balances for fixed points of primitive substitutions. Theor. Comput. Sci. **307**(1), 47–75 (2003)
2. Avgustinovich, S.V., Cassaigne, J., Frid, A.E.: Sequences of low arithmetical complexity. Theor. Inf. Appl. **40**, 569–582 (2006)
3. Avgustinovich, S.V., Fon-Der-Flaass, D.G., Frid, A.E.: Arithmetical complexity of infinite words. Words Lang. Comb. **III**, 51–62 (2003)
4. Blanchet-Sadri, F., Fox, N., Rampersad, N.: On the asymptotic Abelian complexity of morphic words. Adv. Appl. Math. **61**, 46–84 (2014)
5. Cassaigne, J., Fici, G., Sciortino, M., Zamboni, L.Q.: Cyclic complexity of words. J. Comb. Theory Ser. A **145**, 36–56 (2017)
6. Cassaigne, J., Frid, A.E.: On arithmetical complexity of Sturmian words. Theor. Comput. Sci. **380**, 304–316 (2007)
7. Cassaigne, J., Nicolas, F.: Factor complexity. Chapter in: Combinatorics, Automata and Number Theory, Berthé, V., Rigo, M. (eds.) Encyclopedia of Mathematics and its Applications, vol. 135. Cambridge University Press (2010)
8. Cassaigne, J., Richomme, G., Saari, K., Zamboni, L.Q.: Avoiding Abelian powers in binary words with bounded Abelian complexity. Int. J. Found. Comput. Sci. **22**(4), 905–920 (2011)
9. Coven, E.M., Hedlund, G.A.: Sequences with minimal block growth. Math. Syst. Theory **7**, 138–153 (1973)
10. Currie, J., Rampersad, N.: Recurrent words with constant Abelian complexity. Adv. Appl. Math. **47**, 116–124 (2011)
11. Cyr, V., Kra, B.: Nonexpansive $\mathbb{Z}^2$-subdynamics and Nivat's conjecture. Trans. Am. Math. Soc. **367**(9), 6487–6537 (2015)
12. Cyr, V., Kra, B.: Complexity of short rectangles and periodicity. Eur. J. Comb. **52**, 146–173 (2016)
13. de Luca, A.: Sturmian words: structure, combinatorics, and their arithmetics. Theor. Comput. Sci. **183**, 45–82 (1997)

14. Durand, F., Rigo, M.: Multidimensional extension of the Morse-Hedlund theorem. Eur. J. Combin. **34**(2), 391–409 (2013)
15. Ferenczi, S., Mauduit, C.: Transcendence of numbers with a low complexity expansion. J. 1244 Number Theory **67**, 146–161 (1997)
16. Fici, G., Puzynina, S.: Abelian combinatorics on words: a survey. Comput. Sci. Rev. **47**, 100532 (2023)
17. Frid, A.E.: Sequences of linear arithmetical complexity. Theor. Comput. Sci. **339**, 68–87 (2005)
18. Frid, A.: A lower bound for the arithmetical complexity of Sturmian words. Siberian Electron. Math. Rep. **2**, 14–22 (2005). (in Russian, English abstract)
19. Kamae, T., Hui, R.: Maximal pattern complexity of words over l letters. Eur. J. Comb. **27**, 125–137 (2006)
20. Kamae, T., Widmer, S., Zamboni, L.Q.: Abelian maximal pattern complexity of words. Ergodic1283 Theory Dyn. Syst. **35**(1), 142–151 (2015)
21. Kamae, T., Zamboni, L.Q.: Sequence entropy and the maximal pattern complexity of infinite words. Ergodic Theory Dyn. Syst. **22**(4), 1191–1199 (2002)
22. Kamae, T., Zamboni, L.Q.: Maximal pattern complexity for discrete systems. Ergodic Theory Dyn. Syst. **22**, 1201–1214 (2002)
23. Karhumäki, J., Saarela, A., Zamboni, L.Q.: Variations of the Morse-Hedlund theorem for k-Abelian equivalence. Acta Cybern. **23**(1), 175–189 (2017)
24. Karhumäki, J., Saarela, A., Zamboni, L.Q.: On a generalization of Abelian equivalence and complexity of infinite words. J. Comb. Theory Ser. A **120**(8), 2189–2206 (2013)
25. Kari, J., Moutot, E.: Decidability and periodicity of low complexity tilings. Theory Comput. Syst. **67**(1), 125–148 (2023)
26. Kari, J., Szabados, M.: An algebraic geometric approach to Nivat's conjecture. Inf. Comput. **271**, 104481 (2020)
27. Lothaire, M.: Algebraic Combinatorics on Words. Cambridge University Press, Cambridge (2002)
28. Morse, M., Hedlund, G.: Symbolic dynamics. Am. J. Math. **60**, 815–866 (1938)
29. Morse, M., Hedlund, G.: Symbolic dynamics II: Sturmian sequences. Am. J. Math. **62**, 1–42 (1940)
30. Nivat, M.: Invited talk at ICALP 1997
31. Pansiot, J.J.: Complexité des facteurs des mots infinis engendrés par morphismes itérés. In: Paredaens, J. (ed.) ICALP 1984. LNCS, vol. 172, pp. 380–389. Springer, Heidelberg (1984)
32. Parikh, R.J.: On context-free languages. J. ACM **13**(4), 570–581 (1966)
33. Puzynina, S.: Aperiodic two-dimensional words of small Abelian complexity. Electron. J. Comb. **26**(4), 4 (2019)
34. Richomme, G., Saari, K., Zamboni, L.Q.: Abelian complexity in minimal subshifts. J. Lond. Math. Soc. **83**, 79–95 (2011)
35. Richomme, G., Saari, K., Zamboni, L.Q.: Balance and Abelian complexity of the Tribonacci word. Adv. Appl. Math. **45**, 212–231 (2010)
36. Saarela, A.: Ultimately constant abelian complexity of infinite words. J. Autom. Lang. Comb. **14**(3–4), 255–258 (2009)
37. Sander, J., Tijdeman, R.: The rectangle complexity of functions on two-dimensional lattices. Theor. Comput. Sci. **270**, 857–863 (2002)
38. Whiteland, M.A.: Asymptotic Abelian complexities of certain morphic binary words. J. Autom. Lang. Comb. **24**(1), 89–114 (2019)

Succinct Star-Controlled Insertion-Deletion Systems Using Space Separating Normal Forms

Henning Fernau[1] , Lakshmanan Kuppusamy[2] ,
and Indhumathi Raman[3(✉)]

[1] Fachbereich 4 – Abteilung Informatikwissenschaften, Universität Trier,
54286 Trier, Germany
fernau@uni-trier.de
[2] School of Computer Science and Engineering, VIT University,
Vellore 632 014, India
klakshma@vit.ac.in
[3] Department of Computing Technologies, SRM Institute of Science and Technology,
Kattankulathur, Chennai 603203, India
indhumar2@srmist.edu.in

Abstract. Graph-controlled insertion-deletion (GCID) systems are regulated extensions of insertion-deletion systems. At AFL 2023, we introduced *star-controlled* GCID systems as a restriction of GCID systems where there is a special component, namely, a *central* component that will process the string and then send it to any other component that processes another step and then send the string back to the central component. With this restriction, here we obtain three new, different computational completeness results for some typical descriptional complexity measures. These results are crucially based on a variant of Special Geffert normal form (SGNF) of type-0 grammars, that we called space separating SGNF in a paper that appeared in *Natural Computing* in 2019.

Keywords: graph-control · star structure · insertion-deletion systems · computational completeness · descriptional complexity measures · space separating SGNF

1 Introduction

Two basic operations namely *insertion* and *deletion* are frequently used in both linguistics [13] and molecular biology [1,15]. These two fundamental operations were introduced into formal language theory in [11] through a grammatical mechanism called *insertion-deletion system* (shortly termed as ins-del system). The insertion operation refers to inserting a string η between two strings w_1 and w_2, thereby yielding $w_1\eta w_2$ from $w_1 w_2$, whereas the deletion operation is deleting a substring δ from the string $w_1\delta w_2$ to get the resultant string $w_1 w_2$.

One of the important variants of ins-del systems is graph-controlled ins-del (shortly GCID) system which was introduced in [7] and further studied in [9]. In this variant, the rules of the ins-del system are distributed into several *components*. A transition is performed by choosing any applicable rule from the set of rules within the current component and by moving the resultant string to the target component specified in the rule.

Several restrictions of GCID systems have been studied, e.g., matrix ins-del systems [5,16], path-controlled ins-del systems [4] and star-controlled ins-del system [6]. Here, we also consider star-controlled GCID systems (abbreviated as $GCID_S$) where the transitions always toggle between a central and a non-central component. One could correlate this star-structure with a kind of master-slave system where the central component always dispatches work to the slave components who, after finishing their work, report the result back to the master component. This kind of architecture, which describes how the resources are distributed and controlled, is common in network communication, especially with WIFI technology, where the master device serves as the communication hub. $GCID_S$ systems can be correlated with insertion-deletion P systems, pointing to interesting connections to biocomputing, and with matrix insertion-deletion system with binary matrices.

The *descriptional complexity* of a GCID system is measured by its *size* $(k; n, i', i''; m, j', j'')$, where the parameters from left to right denote the following: (i) the number k of components, (ii) the maximal length n of any insertion string, (iii) the maximal lengths i and i' of the left context and right context used in insertion rules, respectively, (iv) the maximal length m of any deletion string, and (v) the maximal lengths j and j' of the left context and right context used in deletion rules, respectively. The sextuple of the last six parameters is known as *ID size*. If $i' = 0$ or $i'' = 0$ ($j' = 0$ or $j'' = 0$), then we say that insertion (deletion) is performed under *one-sided* context. Further, if $i' = i'' = 0$ ($j' = j'' = 0$), then insertion (deletion) is said to be done in a *context-free* manner.

If a $GCID_S$ system is able to describe any recursively enumerable language, then it is said to be *computationally complete*. It is shown in [6] that $GCID_S$ systems of sizes $(k; 1, i', i''; 1, j', j'')$, are not computationally complete for any $k \geq 2$ under the assumption that at every step of derivation, there is a transition from the central component to a non-central component or vice-versa and at no point of derivation the transition stays in the same component. (This restriction looks minor but is crucial, as two components suffice for sizes $(1, 2, 0; 1, 1, 0)$ and $(1, 1, 0; 1, 2, 0)$ and a more relaxed interpretation of star control, as shown in [10].) Further in [6], it is shown that $GCID_S$ systems of sizes $(6; 1, 1, 0; 2, 0, 0)$, $(6; 1, 0, 1; 2, 0, 0)$ and $(4; 2, 1, 1; 1, 0, 0)$ are computationally complete. One may note that in all these systems, deletion is performed in a context-free manner. In this paper, we decrease the number of components from 6 to 5 (and from 4 to 3) at the cost of performing the deletion under a one-sided context to study the computationally completeness of the above $GCID_S$ systems. Moreover, we also prove that, when insertion of string length two is performed in a context-free manner and deletion is performed under a one-sided context, a $GCID_S$ system can describe RE with 4 components. Specifically, we show that:

1. (Theorem 1) RE $=$ $\text{GCID}_S(3; 2, x, y; 1, 1, 0)$ $=$ $\text{GCID}_S(3; 2, x, y; 1, 0, 1)$ for any $x, y \in \{0, 1\}$ with $x + y = 1$.
2. (Theorem 2) RE $= \text{GCID}_S(4; 2, 0, 0; 1, 0, 1) = \text{GCID}_S(4; 2, 0, 0; 1, 1, 0)$.
3. (Theorem 3) RE $= \text{GCID}_S(5; 1, 1, 0; 2, 0, 1) = \text{GCID}_S(5; 1, 0, 1; 2, 1, 0)$.

2   Preliminaries

We assume that the readers are familiar with the standard notations used in formal language theory. Here, we recall a few notations necessary for the understanding of the paper. Let $\mathbb{N}$ denote the set of positive integers, and $[\ell \ldots k] = \{i \in \mathbb{N} : \ell \le i \le k\}$. Given an *alphabet* (finite set) Σ, Σ^* denotes the free monoid generated by Σ. The elements of Σ^* are called *strings* or *words*; λ denotes the empty string. For a string $w \in \Sigma^*$, $|w|$ is the length of w and w^R denotes the reversal (mirror image) of w. L^R and $\mathcal{L}^R$ are also understood for languages L and language families $\mathcal{L}$, respectively.

For the computational completeness results, we use the fact that a recursively enumerable (RE) language can be described by type-0 grammars in a new variant of Special Geffert Normal Form (SGNF) namely *space separating SGNF*.

2.1   Space Separating Special Geffert Normal Form

Definition 1. *A type-0 grammar $G = (N, T, P, S)$ is said to be in SGNF if*

- *N decomposes as $N = N' \cup N''$, where $N'' = \{A, B, C, D\}$ and N' contains at least the two nonterminals S and S';*
- *the only non-context-free rules in P are $AB \to \lambda$ and $CD \to \lambda$;*
- *context-free rules in P are either (i) $S' \to \lambda$, or (ii) $X \to Y_1 Y_2$, where $X \in N' \setminus \{S'\}$ and $Y_1 Y_2 \in ((N' \setminus \{X\})(T \cup \{B, D\})) \cup (\{A, C\}(N' \setminus \{X\}))$.*

The way the normal form is constructed is described in [7] and is based on [8]. We can assume that S' does not appear on the left-hand side of any non-erasing rule. This also means that the derivation in G undergoes two phases. In Phase I, only context-free rules are applied. This phase ends with applying the context-free deletion rule $S' \to \lambda$ (which is the only rule that has S' on its left-hand side). Then only, non-context-free deletion rules $AB \to \lambda$ and $CD \to \lambda$ are applied in Phase II. Notice that the symbol from N', as long as present, separates A and C from B and D; this prevents a premature start of Phase II. One of the features of SGNF derivations is that any string that can be derived can contain at most one substring AB or CD in its so-called *center*. If such a substring is present, the derivation is in Phase II; also, then no nonterminal from N' occurs. In Phase I, exactly one such nonterminal is present (in the center). Therefore, we can differentiate two cases within (ii) for $X, Y \in N' \setminus \{S'\}$ with $X \ne Y$: either, we have a rule $X \to bY$, with $b \in \{A, C\}$, or we have a rule $X \to Yb$, with $b \in T \cup \{B, D\}$.

We write $\Rightarrow_r$ to denote a single derivation step using rule r, and $\Rightarrow_G$ (or $\Rightarrow$ if no confusion arises) denotes a single derivation step using any rule of G. Then, $L(G) = \{w \in T^* \mid S \Rightarrow^* w\}$, where $\Rightarrow^*$ is the reflexive transitive closure of $\Rightarrow$. In [3], we have introduced a variation of SGNF, called *Space Separating Special Geffert Normal Form*, or ssSGNF for short. In that normal form, besides the pairs of nonterminals A, B and C, D, we have a third pair of nonterminals, E, F, within N'', and this normal form is obtained by applying the additional morphism mapping $A \mapsto EA$, $B \mapsto BF$, $C \mapsto EC$ and $D \mapsto DF$. Thus, on top of the rules introduced so far, we have the additional erasing rule $EF \to \lambda$, so that EF is an additional possible center. In rules like $X \to bY$, we have (now) that $b \in \{A, C, E\}$, and in rules like $X \to Yb$, $b \in T \cup \{B, D, F\}$. The main advantage of this normal form is that any sentential form derivable in this grammar will never contain a substring of the form ZZ, where $Z \in \{A, B, C, D, E, F\}$ as the introduction of the symbol E prevents AA and CC that can appear as a substring; likewise, the symbol F prevents BB and DD as substrings. This property will be crucial in *all* of our proofs while simulating the non-context-free rules. Another interesting property is that whenever either $AB \to \lambda$ or $CD \to \lambda$ could be applied, then (only) $EF \to \lambda$ becomes applicable (necessarily). With these details, the normal form ssSGNF is formally defined as follows.

Definition 2. *A type-0 grammar $G = (N, T, P, S)$ is said to be in ssSGNF if*

- *N decomposes as $N = N_0' \cup N_1' \cup N''$, where $N'' = \{A, B, C, D, E, F\}$ and N_0' contains at least the two nonterminals S and S';*
- *the only non-context-free rules in P are $AB \to \lambda$, $CD \to \lambda$ and $EF \to \lambda$;*
- *context-free rules in P are either (i) $S' \to \lambda$, or (ii) $X \to Y_1 Y_2$, where $X \in N_0'\backslash\{S'\}$ and $Y_1 Y_2 \in (N_1'(T \cup \{B, D\})) \cup (\{A, C\}N_1')$, or (iii) $Y \to X_1 X_2$, where $Y \in N_1'$ and $X_1 X_2 \in (N_0'(T \cup \{F\})) \cup (\{E\}N_0')$.*

Notice that by construction, a nonterminal $X \in N' = N_0' \cup N_1'$ cannot be both on the left-hand and on the right-hand side of the same rule.

2.2 Graph-Controlled Insertion-Deletion Systems

Definition 3. *A graph-controlled insertion-deletion system (GCID for short) with k components is a construct $\Pi = (k, V, T, A, H, i_0, F, R)$, where (i) k is the number of components, (ii) V is an alphabet, (iii) $T \subseteq V$ is the terminal alphabet, (iv) $A \subset V^*$ is a finite set of strings, called axioms, present in the initial component, (v) H is a set of labels associated (in a one-to-one manner) to the rules in R, (vi) $i_0 \in [1 \ldots k]$ is the initial component, (vii) $F \subseteq [1 \ldots k]$ is the set of final components and (viii) R is a finite set of rules of the form $l : (i, r, j)$, where $l \in H$ is the label of the rule, r is an insertion rule of the form $(u, \eta, v)_I$, with insertion string η and context (u, v), or deletion rule of the form $(u, \delta, v)_D$, with deletion string δ and context (u, v), where $u, v \in V^*$, $\eta, \delta \in V^+$ and $i, j \in [1 \ldots k]$.*

We now describe how GCID systems work. Applying an insertion rule of the form $(u, \eta, v)_I$ means that the string η is inserted between u and v; this corresponds to the rewriting rule $uv \to u\eta v$. Similarly, applying a deletion rule of the form $(u, \delta, v)_D$ means that the string δ is deleted between u and v; this corresponds to the rewriting rule $u\delta v \to uv$.

A *configuration* of Π is represented by $(w)_i$, where $i \in [1 \ldots k]$ is the index of the current component and $w \in V^*$ is the current string. We also say that w has entered or moved to component Ci. We write $(w)_i \Rightarrow_l (w')_j$ if there is a rule $l : (i, r, j)$ in R, and w' is obtained by applying the insertion or deletion rule r to w. For brevity, we write $(w)_i \Rightarrow (w')_j$ if there is some rule l in R such that $(w)_i \Rightarrow_l (w')_j$. We write $\Rightarrow_*$ for the transitive reflexive closure of $\Rightarrow$ between configurations. The language $L(\Pi)$ generated by Π is defined as

$$L(\Pi) = \{w \in T^* \mid (x)_{i_0} \Rightarrow_* (w)_{i_f} \text{ for some } x \in A \text{ and } i_f \in F\}.$$

The *underlying control graph* of a GCID system Π with k components is defined to be a graph with k nodes labelled $C1$ through Ck and there exists a directed edge from Ci to Cj if there exists a rule of the form (i, r, j) in R of Π. We also associate an undirected graph on k nodes to a GCID system of k components as follows: there is an undirected edge from a node Ci to Cj if there exists a rule of the form (i, r_1, j) or (j, r_2, i) in R of Π where $i \neq j$. We call a GCID system with k components *star-controlled* (denoted as GCID_S) if its underlying undirected control graph has the edge set $\{\{C1, Ci\} \mid i \in [2 \ldots k]\}$, i.e., it is a tree of depth 1. This means that the corresponding directed control graph may contain arcs like $(C1, Ci)$, $(Ci, C1)$, but no self loops (Cj, Cj). The reader is encouraged to consult our AFL paper [6] for simple examples.

A GCID system with exactly one component corresponds to a now classical insertion-deletion (ID) system, without any control mechanism. As transitions from component C to the same component C are prohibited in GCID_S, we can only use computational completeness results for ID systems as follows. We take two (final) components with exactly the same rules of an ID system, so that the toggling between the components does not affect the generated language. This would allow us to transfer several results from [12,14]; relevant to the present study could be: $\text{RE} = \text{GCID}_S(2; 2, 0, 2; 1, 1, 0) = \text{GCID}_S(2; 1, 1, 0; 2, 0, 2) = \text{GCID}_S(2; 2, 0, 0; 1, 1, 1)$, as our new results can be seen as trade-offs.

In [12,14], several insertion-deletion (ID) systems were shown to be computationally complete. However, ID systems of sizes $(2, 1, 1; 1, 1, 0)$, $(2, 1, 1; 1, 0, 1)$, $(2, 0, 0; 1, 1, 0)$, $(2, 0, 0; 1, 0, 1)$, $(1, 1, 0; 2, 0, 1)$ and $(1, 0, 1; 2, 1, 0)$ are not yet known to be computationally complete. If we impose path control as a regulation on these ID systems, which means that we consider graph-controlled systems where the underlying control graph is a path, then it is shown in [4] that such path-controlled insertion-deletion (GCID_P) systems of the above stated sizes are computationally complete with number of components being 3 for the first two sizes and 4 for the last four sizes. If star control is imposed as a regulation, disallowing self-loops in contrast to [10], then we show in this paper that GCID_S systems of the above-mentioned sizes are computationally complete as well, with number of components being $3, 3, 4, 4, 5, 5$, respectively. Actually, the results with three components need one-sided insertion context only. To prove these results, we can deduce the following useful fact from [2] which basically halves the number of proofs we have to write as RE is closed under reversal.

Proposition 1. $\text{GCID}_S(k; n, i', i''; m, j', j'') = [\text{GCID}_S(k; n, i'', i'; m, j'', j')]^R$. for non-negative integers k, n, i', i'', m, j, j''.

3   Computational Completeness Results

In this section, we present our computational completeness results. Each of them makes some use of the ssSGNF that we discussed above. Interestingly, each use of this particular normal form is a bit different. In the first case, we show that ssSGNF form can simplify and improve our argumentation by first explaining how a simulation could work that is based on the 'classical' plain SGNF.

Proposition 2. $\text{RE} = \text{GCID}_S(3; 2, 1, 1; 1, 1, 0)$, $\text{RE} = \text{GCID}_S(3; 2, 1, 1; 1, 0, 1)$.

Table 1. $\text{GCID}_S(3; 2, 1, 1; 1, 1, 0)$ rules simulating the rules of ssSGNF.

Component $C1$	Component $C2$	Component $C3$
$p1.1 : (1, (\lambda, p, X)_I, 2)$	$p2.1 : (2, (p, X, \lambda)_D, 1)$	
$p1.2 : (1, (p, bY, \lambda)_I, 2)$	$p2.2 : (3, (\lambda, p, \lambda)_D, 1)$	
$q1.1 : (1, (\lambda, q, X)_I, 2)$	$q2.1 : (2, (q, X, \lambda)_D, 1)$	
$q1.2 : (1, (q, Yb, \lambda)_I, 2)$	$q2.2 : (2, (\lambda, q, \lambda)_D, 1)$	
$h1.1 : (1, (\lambda, hh', S')_I, 2)$	$h2.1 : (3, (h', S', \lambda)_D, 1)$	
$h1.2 : (1, (h, h', \lambda)_D, 2)$	$h2.2 : (3, (\lambda, h, \lambda)_D, 1)$	
$f1.1 : (1, (A, f', B)_I, 3)$	$f2.1 : (2, (f, f', \lambda)_D, 1)$	$f3.1 : (3, (\lambda, f, A)_I, 1)$
$f1.2 : (1, (f, A, \lambda)_D, 2)$	$f2.2 : (2, (\lambda, f, \lambda)_D, 1)$	
$f1.3 : (1, (f, B, \lambda)_D, 2)$		

Proof. Consider a type-0 grammar $G = (N, T, P, S)$ in ssSGNF as in Definition 2. We construct a GCID_S system $\Pi = (3, V, T, \{S\}, H, 1, \{1\}, R)$ of size $(3; 2, 1, 1; 1, 1, 0)$ such that $L(\Pi) = L(G)$. The set V contains the symbols of G as well as some rule markers. The rules of R are shown in Table 1. For the non-context-free deletion rules, we only provide the case of f-rule simulation, the g-rule and the e-rule are simulated similarly.

In order to prove that $L(G) \subseteq L(\Pi)$, we show that, by simple induction, if $w \Rightarrow w'$ in G, then $(w)_1 \Rightarrow_* (w')_1$ according to Π. The simulation of the rule forms $p : X \to bY$, $q : X \to Yb$ and $h : S' \to \lambda$ are (respectively) shown below. In each case, the intended derivation is presented with $\alpha \in \{EA, EC\}^* \{E, \lambda\}$, $\beta \in \{F, \lambda\} \{BF, DF\}^* T^*$, while $X, Y \in N'$.

- $(\alpha X \beta)_1 \Rightarrow_{p1.1} (\alpha p X \beta)_2 \Rightarrow_{p2.1} (\alpha p \beta)_1 \Rightarrow_{p1.2} (\alpha p b Y \beta)_2 \Rightarrow_{p2.2} (\alpha b Y \beta)_1$.

- $(\alpha X\beta)_1 \Rightarrow_{q1.1} (\alpha q X\beta)_2 \Rightarrow_{q2.1} (\alpha q\beta)_1 \Rightarrow_{q1.2} (\alpha q Y b\beta)_2 \Rightarrow_{q2.2} (\alpha Y b\beta)_1.$
- $(\alpha S'\beta)_1 \Rightarrow_{h1.1} (\alpha h h' S'\beta)_2 \Rightarrow_{h2.1} (\alpha h h'\beta)_1 \Rightarrow_{h1.2} (\alpha h\beta)_2 \Rightarrow_{h2.2} (\alpha\beta)_1.$

The simulation of the rule forms $f : AB \to \lambda$, $g : CD \to \lambda$ and $e : EF \to \lambda$ are similar to each other and hence, we present the f-rule simulation alone below.

$$(\alpha AB\beta)_1 \Rightarrow_{f1.1} (\alpha A f' B\beta)_3 \Rightarrow_{f3.1} (\alpha f A f' B\beta)_1 \Rightarrow_{f1.2}$$
$$(\alpha f f' B\beta)_2 \Rightarrow_{f2.1} (\alpha f B\beta)_1 \Rightarrow_{f1.3} (\alpha f\beta)_2 \Rightarrow_{f2.2} (\alpha\beta)_1.$$

Next, we prove that $L(\Pi) \subseteq L(G)$ by proving that no unintended derivation is possible in Π using induction. Let us first assume that the sentential form $w^1 = \alpha X\beta$ for some $\alpha \in \{EA, EC\}^*\{E, \lambda\}$, $\beta \in \{F, \lambda\}\{BF, DF\}^*T^*$ and $X \in N' = N'_0 \cup N'_1$ is derivable in G and the configuration $(w^1)_1$ is derivable in Π.

Due to the absence of any markers, the following rules are potentially applicable on w^1: $h1.1$, $q1.1$, $p1.1$ and $f1.1$. As w^1 is derivable in G, clearly, AB is not a substring of w^1, making $f1.1$ not applicable.

If we apply $p1.1$ (or $q1.1$) to $w^1 = \alpha X\beta$, then a marker p (q) is inserted to the left of the nonterminal $X \in N'$, resulting in $w^2 = \alpha Xp\beta$ $(\alpha Xq\beta)$ and moving to $C2$. The application of $p2.2$ $(q2.2)$ on w^2 just nullifies the previous application by deleting the marker p (q) inserted in the previous step. This leads us back to the starting point. To proceed further, one has to apply $p2.1$ $(q2.1)$ on w^2 which deletes the nonterminal X sitting on the right of the previously inserted marker. The resultant string $w^3 = \alpha p\beta$ $(\alpha q\beta)$ is then sent back to $C1$. Due to the absence of any nonterminal of N', the only applicable rule is $p1.2$ $(q1.2)$ which inserts the intended bY (Yb) to the right of the marker p (q) and moves the resultant string $w^4 = \alpha pbY\beta$ (αqYb) into $C2$. Due to the absence of the nonterminal X, the only rule application $p2.2$ $(q2.2)$ deletes the marker p (or q) and the resultant intended string $w^5 = \alpha bY\beta$ $(\alpha Yb\beta)$ is sent back to $C1$.

If we apply $h1.1$ on $w^1 = \alpha X\beta$ for $X = S'$, then markers hh' are inserted to the left of S', producing the resultant string $w^2 = \alpha h h' S'\beta$ and moving into $C2$. The only rule that is applicable on w^2 is $h2.1$ since other rules are well guarded by markers. This application of $h2.1$ on w^2 deletes the nonterminal S', thereby moving the resultant string $w^3 = \alpha h h'$ back into $C1$. Due to the absence of any nonterminal of N', the only possible rule application is $h1.2$, followed immediately by an application of $h2.2$ which results in $w^4 = \alpha\beta$. This sequence of derivations faithfully simulates the erasing rule $S' \to \lambda$ of G, thereby transiting from Phase I to Phase II of ssSGNF.

We will now discuss a string w^1 derivable in G and as configuration $(w^1)_1$ in Π, with $w^1 = \alpha\beta$, with $\alpha \in \{EA, EC\}^*$ and $\beta \in \{BF, DF\}^*T^*$.[1] The central (good) substring could either be $EABF$ or $ECDF$, unless some mistake happened upon assembling the string in Phase I. Since the simulation of $g : CD \to \lambda$ and $e : EF \to \lambda$ are similar to the f-rule simulation, we only discuss the correctness of the f-rule simulation in the following where the central part is $EABF$

---

[1] We can assume this special form of w due to ssSGNF, as the description of this normal form makes clear that E alternates with A or C, and similarly, B or D alternate with F.

or more shortly, AB. As $w^1 \in (N'' \cup T)^*$, the only applicable rule is $f1.1$. After its application on $(w^1)_1 = (\alpha'AB\beta')_1$, where $\alpha = \alpha'A$ and $\beta = B\beta'$, we arrive at $(w^2)_3$ with $w_2 = \alpha'Af'B\beta'$. The only applicable rules are $f3.1$ (or $g3.1$ or $e3.1$) that will add a marker f (or g or e) in front of A (or C or E, respectively), within $\alpha'A$, turning it into α'', so that, with $w^3 = \alpha''f'B\beta'$, we arrive at the configuration $(w^3)_1$. Now, the only applicable rule is $f1.2$ (or $g1.2$ or $e1.2$), because none of the symbols B, D, F is immediately to the right of the marker f (or g or e) that was just introduced. This way, α'' is modified to α''' by deleting A (or C or E, respectively) to the right of the introduced marker (or g or e), leading to $w^4 = \alpha'''f'B\beta'$. Alternatively, we could describe the process leading from w^2 to w^4 as replacing one occurrence of A by f (or of C by g or of E by e). In the configuration $(w^4)_2$, potentially applicable rules are $\phi2.i$, with $\phi \in \{f,g,e\}$ and $i \in \{1,2\}$. As all these rules require the presence of marker ϕ, this is only possible if we have applied $\phi3.1$ to produce w^3. Assume that we apply a fitting rule $\phi2.2$ on w^4. Then, the resulting string is sent back to $C1$, where none of the rules is applicable, so that the derivation is stuck. If we want to apply rule $\phi2.1$ on w^4 instead, then $\phi = f$ is fixed, and moreover, it is checked that α''' ends with the marker f, so that $\alpha''' = \alpha'f$. Hence, we arrive at the configuration $(w^5)_1$ with $w^5 = \alpha'fB\beta'$. Now, the only applicable rule is $f1.3$, yielding $(w^6)_2$ with $w^6 = \alpha'f\beta'$. Similarly, $(\alpha'\beta')_1$ as the successor configuration is required as intended.

These arguments inductively show that any terminal string that can be produced with the help of Π is also derivable in G, i.e., $L(\Pi) \subseteq L(G)$. Together with the first part of the proof, we have $L(\Pi) = L(G)$ as claimed. The second part of the theorem follows due to Proposition 1. $\square$

Remark 1. The astute reader might have wondered where exactly we have used the additional combinatorial properties of ssSGNF as opposed to SGNF. Admittedly, the whole construction and proof would have also worked with SGNF instead. This would have been the type of construction that we (and others) would have used to show such computational completeness results in many predecessor papers. However, one of the strengths of this (relatively new) normal form is that it can largely simplify constructions. In the previous theorem, instead of the f-rule simulation presented in Table 1, we could have used

$$f1.1 : (1, (A, B, \lambda)_D, 3) \quad \text{and} \quad f3.1 : (3 : (\lambda, A, \lambda)_D, 1) \tag{1}$$

instead. In other words, we do not use any markers at all for the four rules that simulate the f-rule, g-rule and e-rule.

Why does this idea work?

- As a substring AB (or CD or EF) can only occur in Phase II and also there, only when we really see a sentential form like $w = \alpha AB\beta$ with $\alpha \in \{A, C, E\}^*$ and $\beta \in (\{B, D, F\} \cup T)^*$ (and similarly for the other two substrings), we already know the structure of the string w pretty well.
- This means for $(w)_1 \Rightarrow (w')_3$ that necessarily, $w' = \alpha A\beta$.

– Importantly, in $C3$, only three rules appear: we can delete A, C, E (without context). What happens if we consider some w'' with $(w')_3 \Rightarrow (w'')_1$ where some C or E was deleted, or a 'wrong occurrence' of some A? Then, the derivation will be inevitably get stuck in $C1$, because there, we can only continue with a well-formed string in the center, like AB. After deleting one B from this central part, w'' cannot contain AB (or CD or EF) as a substring if we did anything wrong in $C3$, because in particular ABB cannot be a substring of w by the properties of ssSGNF.

When does this idea work? Every time we use k components for simulating p- q- and h-rules, then we could add an f-rule simulation, using an additional component $C(k+1)$, as described in (1). This guarantees that the rules simulating the context-free part and the rules for the non-context-free simulation cannot interfere. We will see this in Theorem 2. There, we also see how to 'reverse' the construction if we delete using right instead of left context. This means, we use

$$f1.1 : (1, (\lambda, A, B)_D, 3) \quad \text{and} \quad f3.1 : (3 : (\lambda, B, \lambda)_D, 1) \tag{2}$$

instead. Clearly, the overall argument stays the same.

Table 2. Making all important rules explicit for the size $(3; 2, 1, 0; 1, 1, 0)$.

Component $C1$	Component $C2$	Component $C3$
$p1.1 : (1, (\lambda, p, \lambda)_I, 2)$	$p2.1 : (2, (p, X, \lambda)_D, 1)$	
$p1.2 : (1, (p, bY, \lambda)_I, 2)$	$p2.2 : (3, (\lambda, p, \lambda)_D, 1)$	
$q1.1 : (1, (\lambda, q, \lambda)_I, 2)$	$q2.1 : (2, (q, X, \lambda)_D, 1)$	
$q1.2 : (1, (q, Yb, \lambda)_I, 2)$	$q2.2 : (2, (\lambda, q, \lambda)_D, 1)$	
$h1.1 : (1, (\lambda, hh', \lambda)_I, 2)$	$h2.1 : (3, (h', S', \lambda)_D, 1)$	
$h1.2 : (1, (h, h', \lambda)_D, 2)$	$h2.2 : (3, (\lambda, h, \lambda)_D, 1)$	
$f1.1 : (1, (A, B, \lambda)_D, 3)$		$f3.1 : (3, (\lambda, A, \lambda)_D, 1)$

Theorem 1. $\mathrm{RE} = \mathrm{GCID}_S(3; 2, x, y; 1, 1, 0)$ *and* $\mathrm{RE} = \mathrm{GCID}_S(3; 2, x, y; 1, 0, 1)$ *for any* $x, y \in \{0, 1\}$ *satisfying* $x + y = 1$.

Proof. Remark 1 already explained that the marker-free simulation of $AB \to \lambda$ works because of the properties of ssSGNF. Moreover, this clearly also allows to drop the context checks when introducing markers like p, q or hh', as the same condition is also checked upon deletion. We summarize the rules for the convenience of the reader in Table 2 for the size $(3; 2, 1, 0; 1, 1, 0)$. Clearly, one can also introduce the mentioned markers to the right instead of to the left of the nonterminal X (or S') and one can use the variation of Eq. (2). This idea shows the result for the size $(3; 2, 1, 0; 1, 0, 1)$. The other two sizes result from applying Proposition 1.   □

Notice that the following result is a trade-off result with respect to the previous one, as we decrease contexts by one but increase the number of components by one.

Theorem 2. $\mathrm{RE} = \mathrm{GCID}_S(4; 2, 0, 0; 1, 0, 1) = \mathrm{GCID}_S(4; 2, 0, 0; 1, 1, 0)$.

Proof. Consider a type-0 grammar $G = (N, T, P, S)$ in ssSGNF as in Definition 2. We construct a GCID system $\Pi = (4, V, T, \{S\}, H, 1, \{1\}, R)$ of size $(4; 2, 0, 0; 1, 0, 1)$ such that $L(\Pi) = L(G)$. The set V contains the symbols of G as well as some rule markers. We refer to Table 3 for the rules of R. Notice that we use the trick of Eq. (2).

Table 3. $\mathrm{GCID}_S(4; 2, 0, 0; 1, 0, 1)$ rules simulating the rules of ssSGNF

Component $C1$	Component $C2$	Component $C3$	Component $C4$
$p1.1 : (1, (\lambda, pp'', \lambda)_I, 2)$	$p2.1 : (2, (\lambda, X, p)_D, 1)$	$p3.1 : (3, (\lambda, p''', \lambda)_D, 1)$	
$p1.2 : (1, (\lambda, bp', \lambda)_I, 2)$	$p2.2 : (2, (\lambda, p, b)_D, 1)$		
$p1.3 : (1, (\lambda, p'''Y, \lambda)_I, 2)$	$p2.3 : (4, (\lambda, p'', p''')_D, 1)$		
$p1.4 : (1, (\lambda, p', p''')_D, 3)$			
$q1.1 : (1, (\lambda, q, \lambda)_I, 2)$	$q2.1 : (2, (\lambda, X, q)_D, 1)$	$q3.1 : (3, (\lambda, q, Y)_D, 1)$	
$q1.2 : (1, (\lambda, Yb, \lambda)_I, 3)$			
$h1.1 : (1, (\lambda, hh', \lambda)_I, 2)$	$h2.1 : (2, (\lambda, S', h)_D, 1)$	$h3.1 : (3, (\lambda, h, \lambda)_D, 1)$	
$h1.2 : (1, (\lambda, h', \lambda)_D, 3))$			
$f1.1 : (1, (\lambda, A, B)_D, 4)$			$f4.1 : (4, (\lambda, B, \lambda)_D, 1)$

Let $w = \alpha X \beta$ for some $\alpha \in \{EA, EC\}^*(\{E, \lambda\})$, $\beta \in \{F, \lambda\}\{BF, DF\}^*T^*$. The simulations of rules of type q and h are simple and direct. The rule $p : X \to bY$ is simulated as follows.

$$- \ (\alpha X \beta)_1 \ \Rightarrow_{p1.1} \ (\alpha X p p'' \beta)_2 \ \Rightarrow_{p2.1} \ (\alpha p p'' \beta)_1 \ \Rightarrow_{p1.2} \ (\alpha p b p' p'' \beta)_2 \ \Rightarrow_{p2.2}$$
$$(\alpha b p' p'' \beta)_1 \ \Rightarrow_{p1.3} \ (\alpha b p' p'' p''' Y \beta)_2 \ \Rightarrow_{p2.3} \ (\alpha b p' p''' Y \beta)_1 \ \Rightarrow_{p1.4,3.1} \ (\alpha b Y \beta)_1.$$

The simulation of the f-rule, assuming $w = \alpha A B \beta$, for some $\alpha \in \{EA, EC\}^*\{E\}$, $\beta \in \{F\}\{BF, DF\}^*T^*$, is direct.

Next, we show that $L(G) \supseteq L(\Pi)$. As discussed in the previous remark, the non-context-free rule simulations cannot interfere with the context-free rule simulations in Phase I. As we will see, there is also the possibility to *postpone steps* in Phase I, namely rules $p1.4$ and $p3.1$ that are intended to remove the markers p' and p''', respectively. They can be removed later at any time, but without affecting other parts of the simulation, so that we can also assume performing them when intended.

As an induction hypothesis, w be a sentential form that is derivable in G and which obeys $(S)_1 \Rightarrow^* (w)_1$. If w comes from the first phase of the derivation in G, then $w = \alpha X \beta t$ for some $\alpha \in \{A, C, E\}^*$, $X \in N'$, $\beta \in \{B, D, F\}^*$ and $t \in T^*$ (for simplicity). Due to the absence of any markers, the following rules are potentially applicable: (i) $q1.1$ and $q1.2$ for some rule $q : X \to Yb$, (ii) $p1.1$,

$p1.2$ or $p1.3$ for some rule $p : X \rightarrow bY$, or (iii) $h1.1$ for $S' \rightarrow \lambda$. We are not discussing the possibility that $(v)_1$ might correspond to w in the sense that some markers p' and p''' are 'left over' by postponed steps.

If we apply some rule of the form $\zeta 1.1$ to w, with $\zeta \in \{h, q, p\}$, markers will be introduced and the resulting string w' is moved to $C2$, where only deletion rules are available that check out the newly introduced markers. Therefore, we are forced to apply $\zeta 2.1$ now. This guarantees that the correct nonterminal from N' (that forms the left-hand side of the rule to be simulated) was present and was deleted, yielding the resulting string w'' and moving back to $C1$. Let us now distinguish cases for w'':

(a) $\underline{\text{Case } 1} : w'' = \alpha h h' \beta t$: the only applicable rule is $h2.1$, leading to the configuration $(w''')_3$ with $w''' = \alpha h' \beta t$. Now, only $h3.1$ is applicable, giving $(\alpha \beta t)_1$ as intended, correctly simulating the rule $h : S' \rightarrow \lambda$.

(b) $\underline{\text{Case } 2} : w'' = \alpha q \beta t$: the only applicable rule is $q2.1$, leading to the configuration $(w''')_3$ with w''' obtained from w'' by arbitrarily inserting Yb somewhere. However, as $q3.1$ is now the only potentially applicable rule, a successful application of it guarantees that $w''' = \alpha q Y b \beta t$, so that $(\alpha Y b \beta t)_1$ is the subsequent configuration, as intended, correctly simulating the rule $q : X \rightarrow Yb$.

(c) $\underline{\text{Case } 3} : w'' = \alpha p p'' \beta t$: the only applicable rule is $p1.2$, leading to the configuration $(w''')_3$ with w''' obtained from w'' by arbitrarily inserting bp' somewhere. However, w''' could also be obtained from w'' by arbitrarily inserting Yp'' somewhere and moving to $C4$ where no rule is applicable due to the absence of p'''. Hence, we safely assume that w''' was obtained from w'' by arbitrarily inserting bp' somewhere using $p1.2$, which moves the string to $C2$. Let us denote the string w'', with bp' inserted randomly within w'', as w'''. As no symbol from $N' \cup \{p'''\}$ is present, the only applicable rule on w''' in $C2$ is $p2.2$ which deletes the marker p (which was to the left of p'' while inserted) only if it is on the left of b, which guarantees that the rule is applicable only if the previously inserted bp' (by rule $p1.2$) was actually inserted between p and p''. This means $p2.2$ is applicable on w''' only if $w''' = \alpha p b p' p'' \beta t$. On applying $p2.2$, the marker p is deleted and the resulting string $w^4 = \alpha b p' p'' \beta t$ returns to $C1$. Now, we could apply any rule of $p1.z$ for $1 \leq z \leq 3$. If $z = 1, 2$, then the resultant string moves to $C2$ where the derivation is stuck. The rule $p1.4$ cannot be applied due to the absence of p'''. Hence, we have to apply the rule $p1.3$ on w^4: the substring $p'''Y$ is inserted randomly within w^4 and the resultant string moves to $C2$. There, the only applicable rule is $p2.3$ which deletes p'' only if it is on the left of p'''. This guarantees that the rule is applicable only if the previously inserted $p'''Y$ (by rule $p1.4$) was actually inserted after p'', which means $p2.3$ is applicable on w^4 only if $w^4 = \alpha b p' p'' p''' Y \beta t$. On applying $p2.3$, the marker p'' is deleted and the resulting string $w^5 = \alpha b p' p''' Y \beta t$ returns to $C1$. Now, we could apply any rule of $p1.z$ for $1 \leq z \leq 4$. In the cases $p1.2$ or $p1.3$, the resultant string moves to $C2$ where the derivation is stuck. Hence, we either leave p' and p''' in the string to deal with them later at any time in the sense of postponed steps, or we have to apply the rule $p1.4$ on $w^5 = \alpha b p' p''' Y \beta t$ for fruitful continuations: the marker p' (to the left of p''') is deleted and the resultant string $w^6 = \alpha b p''' Y \beta t$ is taken to $C3$. Here, the only applicable rule is $p3.1$ due to the absence of the markers q, h. Applying $p3.1$ on w^6 will delete p''' and the intended string $\alpha b Y \beta t$ is sent back to $C1$.

We should discuss at least one more scenario concerning w^5 a bit more in detail. Namely, what happens if we applied $p1.1$ on $w^5 = \alpha b p' p''' Y \beta t$, leading to $w_6 = \alpha b p' p p'' p''' Y \beta t$ in $C2$? Then, $w_7 = \alpha b p' p p''' Y \beta t$ could be sent back to $C1$, where even $p1.2$ can be applied now (but no other rule with any hope of termination), leading, say, to $(w_8)_2$ with $w_8 = \alpha b p' p b p' p''' Y \beta t$ and further $(w_9)_1$ with $w_9 = \alpha b p' b p' p''' Y \beta t$. However, now the first occurrence of p' is blocked forever from being deleted by the letter b that separates it from p'''. Hence, although the deletion steps appear to be quite deterministic, the insertion steps allow some unintended derivations that are then, however, blocked. It can be checked that $p1.1$ is the only other rule but $p1.4$ that can be applied on w^5 without getting blocked immediately in $C2$. This also proves that there is no *bad scenario* when we postpone the application of $p1.4$ and $p3.1$ but continue with working on the nonterminal Y with some appropriate rules (be them of type p or q). A possible *good scenario* would just apply $p1.4$ and $p3.1$ later, this way returning to the main line of derivation as discussed above. This good scenario is only postponing the application of $p1.4$ and $p3.1$ without any further effect.

For the discussion concerning the second phase of the ssSGNF grammar, we refer to the previous remark.

This concludes our argument concerning the inductive step of the correctness proof of our suggested simulation. Finally, Proposition 1 shows that the class $\mathrm{GCID}_S(4; 2, 0, 0; 1, 1, 0)$ is computationally complete, as well.   □

Our last result makes use of ssSGNF in a different manner: It relies on the fact that, by construction of this normal form, whenever we have a substring AB (in Phase II), then we also expect a substring $EABF$, and similarly, substring CD implies the presence of $ECDF$. This enables another way of marker-free simulation of the non-context-free erasing rules: After deleting AB or CD in $C1$, we can delete EF in another component and return.

We believe that these properties of ssSGNF can be very useful in different regulation scenarios and can be the basis for new or simplified computational completeness results.

Theorem 3. $\mathrm{RE} = \mathrm{GCID}_S(5; 1, 1, 0; 2, 0, 1)$ *and* $\mathrm{RE} = \mathrm{GCID}_S(5; 1, 0, 1; 2, 1, 0)$.

Proof. Consider a type-0 grammar $G = (N, T, P, S)$ in ssSGNF as in Definition 2. We construct a GCID_S system $\Pi = (5, V, T, \{S\}, H, 1, \{1\}, R)$ of size $(5; 1, 1, 0; 2, 0, 1)$ such that $L(\Pi) = L(G)$. The alphabet V contains rule markers, apart from the symbols of G. We refer to Table 4 for the rules of R.

We now prove that $L(G) \subseteq L(\Pi)$ as follows by induction by showing that if $w \Rightarrow w'$ in G, then $(w)_1 \Rightarrow_* (w')_1$ according to Π. Let $w = \alpha X \beta$ for some $\alpha \in \{EA, EC\}^* \{E, \lambda\}$, $\beta \in \{F, \lambda\} \{BF, DF\}^* T^*$. The simulations of $p : X \to bY$ and $q : X \to Yb$ are performed in a very deterministic fashion as follows:

Table 4. $\text{GCID}_S(5; 1, 1, 0; 2, 0, 1)$ rules simulating the rules of ssSGNF.

Component $C1$	Component $C2$	Component $C3$
$p1.1 : (1, (X, p, \lambda)_I, 2)$	$p2.1 : (2, (\lambda, X, p)_D, 1)$	$p3.1 : (3, (p', p^v, \lambda)_I, 1)$
$p1.2 : (1, (p, p', \lambda)_I, 3)$	$p2.2 : (2, (\lambda, p''p''', Y)_D, 1)$	
$p1.3 : (1, (p', b, \lambda)_I, 5)$		
$p1.4 : (1, (\lambda, pp', b)_D, 4)$		
$p1.5 : (1, (p''', p^{iv}, \lambda)_I, 4)$		
$p1.6 : (1, (p''', Y, \lambda)_I, 2)$		
$q1.1 : (1, (X, q, \lambda)_I, 2)$	$q2.1 : (2, (\lambda, X, q)_D, 1)$	$q3.1 : (3, (q', b, \lambda)_I, 1)$
$q1.2 : (1, (q, q', \lambda)_I, 3)$		
$q1.3 : (1, (q', Y, \lambda)_I, 4)$		
$h1.1 : (1, (S', h, \lambda)_I, 2)$	$h2.1 : (2, (\lambda, S'h, \lambda)_D, 1)$	
$f1.1 : (1, (\lambda, AB, \lambda)_D, 2)$	$e2.1 : (2, (\lambda, EF, \lambda)_D, 1)$	
$g1.1 : (1, (\lambda, CD, \lambda)_D, 2)$		
Component $C4$	Component $C5$	
$p4.1 : (4, (p'', p''', \lambda)_I, 1)$	$p5.1 : (5, (b, p'', \lambda)_I, 1)$	
$p4.2 : (4, (\lambda, p^{iv}p^v, \lambda)_D, 1)$		
$q4.1 : (4, (\lambda, qq', Y)_D, 1)$		

$$(\alpha X \beta)_1 \Rightarrow_{p1.1} (\alpha X p \beta)_2 \Rightarrow_{p2.1} (\alpha p \beta)_1 \Rightarrow_{p1.2} (\alpha p p' \beta)_3 \Rightarrow_{p3.1} (\alpha p p' p^v \beta)_1$$
$$\Rightarrow_{p1.3} (\alpha p p' b p^v \beta)_5 \Rightarrow_{p5.1} (\alpha p p' b p'' p^v \beta)_1 \Rightarrow_{p1.4} (\alpha b p'' p^v \beta)_4$$
$$\Rightarrow_{p4.1} (\alpha b p'' p''' p^v \beta)_1 \Rightarrow_{p1.5} (\alpha b p'' p''' p^{iv} p^v \beta)_4 \Rightarrow_{p4.2} (\alpha b p'' p''' \beta)_1$$
$$\Rightarrow_{p1.6} (\alpha b p'' p''' Y \beta)_2 \Rightarrow_{p2.2} (\alpha b Y \beta)_1 .$$
$$(\alpha X \beta)_1 \Rightarrow_{q1.1} (\alpha X q \beta)_2 \Rightarrow_{q2.1} (\alpha q \beta)_1 \Rightarrow_{q1.2} (\alpha q q' \beta)_3 \Rightarrow_{q3.1} (\alpha q q' b \beta)_1$$
$$\Rightarrow_{q1.3} (\alpha q q' Y b \beta)_4 \Rightarrow_{q4.1} (\alpha Y b \beta)_1 .$$

One might wonder that the rule $h : S' \rightarrow \lambda$ could easily be simulated by $(1, (\lambda, S', \lambda)_D, 1)$. However, we emphasize that the target component should be different from the current component in the definition of GCID_S. Hence, we have given a different simulation for this rule. The correctness of the h-rule simulation is direct and simple: $(\alpha S' \beta)_1 \Rightarrow_{h1.1} (\alpha S' h \beta)_2 \Rightarrow_{h2.1} (\alpha \beta)_1$.

In Phase II of ssSGNF, the central substring AB or CD is guarded on the left by E and by F on the right and hence we may regard that $EABF$ or $ECDF$ is the central part. The simulations of $f : AB \rightarrow \lambda$ and $e : EF \rightarrow \lambda$ are together treated as $EABF \rightarrow \lambda$ which is simulated as follows.
Simulating $f : AB \rightarrow \lambda$ and $e : EF \rightarrow \lambda$: $(\alpha EABF \beta)_1 \Rightarrow (\alpha EF \beta)_2 \Rightarrow (\alpha \beta)_1$.
(Similarly, rules g and e.)

This shows that $L(G) \subseteq L(\Pi)$. Next, we prove that $L(\Pi) \subseteq L(G)$ by proving that no unintended derivation is possible in Π using induction.

Let us first assume (by induction) that the sentential form $w^1 = \alpha X \beta$ for some $\alpha \in \{EA, EC\}^* \{E, \lambda\}$, $\beta \in \{F, \lambda\} \{BF, DF\}^* T^*$ and $X \in N'$ is derivable in G and the configuration $(w^1)_1$ is derivable in Π. As long as there is a symbol X from N' between α and β, we will not have substrings of the form AB and CD in the center. This forbids us to apply $f1.1$ or $g1.1$. Due to the lack of markers, only rules of type $p1.1$ or $q1.1$ are applicable.

Applying $q1.1$ to $w^1 = \alpha X\beta$ for some $\alpha \in \{EA, EC\}^*\{E, \lambda\}$, $X \in N'$, the only nonterminal from N', and $\beta \in \{F, \lambda\}\{BF, DF\}^*T^*$, yields the configuration $(w^2)_2$ with $w^2 = \alpha X q\beta$. In $C2$, no rule (except $q2.1$) is applicable since either they are well guarded by markers or due to absence of EF. On applying $q2.1$, we arrive at the configuration $(w^3)_1$ with $w^3 = \alpha q\beta$. Due to the absence of AB or CD or any symbol from N' or any other marker (other than q), only $q1.2$ is applicable on w^3 which inserts q' to the right of q and the resultant string $(w^4)_3$ where $w^4 = \alpha qq'\beta$ moves to $C3$. The required rule markers cause $q3.1$ to be the only applicable rule as desired. Therefore, we arrive at the configuration $(w^5)_1 = (\alpha qq'b\beta)_1$. Clearly, one could apply $q1.2$ again (apart from the intended $q1.3$). On applying $q1.2$ again, with the resultant string $\alpha qq'q'b\beta$, we are back to $C3$. Now, there are two possible subsequent configurations: (a) $(\alpha qq'bq'b\beta)_1$, or (b) $(\alpha qq'q'bb\beta)_1$. In Case (a), we claim that there is no way to delete the second occurrence of q' in the future. Namely, the only way to delete q' is if left to it, q is sitting. But as some $b \in \{B, D, F\} \cup T$ is present to the immediate left of q', there is no way to introduce q later in this position, because the marker q always works as a symbol that replaces the former N'-symbol. Therefore, a derivation following (a) cannot terminate. The situation is different in Case (b). For instance, we can apply $q1.3$ to the string $\alpha qq'q'bb\beta$, followed by $q4.1$. Again, we have two configurations to study: (A) $(\alpha q'Ybb\beta)_1$ or (B) $(\alpha Yq'bb\beta)_1$. In Case (A), we can argue similarly to Case (a) above to see that this configuration cannot lead to a terminal string: left to q' will sit some symbol A or C. Case (B) is indeed different. Assuming that only rules of the form $Z \to b'Z'$ are simulated subsequently, there may be a derivation $Y \Rightarrow^* \gamma X$ with $\gamma \in \{A, C, E\}^+$ that is simulated by the GCID system as intended. Hence, we see now a configuration $(\alpha\gamma Xq'bb\beta)_1$ and then, after a short excursion into $C2$, we see $(\alpha\gamma qq'bb\beta)_1$. Now, we can actually terminate by using the rules $q1.3$ and $q4.1$, leading to $(\alpha\gamma Ybb\beta)_1$. However, we would arrive at the same string if we had followed our intended plan. Then, we could get from $(\alpha Yb\beta)_1$ via $(\alpha\gamma Xb\beta)_1$ to $(\alpha\gamma qb\beta)_1$. Now, after applying $q1.2$ and $q2.2$ as intended, we can also see $(\alpha\gamma qq'bb\beta)_1$ and continue as above. This argument is also valid (by a separate yet straightforward induction) if we happen to produce a string $(\alpha q(q')^k b^k \beta)_1$ for an arbitrary $k > 1$. Therefore, we can avoid this process that we call *rule inversion*, and always follow our standard derivation instead. We can hence assume that we apply $q1.3$ to w^5 as desired. Therefore, we arrive at the configuration $(w^5)_1 = (\alpha qq'Yb\beta)_4$. On applying the only applicable rule $q4.1$, we arrive at $(\alpha Yb\beta)_1$ as intended, proving the inductive step in this case.

Applying $p1.1$ to $w^1 = \alpha X\beta$ for some $\alpha \in \{EA, EC\}^*\{E, \lambda\}$, $X \in N'$, the only nonterminal from N', and $\beta \in \{F, \lambda\}\{BF, DF\}^*T^*$, will insert a marker p to the right of X, yielding $(w^2)_2 = (\alpha Xp\beta)_2$. Recall that we are trying to simulate the rule $p : X \to bY$ for some $X, Y \in N'$ and $b \in \{A, C, E\}$. In $C2$, since all rules (except $p2.1$) are guarded by markers other than p and due to the absence of EF, the only applicable rule on w^2 is $p2.1$ which deletes the nonterminal X, yielding a string $w^3 = \alpha p \beta$, i.e., we arrive at the configuration $(w^3)_1$. Since X is deleted in the previous step and there is no p', p''', the only applicable rule is $p1.2$ which inserts a p' after p, yielding the configuration $(w^4)_3 = (\alpha p p' \beta)_3$. In $C3$, guarded by rule markers, we have to apply $p3.1$ as intended. Hence, we arrive at $(w^5)_1 = (\alpha p p' p^v \beta)_1$. If we re-apply $p1.2$, we achieve an imbalance of the number of occurrences of p and p' (as discussed the case for the q-rule simulation). This is problematic insofar as pp' is deleted together. Also, we would have to then re-apply $p3.1$ again, creating another imbalance. This brings us to the conclusion that we should apply $p1.3$ to $(w^5)_1$.

Hence, we arrive at $(w^6)_5 = (\alpha p p' b p^v \beta)_5$, with $b \in \{A, C, E\}$. In $C5$, we have to apply a rule that puts some marker r'' to the right of an occurrence of b. As $b \in \{A, C, E\}$, the b occurring between p' and p^v is the rightmost of all occurrences of A, C, E within w^6. Let us first discuss what happens if we do apply some $r5.1$ (but possibly $r \neq p$) to this described rightmost occurrence and mark the situation when some b within α is affected as $(*)$, not to forget its discussion. We get to $(w^7)_1 = (\alpha p p' b r'' p^v \beta)_1$. Now, we could also apply $p1.2$ or $p1.3$, and finally also $p1.4$ (as intended). If we apply rule $p1.2$, we again create an imbalance concerning p/p'. Let us defer the discussion of applying $p1.3$ at this configuration $(w^7)_1$ a bit as $(+)$; we rather discuss applying $p1.4$. We arrive at the configuration $(w^8)_4 = (\alpha b r'' p^v \beta)_4$. Now, only $r4.1$ would be applicable, leading to $(w^9)_1 = (\alpha b r'' r''' p^v \beta)_1$. We are now in safer waters, as we have to use rule $r1.5$ to get to $(w^{10})_4 = (\alpha b r'' r''' r^{iv} p^v \beta)_4$, because if we apply $p1.6$ directly, we have no chance to delete p^v in the future. If we apply $r4.1$ again on w^{10}, we create an imbalance between the number of r'' and r''', but this balance is necessary for deleting these markers in $C2$. By using $r4.2$ alternatively on w^{10}, one can see that the only chance to continue the route is when we have $r = p$. In that case, we move to $C1$ with $w^{11} = \alpha b p'' p''' \beta$. If we now re-apply $p1.5$, at $C4$, we have to apply $p4.1$ and create an imbalance between p'' and p''', hence preventing us from a terminating derivation. Hence, we have to discuss applying $p1.6$ as intended. We enter $C2$ with $w^{12} = \alpha b p'' p''' Y \beta$. Due to the absence of any markers, other than p'' and p''', we apply $p2.2$ as intended, finally getting to the configuration $(w^{12})_1 = (\alpha b Y \beta)_1$ as desired.

In order to conclude that the induction step has been shown, we still have to consider two scenarios, marked as $(*)$ and $(+)$ above. In $(+)$, we look at $(w^7)_1 = (\alpha p p' b r'' p^v \beta)_1 \Rightarrow_{p1.3} (\alpha p p' b b r'' p^v \beta)_5$. Assume we apply a rule $s5.1$ next. As the case when we find $b \in \{A, C, E\}$ within α is similar to the discussion $(*)$ that is still to come, we focus on two cases of configurations: (1) $(\alpha p p' b s'' b r'' p^v \beta)_1$ or (2) $(\alpha p p' b b s'' r'' p^v \beta)_1$. In both configurations, we can again apply $p1.3$, but this makes the whole case fail even more. We can now derive (under the conclusion that $r = p$) in the same way as in the main line of derivation, leading to $(\alpha b s'' b Y \beta)_1$ (Case (1)) or to $(\alpha b b s'' Y \beta)_1$ (Case (2)). In both cases, there is no way to make use of s'', because this means we have to move to $C4$, or we mis-use another p-type rule at some point, when $p1.4$ makes us enter

$C4$ again, but then continuing with the s-markers (using $s4.1$). Let us clarify this by assuming that we simulate $t : Y \rightarrow b'Y'$ next. Following the standard simulation up to $t1.4$, we get $(\alpha bs''bb't''t^v\beta)_4$ (Case (1)) or $(\alpha bbs''b't''t^v\beta)_4$ (Case (2)). We could now use $s4.1$, $s1.6$ and $s2.2$ to introduce another nonterminal from N' at the position of s'', but behold: we have now another left-over double-primed marker t'' whose removal can only be achieved by switching between two rule simulations in the 'next round'. Therefore, we will never be able to terminate this derivation.

For scenario $(*)$, we reconsider $(w^6)_5 = (\alpha pp'bp^v\beta)_5$, with $\alpha = \alpha_1 b\alpha_2$, so that for a suitable rule r that should introduce $Z \in N'$, $(w^7)_1 = (\alpha_1 br''\alpha_2 pp'bp^v\beta)_1$. We could try to continue with $(w^7)_1 \Rightarrow_{p1.4}$

$$(\alpha_1 br''\alpha_2 bp^v\beta)_4 \Rightarrow_{r4.1,r1.6} (\alpha_1 br''r'''Z\alpha_2 bp^v\beta)_2 \Rightarrow_{r2.2} (\alpha_1 bZ\alpha_2 bp^v\beta)_1$$

but then there is never a chance to lose p^v again . Therefore, also this scenario will never see a derivation producing a terminal string.

Applying $h1.1$ to $w^1 = \alpha X\beta$ for some $\alpha \in \{EA, EC\}^*\{E, \lambda\}$, $X \in N'$, the only nonterminal from N', and $\beta \in \{F, \lambda\}\{BF, DF\}^*T^*$, yields the configuration $(w^2)_2$ with $w^2 = \alpha S'h\beta$. In $C2$, the only applicable rule is $h2.1$ which deletes $S'h$ and the resultant string $w^3 = \alpha\beta$ is moved back to $C1$. The back-to-back application of $h1.1, h2.1$ simulates the rule $S' \rightarrow \lambda$ of G which enables the transition from Phase I to Phase II.

We are now discussing a string w derivable in G and as configuration $(w)_1$ in Π, with $w = \alpha\beta$, with $\alpha \in \{EA, EC\}^*$ and $\beta \in \{BF, DF\}^*T^*$; see Footnote 1. The central (good) substring could either be $EABF$ or $ECDF$. The application of $f1.1$ (or $g1.1$) deletes the central AB (or CD) which yields the resultant string $(w')_2 = (\alpha EF\beta)_2$. The rule $e2.1$ is deterministically applied to delete the central EF yielding (again) $(w)_1 = (w'')_1 = \alpha\beta$ back into $C1$ paving way to start another simulation of $AB \rightarrow \lambda$ and $EF \rightarrow \lambda$ or $CD \rightarrow \lambda$ and $EF \rightarrow \lambda$. Any other (wrong) forms of central parts (like $EADF$) will let the derivation inevitably get stuck.

This concludes our argument concerning the inductive step of the correctness proof of our suggested simulation. Finally, Proposition 1 shows that GCID_S systems of size $(5; 1, 0, 1; 2, 1, 0)$ are computationally complete, as well.   □

4   Summary and Open Problems

In this paper, we examined the computational power of graph-controlled ins-del systems with a star as a control graph. RE characterizations are by now known for several GCID_S systems. More specifically, the sizes $(6; 1, 1, 0; 2, 0, 0)$, $(6; 1, 0, 1; 2, 0, 0)$ and $(4; 2, 1, 1; 1, 0, 0)$ suffice by [6], while we added sizes $(3; 2, 1, 0; 1, 1, 0)$, $(3; 2, 0, 1; 1, 0, 1)$, $(3; 2, 0, 1; 1, 1, 0)$, $(3; 2, 1, 0; 1, 0, 1)$, $(4; 2, 0, 0;$ $1, 0, 1)$, $(4; 2, 0, 0; 1, 1, 0)$, $(5; 1, 1, 0; 2, 0, 1)$ and $(5; 1, 0, 1; 2, 1, 0)$ to this list in this paper. In some cases at least, the number of components that we need is relatively big. It is not clear at all where exactly the Pareto frontier of computational completeness lies for star-controlled systems. Further research is needed here. In particular, in the cases where we used five or six components in our simulations, it could well be that less components are also sufficient to generate every recursively enumerable language.

On the technical side, the space separating SGNF seems to be quite important to obtain our results. We think that this could be an indication that this normal form could be very useful in other contexts concerning computational completeness proof for variants of insertion-deletion systems. We saw already two quite different uses of the properties of ssSGNF, mainly relying on two different combinatorial properties of these normal forms. Possibly, there are more and other exploits. Finally, one should not forget that it might be desirable to create other variants of SGNF as a tool for getting more computational completeness results in the context of insertion-deletion systems.

Acknowledgements. We are indebted to the reviewers of MCU, in particular, as they spotted some problems in a previous construction as submitted to the conference. Thoroughly reconsidering our approach has even led to improved results.

References

1. Benne, R. (ed.): RNA Editing: The Alteration of Protein Coding Sequences of RNA. Ellis Horwood (1993)
2. Fernau, H., Kuppusamy, L., Raman, I.: On the computational completeness of graph-controlled insertion-deletion systems with binary sizes. Theor. Comput. Sci. **682**, 100–121 (2017)
3. Fernau, H., Kuppusamy, L., Raman, I.: Computational completeness of simple semi-conditional insertion-deletion systems of degree (2, 1). Nat. Comput. **18**(3), 563–577 (2019)
4. Fernau, H., Kuppusamy, L., Raman, I.: On path-controlled insertion-deletion systems. Acta Informatica **56**(1), 35–59 (2019)
5. Fernau, H., Kuppusamy, L., Raman, I.: On the generative capacity of matrix insertion-deletion systems of small sum-norm. Nat. Comput. **20**(4), 671–689 (2021). https://doi.org/10.1007/s11047-021-09866-y
6. Fernau, H., Kuppusamy, L., Raman, I.: When stars control a grammar's work. In: Gazdag, Z., Iván, S., Kovásznai, G. (eds.) Proceedings of the 16th International Conference on Automata and Formal Languages, AFL. EPTCS, vol. 386, pp. 96–111. Open Publishing Association (2023)
7. Freund, R., Kogler, M., Rogozhin, Y., Verlan, S.: Graph-controlled insertion-deletion systems. In: McQuillan, I., Pighizzini, G. (eds.) Proceedings Twelfth Annual Workshop on Descriptional Complexity of Formal Systems, DCFS. EPTCS, vol. 31, pp. 88–98. Open Publishing Association (2010)
8. Geffert, V.: Normal forms for phrase-structure grammars. RAIRO Informatique théorique et Applications/Theor. Inform. Appl. **25**, 473–498 (1991)
9. Ivanov, S., Verlan, S.: About one-sided one-symbol insertion-deletion P systems. In: Alhazov, A., Cojocaru, S., Gheorghe, M., Rogozhin, Y., Rozenberg, G., Salomaa, A. (eds.) Membrane Computing - 14th International Conference, CMC 2013. LNCS, vol. 8340, pp. 225–237. Springer, Cham (2014)

10. Ivanov, S., Verlan, S.: Universality and computational completeness of controlled leftist insertion-deletion systems. Fund. Inform. **155**(1–2), 163–185 (2017)
11. Kari, L., Thierrin, G.: Contextual insertions/deletions and computability. Inf. Comput. **131**(1), 47–61 (1996)
12. Krassovitskiy, A., Rogozhin, Y., Verlan, S.: Further results on insertion-deletion systems with one-sided contexts. In: Martín-Vide, C., Otto, F., Fernau, H. (eds.) LATA 2008. LNCS, vol. 5196, pp. 333–344. Springer, Heidelberg (2008). https://doi.org/10.1007/978-3-540-88282-4_31
13. Marcus, S.: Contextual grammars. Rev. Roumaine Math. Pures Appl. **14**, 1525–1534 (1969)
14. Matveevici, A., Rogozhin, Y., Verlan, S.: Insertion-deletion systems with one-sided contexts. In: Durand-Lose, J., Margenstern, M. (eds.) MCU 2007. LNCS, vol. 4664, pp. 205–217. Springer, Heidelberg (2007). https://doi.org/10.1007/978-3-540-74593-8_18
15. Păun, Gh., Rozenberg, G., Salomaa, A.: DNA Computing: New Computing Paradigms. Springer, Cham (1998)
16. Petre, I., Verlan, S.: Matrix insertion-deletion systems. Theor. Comput. Sci. **456**, 80–88 (2012)

On Switching Finite State Automata

Joss Chapman[1], Markus Holzer[2(✉)], and Petra Wolf[3]

[1] Diamond Age Technology LLC, 15714 Crestbrook Dr., Houston, TX 77059, USA
[2] Institut für Informatik, Universität Giessen, Arndtstr. 2, 35392 Giessen, Germany
holzer@informatik.uni-giessen.de
[3] LaBRI, CNRS, Université de Bordeaux,
351, cours de la Libération, 33405 Talence Cedex, France
mail@wolfp.net

Abstract. We introduce the concept of switch transitions for finite state machines. Roughly speaking, a switch transition branches and connects one state (source) with two states (targets), and changes which state it goes to every time it is used. In this way, a switching finite automaton remembers besides the current state also for each switch transition where it points to—this can be seen as an additional bit of memory for each switch transition. We study the accepting capacity of switching automata and show that they are exponentially more succinct than ordinary finite automata. Moreover, the computational complexity of these devices are investigated for standard problems from formal language theory. Here it turns out that some lower bounds can be deduced from problems on regular like expressions with squaring. This is due to the fact that one can construct a linear size switching automaton equivalent to a regular like expression with squaring.

1 Introduction

In the realm of computer science and formal language theory, finite state machines serve as fundamental models [5,8] for representing computational processes. Traditionally, finite state device computations move between states based on input symbols, providing a simplistic yet powerful framework for various applications. However, for some applications finite automata are not powerful enough. Thus, since the very beginning of automata theory advancements have led to the introduction of a novel concepts such as bounded height pushdown stores, pushdown stores in general, or other even more general storage mechanisms in order to improve the succinctness and/or the capability of the original devices. Here, we will study a new concept that is based on a dynamic behavior of the transitions, that are allowed to change their destination in a specific manner after use—compare with [2]. Switching transitions, an addition to the traditional finite state automata framework, change the way machines traverse states. Unlike conventional transitions that connect one state to another,

P. Wolf—Supported by the French ANR, project ANR-22-CE48-0001 (TEMPOGRAL).

switch transitions branch out, connecting a source state to two distinct target states. What distinguishes switch transitions is their dynamic nature; with each use, they alternate between the connected states, effectively introducing an additional layer of memory to the machine. We embark on a comprehensive exploration of switching finite automata, shedding light on their unique properties and computational capabilities. Our primary focus lies in understanding the accepting capacity of these automata and contrasting them with conventional finite automata. Our findings reveal that switching automata offer exponential improvements in succinctness over their traditional counterparts. Furthermore, we delve into the computational complexity of switching automata by investigating their performance on standard problems in formal language theory. Notably, we uncover intriguing connections between switching automata and regular-like expressions with squaring operations. By demonstrating a close connection between regular-like expressions with squaring and linear-size switching automata, we establish lower bounds for computational problems, illuminating the rich interplay between memory augmentation and computational efficiency.

2 Definitions

We assume the reader to be familiar with the basics in computational complexity theory as contained in [6]. In particular we recall the inclusion chain:

$$\mathsf{ALOGTIME} \subseteq \mathsf{NL} \subseteq \mathsf{NP} \subseteq \mathsf{PSPACE} \subseteq \mathsf{EXPSPACE}.$$

Here, $\mathsf{ALOGTIME}$ denotes the class of problems solvable by alternating Turing machines in logarithmic time. Moreover, NL (NP, respectively) refers to the class of languages accepted by nondeterministic Turing machines with logarithmic space (polynomial time, respectively). Finally, PSPACE refers to the class of languages accepted by deterministic or nondeterministic Turing machines in polynomial space [9] and $\mathsf{EXPSPACE}$ is a short hand notation for $\bigcup_k \mathsf{NSPACE}(2^{n^k})$. If not stated otherwise, hardness is always meant w.r.t. deterministic logspace bounded many-one reductions, $\leq$ for short.

In the following, we present a generalization of finite state automata called *switching finite state automata*. We begin with introducing a non-deterministic version. We call $\mathcal{S} = (Q, \Sigma, \delta, q_0, F)$ a *switching non-deterministic finite automaton* (SNFA for short), if Q is a finite set of states, Σ is a finite alphabet, $\delta \subseteq Q \times (\Sigma \cup \{\varepsilon\}) \times Q^2$ is a transition relation allowing for ε transitions, where ε is the empty word, $q_0 \in Q$ is the initial state and $F \subseteq Q$ is a set of final states. We call $\delta^{\lozenge} = \{(q, \sigma, p, p) \in \delta\}$ the set of *ordinary* transitions of $\mathcal{S}$ and $\delta^{\curlyvee}$ refers to the *switching* transitions of $\mathcal{S}$; obviously $\delta^{\curlyvee} = \delta \setminus \delta^{\lozenge}$. We further call $\kappa = |\delta \setminus \delta^{\lozenge}| = |\delta^{\curlyvee}|$ the *switching degree* of $\mathcal{S}$. Next, we describe how $\mathcal{S}$ acts on input words. Therefore, we define a configuration of $\mathcal{S}$ as a tuple $(q, \nu) \in Q \times (\mathbb{U} \cup \mathbb{B})^{\delta}$ where $\mathbb{B} = \mathbb{Z}/2\mathbb{Z}$ is the ring of integers modulo 2, and $\mathbb{U} = \mathbb{Z}/1\mathbb{Z}$ is the ring of integers modulo 1, and ν is a function from the set δ into $(\mathbb{U} \cup \mathbb{B})$ where $\delta^{\lozenge} \to \mathbb{U}$, and $\delta \setminus \delta^{\lozenge} \to \mathbb{B}$. We interpret a configuration (q, ν) as $\mathcal{S}$

being in the state q, and ν describing the current configuration of the switch transitions of $\mathcal{S}$. For a configuration (q, ν) and $\sigma \in \Sigma \cup \{\varepsilon\}$ we simply write $(q, \nu) \xrightarrow{\sigma} (q', \nu')$ if for some $p \in Q$,

1. either $(q, \sigma, q', p) \in \delta$, and $\nu((q, \sigma, q', p)) = 0$, and in addition $\nu'((q, \sigma, q', p)) = \nu((q, \sigma, q', p)) + 1$ with addition in the codomain of ν, and $\nu'(t) = \nu$ for $t \neq (q, \sigma, q', p)$;
2. or $(q, \sigma, p, q') \in \delta$, and $\nu((q, \sigma, p, q')) = 1$, and $\nu'((q, \sigma, p, q')) = \nu((q, \sigma, p, q')) + 1$ with addition in the codomain of ν, and $\nu'(t) = \nu$ for $t \neq (q, \sigma, p, q')$.

We denote with $\rightarrow$ the reflexive transitive closure of the union of $\xrightarrow{\sigma}$ over all $\sigma \in \Sigma \cup \{\varepsilon\}$. The input words on top of $\rightarrow$ are concatenated accordingly, so that $\rightarrow = \bigcup_{w \in \Sigma^*} \xrightarrow{w}$. We call (q_0, ν_0) with $\nu_0(t) = 0$ for all $t \in \delta$ the *start* configuration of $\mathcal{S}$. We call (q, ν) with $q \in F$ an *accepting* configuration. We denote with $\mathcal{L}(\mathcal{S})$ the *language* accepted by $\mathcal{S}$ consisting of all words $w \in \Sigma^*$ for which there exists an accepting configuration (q, ν) with $(q_0, \nu_0) \xrightarrow{w} (q, \nu)$. If for an accepting configuration (q, ν) it holds that $\nu(t) = 0$ for all $t \in \delta$, we call (q, ν) an *accepting reset configuration*. We denote with $\mathcal{R}(\mathcal{S})$ the *reset language* accepted by $\mathcal{S}$ consisting of all words $w \in \Sigma^*$ for which there exists an accepting *reset* configuration (q, ν_0) with $(q_0, \nu_0) \xrightarrow{w} (q, \nu_0)$. By definition $\mathcal{R}(\mathcal{S}) \subseteq \mathcal{L}(\mathcal{S})$ holds.

Next, we define a *deterministic* version of a switching finite automaton. We call an SNFA $\mathcal{S} = (Q, \Sigma, \delta, q_0, F)$ a *switching deterministic finite automaton* (SDFA for short) if for all $q \in Q$ it holds that

1. if $(\{q\} \times \Sigma \times Q^2) \cap \delta \neq \emptyset$, then $(\{q\} \times \{\varepsilon\} \times Q^2) \cap \delta = \emptyset$, and
2. $(\{q\} \times \{\sigma\} \times Q^2) \cap \delta \leq 1$ for all $\sigma \in \Sigma \cup \{\varepsilon\}$.

The accepted language and the reset language are similarly defined as for SNFAs.

If for an SNFA $\mathcal{S}$ it holds that $\delta \setminus \delta^{\lozenge} = \emptyset$, i.e., for all transitions, both endpoints are identical, then we call $\mathcal{S}$ a *non-deterministic finite automaton* (NFA for short). In this case, we might also identify $\mathcal{S}$ with the *ordinary* NFA $\mathcal{A} = (Q, \Sigma, \delta_\mathcal{A}, q_0, F)$ where Q, Σ, q_0, and F are as for $\mathcal{S}$, but $\delta_\mathcal{A} \subseteq Q \times (\Sigma \cup \{\varepsilon\}) \times Q$ projects the fourth component of δ onto the third. Observe, that our NFAs are allowed to use spontaneous transitions, i.e., ε-moves. We further call $\mathcal{S}$ a *deterministic finite automaton* (DFA for short) if $(Q \times \{\varepsilon\} \times Q^2) \cap \delta = \emptyset$ and $|\{(p, \sigma, q, q) \mid q \in Q\}| \leq 1$ for all $\sigma \in \Sigma$ and $p \in Q$. Again, we might identify an SDFA $\mathcal{S}$ with the *ordinary* DFA $\mathcal{A} = (Q, \Sigma, \delta_\mathcal{A}, q_0, F)$ where the fourth component of δ is projected onto the third. Note that DFAs do *not* have spontaneous or ε-transitions, as usually in the literature. Moreover, by definition the DFA is allowed to be partial. Observe, that for NFAs and DFAs, the accepted reset language coincides with the accepted language. For an *ordinary* NFA $\mathcal{A} = (Q, \Sigma, \delta_\mathcal{A}, q_0, F)$ we define a configuration of $\mathcal{A}$ as a single state q and write $q \xrightarrow{\sigma} p$ if $(q, \sigma, p) \in \delta_\mathcal{A}$. Again, we denote with $\rightarrow$ the reflexive transitive closure of $\xrightarrow{\sigma}$ over all $\sigma \in \Sigma \cup \{\varepsilon\}$ and concatenate input words on top of $\xrightarrow{w}$. Note that every ordinary NFA can be associated with an (S)NFA by extending $\delta_\mathcal{A}$ to $\delta \subseteq Q \times \Sigma \cup \{\varepsilon\} \times Q^2$ by duplicating the third component of $\delta_\mathcal{A}$ (the same holds for DFAs w.r.t. (S)DFAs).

In order to explain our notation we give an example:

Example 1. Consider the SNFA $\mathcal{S} = (Q, \{a\}, \delta, q_0, F)$ with state set $Q = \{0, 1, 2\}$, transition relation

$$\delta = \{(0, a, 1, 1), (1, a, 0, 2), (2, a, 0, 0)\},$$

initial state $q_0 = 0$, and the set of final states $F = \{0\}$. The SNFA $\mathcal{S}$ has 3 transitions, where 2 are ordinary ones, which induces that the switching degree κ is equal to 1. In fact the SNFA $\mathcal{S}$ is a SDFA indeed. A drawing of the switching automaton is depicted in Fig. 1. Next consider the word a^{10} as input to $\mathcal{S}$.

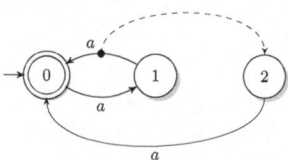

Fig. 1. Switching automaton $\mathcal{S}$. The switch transition $t = (1, a, 0, 2)$ is depicted with a solid and dashed (split) edge. The solid transition corresponds to ν_0, while the dashed one to ν_1.

To discuss the sequence of configurations, we define two functions ν_0 and ν_1 on the transitions of the SNFA $\mathcal{S}$ as follows:

$$\nu_0(t) = 0 \quad \text{and} \quad \nu_1(t) = \begin{cases} 1 & \text{if } t = (1, a, 0, 2) \\ 0 & \text{otherwise.} \end{cases}$$

Then we find the accepting computation

$$(0, \nu_0) \xrightarrow{a} (1, \nu_0) \xrightarrow{a} (0, \nu_1) \xrightarrow{a} (1, \nu_1) \xrightarrow{a} (2, \nu_0) \xrightarrow{a} (0, \nu_0)$$
$$\xrightarrow{a} (1, \nu_0) \xrightarrow{a} (0, \nu_1) \xrightarrow{a} (1, \nu_1) \xrightarrow{a} (2, \nu_0) \xrightarrow{a} (0, \nu_0).$$

Thus, $a^{10} \in \mathcal{L}(\mathcal{S})$ and moreover, because the last configuration is $(0, \nu_0)$, we also have that $a^{10} \in \mathcal{R}(\mathcal{S})$. By the above given computation it is also easy to see that the words ε, a^2, a^5, and a^7 are members of $\mathcal{L}(\mathcal{S})$, but not all of these words belong to $\mathcal{R}(\mathcal{S})$. In fact only the words ε and a^5 are in $\mathcal{R}(\mathcal{S})$. With a little bit more effort one can show that

$$\mathcal{L}(\mathcal{S}) = (\varepsilon + a^2)(a^5)^* \quad \text{and} \quad \mathcal{R}(\mathcal{S}) = (a^5)^*.$$

It is worth mentioning that any ordinary finite automaton requires at least 5 states for accepting either $\mathcal{L}(\mathcal{S})$ or $\mathcal{R}(\mathcal{S})$.   □

3   Basics on Switching Automata

We start with some basics on switching automata. In the definition of the accepted language or the reset language of an SNFA we have arbitrarily chosen ν_0 as part of the starting configuration. We show that this is not essential in the definition. To this end we argue as follows: for an SNFA $\mathcal{S} = (Q, \Sigma, \delta, q_0, F)$ and a transition $t \in \delta$ we define $\mathcal{S}_t = (Q, \Sigma, \delta_t, q_0, F)$ with $\delta_t = (\delta \setminus \{t\}) \cup \{t^{\circlearrowleft}\}$, where $t^{\circlearrowleft}$ refers to the transition (q, a, p, q'), if $t = (q, a, q', p)$. Note that $\mathcal{S}_t$ is deterministic if $\mathcal{S}$ is deterministic. For the computations of $\mathcal{S}$ and $\mathcal{S}_t$ we find the following situation, which can be shown by induction on the length of the computation—the tedious details are left to the reader.

Lemma 2. *Let* $\mathcal{S} = (Q, \Sigma, \delta, q_0, F)$ *be an SNFA or SDFA, transition* $t \in \delta$, *and* $\mathcal{S}_t = (Q, \Sigma, \delta_t, q_0, F)$ *be the switching automata of same type (nondeterministic or deterministic) defined as above. Then*

$$(q, \nu) \xrightarrow{w}_{\mathcal{S}} (p, \nu') \quad \textit{if and only if} \quad (q, \nu_t) \xrightarrow{w}_{\mathcal{S}_t} (p, \nu'_t),$$

for some $w \in \Sigma^*$, *where* $\nu, \nu' \in (\mathbb{U} \cup \mathbb{B})^{\delta}$, $\nu_t, \nu'_t \in (\mathbb{U} \cup \mathbb{B})^{\delta_t}$, *and* ν *coincides with* ν_t (ν' *coincides with* ν'_t, *respectively) on all transitions, except for* t *or* $t^{\circlearrowleft}$, *where we have* $\nu_t(t^{\circlearrowleft}) = \nu(t) + 1$ ($\nu'_t(t^{\circlearrowleft}) = \nu'(t) + 1$, *respectively).* $\qquad\square$

The previous lemma allows us to deduce for switching automata the restriction to the ν_0 function in the starting configuration and accepting reset configuration is no limitation at all. Next we show that with switching automata one can only accept regular languages. To this end it suffices to show how to convert a switching automaton to an ordinary finite state automaton.

Theorem 3. *Let* $\mathcal{S}$ *be a n-state SNFA with switching degree* κ. *Then there are NFAs* $\mathcal{A}_{\mathcal{L}}$ *and* $\mathcal{A}_{\mathcal{R}}$ *both with at most* $n \cdot 2^{\kappa}$ *states such that* $\mathcal{L}(\mathcal{A}_{\mathcal{L}}) = \mathcal{L}(\mathcal{S})$ *and* $\mathcal{L}(\mathcal{A}_{\mathcal{R}}) = \mathcal{R}(\mathcal{S})$. *The statement remains valid for deterministic devices, too.*

Proof. We only prove the statement for the nondeterministic case. Let $\mathcal{S} = (Q, \Sigma, \delta, q_0, F)$. We define the NFAs

$$\mathcal{A}_{\mathcal{L}} = (Q \times (\mathbb{U} \cup \mathbb{B})^{\delta}, \Sigma, \delta', (q, \nu_0), F_{\mathcal{L}})$$

and

$$\mathcal{A}_{\mathcal{R}} = (Q \times (\mathbb{U} \cup \mathbb{B})^{\delta}, \Sigma, \delta', (q, \nu_0), F_{\mathcal{R}}),$$

where $((q, \nu), \sigma, (q', \nu')) \in \delta'$ if for some $p \in Q$ and $\sigma \in \Sigma \cup \{\varepsilon\}$, either $(q, \sigma, q', p) \in \delta$, and $\nu((q, \sigma, q', p)) = 0$, and $\nu'((q, \sigma, q', p)) = \nu((q, \sigma, q', p)) + 1$ with addition in the codomain of ν, and $\nu'(t) = \nu$ for $t \neq (q, \sigma, q', p)$; or $(q, \sigma, p, q') \in \delta$, and $\nu((q, \sigma, p, q')) = 1$, and $\nu'((q, \sigma, p, q')) = \nu((q, \sigma, p, q')) + 1$ with addition in the codomain of ν, and $\nu'(t) = \nu$ for $t \neq (q, \sigma, p, q')$. This completes the description of the transitions in δ'; thus no other transitions belong to δ'. Finally, the set of final states is defined as

$$F_{\mathcal{L}} = F \times (\mathbb{U} \cup \mathbb{B})^{\delta}$$

and

$$F_{\mathcal{R}} = F \times \{\nu_0\},$$

where $\nu_0(t) = 0$, for all $t \in \delta$. It is easy to see that both automata have at most $n \cdot 2^\kappa$ number of states, because every $\nu \in (\mathbb{U} \cup \mathbb{B})^\delta$ maps every transition in $\delta^{\emptyset}$ to 0, while for all other transitions in $\delta \setminus \delta^{\emptyset}$ we can choose between 0 and 1; hence there are 2^κ possibilities for ν, where κ refers to the switching degree, i.e., $\kappa = |\delta \setminus \delta^{\emptyset}|$.

By construction one can show by induction on the length of the computation that

$$(q, \nu) \xrightarrow{\sigma_1 \sigma_2 \ldots \sigma_n}_{\mathcal{S}} (p, \nu') \quad \text{if and only if} \quad (q, \nu) \xrightarrow{\sigma_1 \sigma_2 \ldots \sigma_n}_{\mathcal{A}} (p, \nu'), \qquad (1)$$

for $q, p \in Q$, $\nu, \nu' \in (\mathbb{U} \cup \mathbb{B})^\delta$, and $\sigma_1, \sigma_2, \ldots, \sigma_n \in \Sigma \cup \{\varepsilon\}$, where $\mathcal{A}$ stands either for $\mathcal{A}_{\mathcal{L}}$ or $\mathcal{A}_{\mathcal{R}}$, respectively. By the property (1) and the choice of the set of final states of the NFAs $\mathcal{A}_{\mathcal{L}}$ and $\mathcal{A}_{\mathcal{R}}$ we can deduce that (i) $w \in \mathcal{L}(\mathcal{S})$ if and only if $w \in \mathcal{L}(\mathcal{A}_{\mathcal{L}})$ and (ii) $w \in \mathcal{R}(\mathcal{S})$ if and only if $w \in \mathcal{L}(\mathcal{A}_{\mathcal{R}})$, which proves that $\mathcal{L}(\mathcal{A}_{\mathcal{L}}) = \mathcal{L}(\mathcal{S})$ and $\mathcal{L}(\mathcal{A}_{\mathcal{R}}) = \mathcal{R}(\mathcal{S})$. □

Next we show an exponential lower bound for the conversion of switching automata to ordinary automata of the same kind (deterministic or nondeterministic) already for unary languages.

Theorem 4. *Let $n \geq 2$ and $\kappa = n - 2$. Then $3 \cdot 2^\kappa - 1$ states are necessary in the worst case for any NFA accepting the language $\mathcal{L}(\mathcal{S})$ or $\mathcal{R}(\mathcal{S})$ of an n-state unary SNFA $\mathcal{S}$ with switching degree κ accepting a finite language. The statement remains valid for deterministic devices, too.*

Proof. Define the unary SNFA $\mathcal{S}_n = (Q_n, \{a\}, \delta_n, q_0, F_n)$ with $Q_n = \{1, 2, \ldots, n\}$ and $q_0 = 1$. Moreover, let $F_n = \{n\}$ and the transitions are defined as follows:

$$\delta_n = \{(1, a, 2, 2)\} \cup \{(i, a, 1, i+1) \mid 2 \leq i \leq n-1\}.$$

Note that $\kappa = n-2$ and that $\mathcal{S}_n$ is in fact an SDFA. The switching automaton $\mathcal{S}_n$ for the case $n = 4$ and hence $\kappa = 2$ is shown in Fig. 2. By induction on the number of states one shows that for the SNFA $\mathcal{S}_n$ it holds

$$\mathcal{L}(\mathcal{S}_n) = \mathcal{R}(\mathcal{S}_n) = \{a^{3 \cdot 2^\kappa - 2}\}.$$

For $n = 2$ it obviously holds that $\mathcal{L}(\mathcal{S}_2) = \mathcal{R}(\mathcal{S}_2) = \{a^{3 \cdot 2^0 - 2}\} = \{a\}$ because of the single step computation $(1, \nu_0) \xrightarrow{a} (2, \nu_0)$. In the induction step from n to $n+1$ we argue as follows: for every word w in $\mathcal{L}(\mathcal{S}_{n+1})$ ($\mathcal{R}(\mathcal{S}_{n+1})$, respectively) we find a computation in the automaton $\mathcal{S}_{n+1}$ that can be split by the construction of $\mathcal{S}_{n+1}$ and the induction hypothesis into the computation

1. $(1, \nu_0) \xrightarrow{a^{3 \cdot 2^\kappa - 2}} (n, \nu_0)$,
2. followed by the single step $(n, \nu_0) \xrightarrow{a} (1, \nu_0')$,

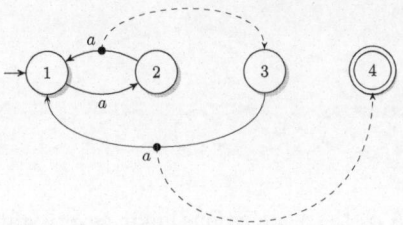

Fig. 2. The unary switching automaton $\mathcal{S}_n$ for $n = 4$ and switching degree $\kappa = n - 2$, that is, $\kappa = 2$, where any NFA or DFA accepting the language $\mathcal{L}(\mathcal{S}_n)$ or $\mathcal{R}(\mathcal{S}_n)$ requires at least $3 \cdot 2^{n-2} - 1$ states. The sink state of $\mathcal{S}_n$ is not shown.

3. continued by the computation $(1, \nu_0') \xrightarrow{a^{3 \cdot 2^{\kappa} - 2}} (n, \nu_0')$, and
4. finally $(n, \nu_0') \xrightarrow{a} (n + 1, \nu_0)$,

where ν_0 coincides with ν_0' on all transitions, except for $t = (n, a, 1, n+1)$, where we have $\nu_0(t) = 0$ and $\nu_0'(t) = 1$. Thus, $(1, \nu_0) \xrightarrow{a^{3 \cdot 2^{\kappa+1} - 2}} (n + 1, \nu_0)$ because $3 \cdot 2^{\kappa} - 2 + 1 + 3 \cdot 2^{\kappa} - 2 + 1 = 3 \cdot 2^{\kappa+1} - 2$ and therefore $\mathcal{L}(\mathcal{S}_{n+1}) = \mathcal{R}(\mathcal{S}_{n+1}) = \{a^{3 \cdot 2^{\kappa+1} - 2}\}$. Since any DFA or NFA accepting the unary finite language $\{a^{3 \cdot 2^{\kappa} - 2}\}$ requires at least $3 \cdot 2^{\kappa} - 1$ states the stated claim follows. □

When considering languages over an alphabet that is at least binary, we can do slightly better w.r.t. the number of states compared to the previous theorem.

Theorem 5. *Let $n \geq 1$ and κ with $0 \leq \kappa \leq n$. Then $n \cdot 2^{\kappa}$ states are sufficient and necessary in the worst case for any DFA accepting the language $\mathcal{L}(\mathcal{S})$ or $\mathcal{R}(\mathcal{S})$ of an n-state SDFA $\mathcal{S}$ with switching degree κ.*

Proof. The upper bound of $n \cdot 2^{\kappa}$ is immediate by Theorem 3. Thus, it remains to show that this is also a lower bound. To this end we argue as follows: let $\mathcal{S} = (Q, \{a, b, c\}, \delta, q_0, F)$ be an SDFA with $Q = \{1, 2, \ldots n\}$ and $q_0 = 1$. Moreover, let $F = \{1\}$ and the transitions are defined as follows:

$$\delta = \{(i, a, i + 1, i) \mid 1 \leq i \leq \kappa\} \cup \{(i, a, i + 1, i + 1) \mid \kappa < i < n\}$$
$$\cup \{(n, a, 1, 1) \mid \kappa < n\} \cup \{(n, a, 1, n) \mid \kappa = n\}$$
$$\cup \{(i, b, i + 1, i + 1) \mid 1 \leq i < n\} \cup \{(n, b, 1, 1)\}$$
$$\cup \{(i, c, 1, 1) \mid 1 \leq i \leq n\}.$$

The switching automaton $\mathcal{S}$ for the case $\kappa = 2$ is depicted in Fig. 3.

The DFA constructed in the proof of Theorem 3 has state set $Q \times (\mathbb{U} \cup \mathbb{B})^{\delta}$ and the initial state $(1, \Delta_0)$, where $\Delta_0(t) = 0$, for every transition $t \in \delta$ of the SDFA $\mathcal{S}$. We refer to the transitions of the constructed DFA as δ'.

In case $\kappa = 0$, the SDFA $\mathcal{S}$ is an ordinary DFA, which is obviously minimal, since all states (i, Δ_0), for $1 \leq i \leq n$, are reachable from the initial state $(1, \Delta_0)$ by reading the word b^{i-1}, and every pair of different states (i, Δ_0) and (j, Δ_0)

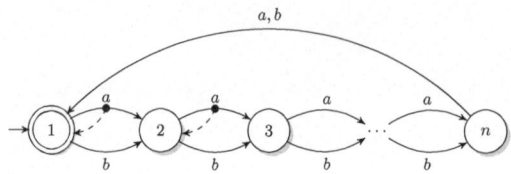

Fig. 3. The n-state SDFA $\mathcal{S}$ (the c-transitions linking every state with the initial state 1 are not shown) with switching degree $\kappa = 2$, where any DFA accepting language $\mathcal{L}(\mathcal{S})$ or $\mathcal{R}(\mathcal{S})$ requires at least $n \cdot 2^{\kappa} = n \cdot 2^2 = 4 \cdot n$ states.

with $i \neq j$ is distinguishable by reading the word b^{n+1-i}. No other states are reachable, since no switch transition exists and thus Δ_0 cannot be modified. Thus, the SDFA $\mathcal{S}$ is minimal.

Now assume that $1 \leq \kappa \leq n$. Let $t_1, t_2, \ldots, t_\kappa$ in $\delta \backslash \delta^{\emptyset}$ be the switch transitions of the SDFA $\mathcal{S}$, where $t_i \in \{i\} \times \{a\} \times Q^2$. Before we show that every state (i, Δ) with $1 \leq i \leq n$ and $\Delta \in (\mathbb{U} \cup \mathbb{B})^{\delta}$ is reachable in the constructed DFA we take a look at how to modify Δ by reading appropriate words. For the switch transitions of the SDFA $\mathcal{S}$ and $\Delta \in (\mathbb{U} \cup \mathbb{B})^{\delta}$ define the words

$$w_{t_j, \Delta} = \begin{cases} b & \text{if } \Delta(t_j) = 0 \\ a & \text{if } \Delta(t_j) = 1. \end{cases}$$

Then we find the computation

$$(1, \Delta_0) \xrightarrow{w_{t_1, \Delta}} (2, \Delta_1) \xrightarrow{w_{t_2, \Delta}} \ldots$$

$$\ldots \xrightarrow{w_{t_{\kappa-1}, \Delta}} (\kappa, \Delta_{\kappa-1}) \xrightarrow{w_{t_\kappa, \Delta}} (\kappa', \Delta_\kappa) = \begin{cases} (\kappa+1, \Delta) & \text{if } \kappa < n, \\ (1, \Delta) & \text{otherwise,} \end{cases}$$

where $\Delta_k(t) = 0$, for $t \in \delta \backslash \{t_1, t_2, \ldots, t_k\}$, and $\Delta_k(t) = \Delta(t)$, otherwise. that by construction Δ_κ is equal to Δ. Now we are ready to show that every state (i, Δ) is reachable. We start in $(1, \Delta_0)$ and read the word $w = w_{t_1, \Delta} w_{t_2, \Delta} \cdots w_{t_\kappa, \Delta}$, which leads us to state $(\kappa+1, \Delta)$, if $\kappa < n$, or $(1, \Delta)$, otherwise. In the former case we further read $b^{n-\kappa+i-1}$ and in the latter case the word b^{i-1}, which leads us in both cases to the state (i, Δ) in question, because the second component of a state is not changed by reading letters b at all. Thus, all states of the corresponding DFA are reachable (by words only using letters a and b).

It remains to show that two different states (i, Δ) and (i', Δ') are distinguishable in the constructed DFA. We start by showing dinstinguishability of states with respect to the *accepted language* $\mathcal{L}(\mathcal{S})$. We consider two cases:

1. First assume that $i \neq i'$. Without loss of generality let $1 \leq i < i' \leq n$. Then we find that $(i, \Delta) \xrightarrow{b^{n+1-i}} (1, \Delta)$ is an accepting computation while $(i', \Delta') \xrightarrow{b^{n+1-i}} (i' - i + 1, \Delta')$ is not. Hence, the states (i, Δ) and (i', Δ') are distinguishable in the DFA.

2. Next assume $i = i'$ and $\Delta \neq \Delta'$. Here, $\Delta \neq \Delta'$ means that there is a switch transition t_j such that $\Delta(t_j) \neq \Delta'(t_j)$. Without loss of generality we may assume that $\Delta(t_j) = 0$ and $\Delta'(t_j) = 1$. Reading the word $b^{n+1-i}ab^{j-1}a$ leads to the first case analyzed above, because

$$(i, \Delta) \xrightarrow{b^{n+1-i}a} (1, \Delta) \xrightarrow{b^{j-1}} (j, \Delta) \xrightarrow{a} (j', \Delta''),$$

where $j' = j + 1$, if $1 \leq j < n$, and $j' = 1$, otherwise, and

$$(i, \Delta') = (i', \Delta') \xrightarrow{b^{n+1-i}a} (1, \Delta') \xrightarrow{b^{j-1}} (j, \Delta') \xrightarrow{a} (j'', \Delta'''),$$

where $j'' = j$, for appropriate Δ'' and Δ'''. In fact Δ'' (Δ''', respectively) is equal to Δ (Δ', respectively) except for t_j, where $\Delta''(t_j) = 1$ ($\Delta'''(t_j) = 0$, respectively). Observe, that $j' \neq j''$ and we are left with the first case above. This shows that also in this case the originally given states are distinguishable in the constructed DFA.

For the dinstinguishability of the DFA states with respect to the *reset language* we also consider two cases and argue as follows—again we assume that we have two different states (i, Δ) and (i', Δ') of the DFA:

1. Assume that $i = i'$. Hence, $\Delta \neq \Delta'$. Define $k = |\{\Delta(t) = 1 \mid t \in \delta\}|$. Then we consider the following subcases:
   (a) Let $k = 0$. Then $\Delta = \Delta_0$ and we are done by reading the word b^{n+1-i} resulting in the states $(1, \Delta_0)$, for (i, Δ), and $(1, \Delta')$, for (i', Δ'). Since $\Delta \neq \Delta'$, the first state $(1, \Delta_0)$ is accepting, while the latter state $(1, \Delta')$ is *not* accepting. Hence, the original states are distinguishable w.r.t. the reset language.
   (b) Finally, let $k \geq 1$. We show how to reduce k by 1. Let t_j satisfy $\Delta(t_j) = 1$. Then we find

$$(i, \Delta) \xrightarrow{b^{n+1-i}b^{j-1}ac} (1, \Delta'') \quad \text{and} \quad (i', \Delta') \xrightarrow{b^{n+1-i}b^{j-1}ac} (1, \Delta'''),$$

   where obviously $\Delta'' \neq \Delta'''$ since only the value for the switch transition t_j is changed and $|\{\Delta(t) = 1 \mid t \in \delta\}| = k - 1$. Hence, Δ'' is one step closer to Δ_0 compared to Δ. Thus, with the new states $(1, \Delta'')$ and $(1, \Delta''')$ we are back to the original situation, but now with the value $k - 1$. Thus, we conclude that the original states are distinguishable in the DFA w.r.t. the reset language.

2. Let $i \neq i'$. Without loss of generality assume that $1 \leq i < i' \leq n$. Then we consider two subcases for Δ and Δ':
   (a) If $\Delta \neq \Delta'$ we simply read the letter c and we are left with the states $(1, \Delta)$ and $(1, \Delta')$, where the above case applies since by assumption $\Delta \neq \Delta'$.
   (b) In case $\Delta = \Delta'$ we read the word $b^{n+1-i}c$. Then $(i, \Delta) \xrightarrow{b^{n+1-i}ac} (1, \Delta'')$ and $(i', \Delta') \xrightarrow{b^{n+1-i}ac} (1, \Delta''')$, where Δ'' coincides with Δ except for the switch transition t_1, while Δ''' still coincides with Δ on t_1. Thus, $\Delta'' \neq \Delta'''$ and then the above case on the states $(1, \Delta'')$ and $(1, \Delta''')$ applies.

This shows the stated claim for the accepted and the reset language.   □

Increasing the number of switch transitions eventually results in a switching automaton, where certain states can only be reached *via* switch transitions. For a binary language this situation is reached if $\kappa = n+1$. In this case not all states in the constructed equivalent ordinary finite automaton remain reachable—see Fig. 4. Let $t_\ell = (p_\ell, a, q, q_\ell)$ and $t_r = (p_r, b, q, q_r)$. Then state q is only reachable

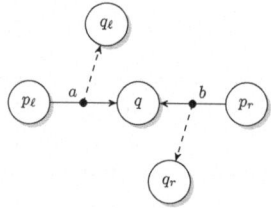

Fig. 4. Principle situation for a state q in the switching automaton to induce unreachable states with first component q in the constructed equivalent DFA.

in the switching automaton if $\Delta(t_\ell) = 0$ or $\Delta(t_r) = 0$. Hence, for a state (q, Δ) to become reachable in the constructed DFA, the above given condition must be satisfied, i.e., $\Delta(t_\ell) = 0$ or $\Delta(t_r) = 0$. Thus, instead of four states having q as a first component only three states with first component q are possibly reachable. Since several of these scenarios may overlap the counting of reachable states is involved and left for further investigation.

4   Computational Complexity

Here, we prove a few results on the computation complexity of some standard problems from formal language theory if the input is a switching finite automaton. For some of the presented results we use a close connection between regular like expressions with squaring and switching automata. Recall, that for every regular expression one can construct an equivalent NFA by, e.g., the Thompson construction [11]. Thompson's construction amounts to the recursive connection of sub-automata *via* ε-transitions—see Figs. 5 and 6. These sub-automata are connected in parallel for the union, in series for the concatenation, and in an iterative fashion for the Kleene star. This yields an NFA with ε-transitions with at most $2n$ states and at most $4n$ transitions, where n is the size of the regular

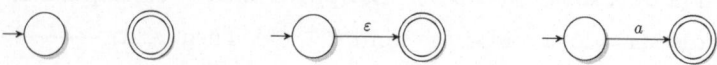

Fig. 5. The NFA sub-automata for the three basic cases of regular expressions: (left) $R = \emptyset$, (middle) $R = \varepsilon$, and (right) $R = a$.

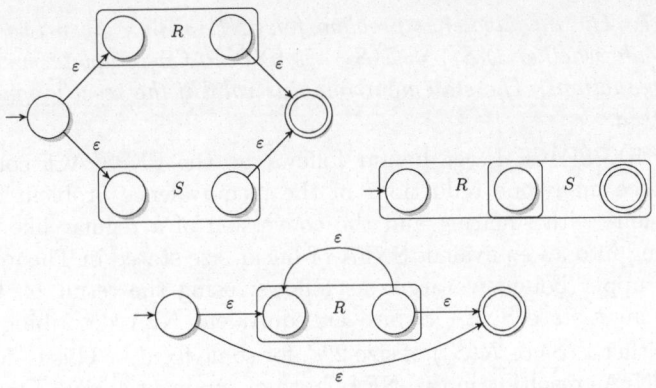

Fig. 6. The NFA sub-automata for the (top left) union $R + S$, (top right) concatenation $R \cdot S$, and (lower mid) Kleene star R^* of regular expressions.

expression. Hence, the equivalent NFA is of size at most $O(n)$. We utilize this construction for regular like expressions with squaring. To this end we only have to explain how the squaring operation is implemented for a regular expression R^2 on a switching automaton—see Fig. 7. It is straight forward, that this construction results in an equivalent SNFA, regardless whether we consider the accepted or the reset language. Here, the same upper bounds as for the original Thompson construction for ordinary regular expressions applies. Hence, the SNFA is of size at most $O(n)$, where n is now the size of the regular expression with squaring. Thus, we can summarize:

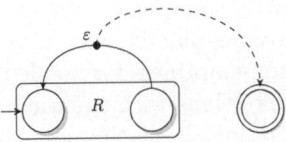

Fig. 7. The recursive construction for the squaring operation R^2 on a regular like expression R.

Theorem 6. *Let R be a regular like expression with squaring of size n. Then there is an equivalent SNFA $\mathcal{S}$, i.e., $\mathcal{L}(R) = \mathcal{L}(\mathcal{S})$ of size at most $O(n)$ that can be constructed by a deterministic logspace bounded Turing machine. The same holds true if one considers the reset language $\mathcal{R}(\mathcal{S})$.*   □

Now we are ready to prove the following result, which is based on the inequivalence problem for regular expressions with squaring that is known to be **EXPSPACE**-complete [10]—recall that **EXPSPACE** is an abbreviation for the complexity class $\bigcup_k \mathsf{NSPACE}(2^{n^k})$:

Theorem 7. *The inequivalence problem for SNFAs, i.e., given two SNFAs S_1 and S_2, decide whether $\mathcal{L}(S_1) \neq \mathcal{L}(S_2)$, is* EXPSPACE-*complete w.r.t. logspace many-one reductions. The statement remains valid if the reset language is considered instead.*

Proof. The EXPSPACE lower bound follows by the EXPSPACE-completeness w.r.t. logspace many-one reductions of the inequivalence problem for regular like expressions with squaring and the conversion of a regular like expression with squaring into an equivalent SNFA of linear size stated in Theorem 6.

For the upper bound we argue as follows: using the result of Theorem 3 we convert an n-state SNFA S into an equivalent NFA describing the same language (either $\mathcal{L}(S)$ or $\mathcal{R}(S)$) of size 2^{n^k}, for some fixed k. This is done for the two input SNFAs resulting in two NFAs both of exponential size. Then checking inequivalence on the exponential size NFAs can be done within (deterministic) polynomial space with respect to the actual input length, which is exponential. Hence, the whole algorithm runs in exponential space. Thus, inequivalence for SNFAs can be verified in EXPSPACE. This proves the stated claim.   □

By similar arguments as in the previous proof we find also EXPSPACE-completeness for the non-universality problem for SNFAs (also known as the non-emptiness complementation problem). Recall that the non-universality problem for regular like expressions with squaring is EXPSPACE-complete [10].

Theorem 8. *The non-universality problem for SNFAs, that is, given a SNFA S with input alphabet Σ, decide whether $\mathcal{L}(S) \neq \Sigma^*$, is* EXPSPACE-*complete w.r.t. logspace many-one reductions. The statement remains valid if the reset language is considered instead.*   □

It is worth mentioning that the non-emptiness problem for regular expressions and regular like expressions with squaring belongs to ALOGTIME. This is seen as follows: we first show that both regular expression problems are equivalent w.r.t. AC^0-reductions. Obviously non-emptiness for regular expressions reduces to non-emptiness for regular like expressions with squaring. Conversely, consider a regular like expression with squaring. Replacing all squaring operations R^2 by R, for each subexpression R results in an ordinary regular expression that describes a non-empty set if and only if the original regular like expression with squaring refers to a non-empty set. This is based on the obvious fact that $L(R^2) \neq \emptyset$ if and only if $L(R) \neq \emptyset$, for any regular (like) expression. It remains to show that non-emptiness for regular expressions belongs to ALOGTIME. To this end we construct a Boolean formula f_R for a regular expression R as follows: if $R = \emptyset$ ($R = \varepsilon$ or $R = a$, respectively), then the Boolean formula f_R is 0 (1, respectively). In case $R = S + T$ ($R = S \cdot T$, $R = (S^*)$, respectively), then inductively we have Boolean formulas f_S and f_T for S and T, and we define the Boolean formula f_R for R to be $f_S \vee f_T$ ($f_S \wedge f_T$, 1, respectively). Then it is easy to see that the regular expression R satisfies $L(R) \neq \emptyset$ if and only if the Boolean formula value problem for the constructed formula f_R for R has a positive answer, i.e., the formula f_R evaluates to 1. Since the Boolean formula value problem belongs to ALOGTIME by [1], the stated result follows.

Theorem 9. *The non-emptiness problem for regular expressions and regular expressions with squaring both belong to* ALOGTIME.   □

When considering switching automata the situation completely changes. For these devices the non-emptiness problem becomes NP-hard.

Theorem 10. *The non-emptiness problem for SNFAs, that is, given a SNFA $\mathcal{S}$ with input alphabet Σ, decide whether $\mathcal{L}(\mathcal{S}) \neq \emptyset$, is* NP-*hard and contained in* PSPACE. *The* PSPACE *upper bound remains valid if the reset language is considered instead.*

The reader may have noticed, that the above statement on switching automata does not say anything about a lower bound for the reset language. The only lower bound that we know at the moment is the lower bound for the problem in question for NFAs, which is NL-hardness—see, e.g., [4]. Whether the proof given below also generalizes to the case of reset languages is left open.

Proof. The containment in PSPACE is seen as follows: Let $\mathcal{S}$ be an SNFA. We use the fact that PSPACE = NPSPACE by Savitch [9] to guess a word that is accepted by $\mathcal{S}$ on the fly. During this computation, we do not store the guessed word, but only the current configuration consisting of the active state and the status Δ of the switch transitions. Hence, we only use polynomial space. In the case of $\mathcal{L}(\mathcal{S})$ we return yes as soon as we reach an accepting configuration; in the case of $\mathcal{R}(\mathcal{S})$ we return yes if we reach an accepting reset configuration.

It remains to show NP-hardness for the problem in question. To this end we reduce an NP-complete variant of 3SAT to the non-emptiness problem for SNFAs. Let

$$F = C_1 \wedge C_2 \wedge \ldots \wedge C_m$$

be a Boolean formula in 3CNF with n variables $x_1, x_2, \ldots, x_n$ and m clauses, where each variable appears at most four times—this problem remains NP-complete as shown in [12]. The main ingredient for the SNFA construction is a gate-keeper sub-automaton, which is depicted in Fig. 8. We assume that all transitions of the whole SNFA are labeled by the letter a; thus the automaton is unary. The gate-keeper sub-automaton can be traversed from left to right. Then the switch transition turns and it cannot be traversed from left to right anymore. Instead a traversal from top to bottom is possible. If it is traversed

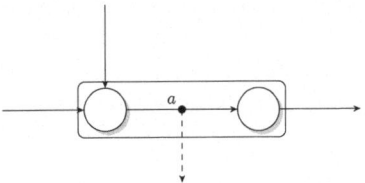

Fig. 8. Gate-keeper sub-automaton. The first and the last state of the gate-keeper are shown on the left and right, respectively.

in this way, the switch transition turns again, and traversal from left to right is possible again (this last behavior will not be used by our construction). The name gate-keeper comes from the behavior of this sub-automaton since the first pass from left to right opens the "door," i.e., the traversal from top to bottom, and it will be closed after a passage through it. Next we arrange four gate-keeper sub-automata in left to right fashion by identifying the last state of a gate-keeper sub-automaton with the first state of the next gate-keeper. In this way we get four doors aligned, numbered from left to right by 1 up to 4, which can be opened by a single pass from left to right. Let us call this sub-automaton a door-hallway. Then we construct for every variable x_i, for $1 \leq i \leq n$, a sub-automaton that uses a nondeterministic state that chooses between two door-hallways, one at the top and the other at the bottom. The last states in both door-hallways are identified and connected to a state, which has a switch transition that continues to the right and switches to a dead state. The schematic drawing of this sub-automaton is shown in Fig. 9—here the door entries and exits are not shown.   If the upper

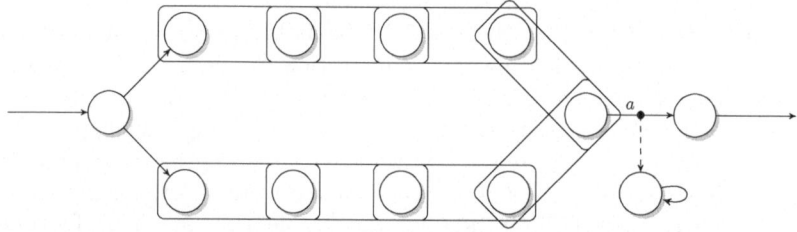

Fig. 9. Schematic drawing of the sub-automaton for a variable x_i, for $1 \leq i \leq n$, constructed from eight gate-keeper sub-automata (four gate-keeper each on top and bottom). The first and last state are shown on the left and right, respectively.

strand of the sub-automaton for variable x_i, for $1 \leq i \leq n$, is used we assume that the variable is set to *true*, while it is set to *false* otherwise, i.e., the lower strand is used. Thus, by combining these variable-sub-automata in sequence, by identifying the last state with the first state of the next sub-automaton, we can simulate the assignment to the variables x_1, x_2, up to x_n in sequence.

Next we have to verify, whether the formula evaluates to *true*. To this end we use sub-automata for the clauses C_i, for $1 \leq i \leq m$, which are arranged in sequence. Let $C_i = (\ell_{i,1} \vee \ell_{i,2} \vee \ell_{i,3})$ be a clause with literals $\ell_{i,j}$, for $1 \leq j \leq 3$. The sub-automaton for this clause consists of two states (first and last state) that are connected by the transitions as follows: the first state is nondeterministic and three transitions go to the corresponding entries of the doors in the appropriate variable sub-automaton in the way that whenever $\ell_{i,j} = x_k$ ($\ell_{i,j} = \overline{x}_k$, respectively) and it is the rth appearance (from left to right in the formula F) then the transition goes to the entry of the rth door in the top door-hallway (bottom door-hallway, respectively) in the variable sub-automaton responsible for variable x_k. Moreover, the respective door exit is connected to the last state of the appropriate clause C_i sub-automaton. Then it is easy to see that whenever one wants to satisfy a clause with one of its literals, one has to pass trough the corresponding door in the variable sub-automaton, which has to be opened in the first pass trough these sub-automata. If the door is closed, then one passes trough the whole door-hallway until one reaches the last switch transition in the variable sub-automaton that points to the non-accepting sink. In this way, one can check whether a particular clause C_i is satisfied by the previously chosen assignment of the variables.

Finally, non-used door exits, regardless of whether these exits are in the top or bottom door-hallway are connected to the non-accepting sink state. Moreover, the last state of the clause sub-automaton responsible for C_m is made accepting. This completes the construction of the SNFA for the formula F. It is easy to see that this SNFA can be made deterministic (and complete) by using different letters for the nondeterministic choices.

The construction of the SNFA can be done by a deterministic logspace bounded Turing machine, and it is easy to see by the above description that the formula F is satisfiable if and only if the language accepted by the SNFA is non-empty. Therefore, the non-emptiness problem for language acceptance of SNFAs is NP-hard.   □

For the next problem we have a similar situation as in the previous statement. The upper bound follows along similar lines as in the proof above, and the lower bound is immediate, since the word that witnesses the non-emptiness of the given SNFA is unary and can be chosen as a^n, where n is the number of states of the constructed SNFA. Thus, we have the following result:

Theorem 11. *The membership problem for SNFAs, i.e., given a SNFA S and a word w, decide whether $w \in \mathcal{L}(S)$, is NP-hard and contained in PSPACE. The NP-hardness holds even for unary SNFAs, and the PSPACE upper bound remains valid if the reset language is considered instead.*   □

Let us summarize our findings on the computational complexity of the considered problems on SNFAs in Table 1. For comparison reasons also results for NFAs, regular expressions, and regular expressions with squaring are listed. For some of these results see, e.g., [3,4,7,10].

Table 1. Computational complexity results of some standard problems for NFAs, SNFAs (reset and accepted language), regular expressions, and regular expressions with squaring. If not otherwise stated, an entry indicates a completeness result; otherwise upper and/or lower bounds are given. Here, LOGCFL refers to the class of languages that are reducible to context-free languages *via* deterministic logspace many-one reductions.

	NFA	SNFA	regex	regex^2
non-emptiness	NL	NL (reset) $\Big\}$ $\leq \cdot \in$ PSPACE	$\cdot \in$ ALOGTIME	
membership		NP (accept)	NL	NL $\leq \cdot \in$ LOGCFL
non-universality	PSPACE	EXPSPACE	PSPACE	EXPSPACE
inequivalence				

5 Conclusions

We have introduced switching automata as a natural generalization of ordinary finite automata and studied them from a descriptional and computational complexity point of view. In this way we have obtained a series of interesting results on a device that may be exponentially more succinct than ordinary finite state devices. Nevertheless, there are fundamental problems that remain open such as for instance, the role of spontaneous switch transitions w.r.t. the descriptional and computational complexity. Moreover, also the exact relation between the accepted language of an SNFA and the reset language remains open for the two studied perspectives. This question is also open for SDFAs. In particular, are computational complexity problems defined for SDFAs easier than those for SNFAs? We think that SNFAs or SDFAs are a natural host for a variety of interesting and challenging problems that are worth being investigated further.

References

1. Buss, S.R.: The Boolean formula value problem is in ALOGTIME. In: Proceedings of the 19th Annual ACM Symposium on Theory of Computing, pp. 123–131. ACM, New York City (1987). https://doi.org/10.1145/28395.28409
2. Holzer, M., Kutrib, M.: Automata that may change their mind. In: Freund, R., Hospodár, M., Jirásková, G., Pighizzini, G. (eds.) Proceedings of the 10th International Workshop on Non-Classical Models of Automata and Applications, vol. 332, pp. 83–98 in books@ocg.at, Österreichische Computer Gesellschaft, Košice, Slovakia (2018)
3. Hunt, H.B., III.: Observations on the complexity of regular expressions problems. J. Comput. Syst. Sci. **19**, 222–236 (1979). https://doi.org/10.1016/0022-0000(79)90002-3
4. Jiang, T., Ravikumar, B.: A note on the space complexity of some decision problems for finite automata. Inform. Process. Lett. **40**, 25–31 (1991). https://doi.org/10.1016/S0020-0190(05)80006-7
5. Kleene, S.C.: Representation of events in nerve nets and finite automata. In: Shannon, C.E., McCarthy, J. (eds.) Automata Studies, Annals of Mathematics Studies, vol. 34, pp. 2–42. Princeton University Press (1956)

6. Papadimitriou, C.H.: Computational Complexity. Addison-Wesley (1994)
7. Petersen, H.: The membership problem for regular expressions with intersection is complete in LOGCFL. In: Alt, H., Ferreira, A. (eds.) Proceedings of the 19th International Symposium on Theoretical Aspects of Computer Science. LNCS, vol. 2285, pp. 513–522. Springer, Antibes - Juan les Pins, France (2002). https://doi.org/10.1007/3-540-45841-7_42
8. Rabin, M.O., Scott, D.: Finite automata and their decision problems. IBM J. Res. Dev. **3**, 114–125 (1959). https://doi.org/10.1147/rd.32.0114
9. Savitch, W.J.: Relationships between nondeterministic and deterministic tape complexities. J. Comput. Syst. Sci. **4**(2), 177–192 (1970). https://doi.org/10.1016/S0022-0000(70)80006-X
10. Stockmeyer, L.J., Meyer, A.R.: Word problems requiring exponential time. In: Proceedings of the 5th Symposium on Theory of Computing, pp. 1–9 (1973). https://doi.org/10.1145/800125.804029
11. Thompson, K.: Regular expression search algorithm. Commun. ACM **11**(6), 419–422 (1968). https://doi.org/10.1145/363347.363387
12. Tovey, C.A.: A simplified NP-complete satisfiability problem. Discret. Appl. Math. **8**, 85–89 (1984). https://doi.org/10.1016/0166-218X(84)90081-7

Computing Threshold Circuits with Void Reactions in Step Chemical Reaction Networks

Rachel Anderson[1], Alberto Avila[1], Bin Fu[1], Timothy Gomez[2], Elise Grizzell[1], Aiden Massie[1], Gourab Mukhopadhyay[1], Adrian Salinas[1], Robert Schweller[1], Evan Tomai[3], and Tim Wylie[1(✉)]

[1] University of Texas Rio Grande Valley, Edinburg, TX 78539-2999, USA
timothy.wylie@utrgv.edu
[2] Massachusetts Institute of Technology, Cambridge, MA 02139, USA
[3] University of Texas Dallas, Richardson, TX 75080-3021, USA

Abstract. We introduce a new model of *step* Chemical Reaction Networks (step CRNs), motivated by the step-wise addition of materials in standard lab procedures. Step CRNs have ordered reactants that transform into products via reaction rules over a series of steps. We study an important subset of weak reaction rules, *void* rules, in which chemical species may only be deleted but never changed. We demonstrate the capabilities of these simple limited systems to simulate threshold circuits and compute functions using various configurations of rule sizes and step constructions, and prove that without steps, void rules are incapable of these computations, which further motivates the step model. Additionally, we prove the coNP-completeness of verifying if a given step CRN computes a function, holding even for $O(1)$ step systems.

1 Introduction

Chemical Reaction Networks (CRNs) are one of the most established and longest studied models of self-assembly [6,7]. CRNs originate in attempting to model chemical interactions as molecular species that react and create products from the reaction. This can be represented as an original number of each species and a set of replacement rules. The fundamental nature of the model is evident in the independent inception of equivalent models in multiple areas of research through other motivations [13], such as Vector Addition Systems (VASs) [19] and Petri-Nets [21]. Further, Population Protocols [3] are a restricted version where the number of input and output elements are each two.

Step CRNs. We propose and investigate an important but straightforward extension to the CRN model (and VASs, Petri-Nets) motivated by the desire to reflect standard laboratory and medical practices (and multi-step distributed processes). The *Step* CRN model augments the CRN model with a sequence of

This research was supported in part by National Science Foundation Grant CCF-2329918.

discrete steps where an additional specified amount of chemical species is combined with the existing CRN after running the system to completion. Our goal is to explore the computational power of Step CRNs using highly restricted classes of CRN rules that would otherwise be computationally weak. In particular, we consider the problem of implementing the powerful, computationally universal class of *Threshold Circuits* (*TC*) using only *void* rules, a class of rules that are provably weak without a step augmentation (Theorem 3).

Void Rules. We study the computational power of Step CRNs under an extremely simple subset of CRN rules termed *void* rules [1]. General CRN rules are powerful since they allow the removal, addition, and replacement of species. Impressively, these rules have successful experimental implementations using DNA strand replacement mechanisms [26]. However, implementing this level of generality requires sophisticated, and large, DNA complexes that incur practical errors and constitute one of the primary hurdles limiting the scalable implementation of molecular computing schemes [11,28].

Here, we focus on *void* rules, a class of rules that utilize only the *removal* feature of CRN rules. Note that by removal, we simply mean that both elements can no longer be used, which may be that they become some species that is easily filtered. While simpler, the class of pure void rulse is unable to compute even simple functions such as the CNOT gate (Theorem 3). We show that void rules become computationally powerful in the step model with just tri-molecular or bi-molecular interactions. Specifically, that *TC*s can be simulated with void rules using a number of steps linear in the circuit's depth.

Our Contributions. Table 1 has an overview of the main results of this paper beyond the introduction of the model and simulation definitions. The most important results are the ability to simulate the class of *TC* by simulating AND, OR, NOT, and MAJORITY gates through a restrictive definition of simulation while only using small void rules.

In Sect. 2, we define Step Chemical Reaction Networks and what it means to compute a function. Following, in Sect. 3, we show how to simulate the class of *TC* with void rules of size $(3,0)$ using $O(D \log f)$ steps, where D is the depth of the circuit and f denotes the maximum fan-out of the circuit. In Sect. 4, we achieve the same result using both $(2,0)$ and $(2,1)$ rules and a slightly more efficient step complexity of $O(D)$. We then use exclusively $(2,1)$ rules to achieve this same result by adding a factor of $\log F_{maj}$ to the steps, where F_{maj} is the maximum fan-in of majority gates. In Sect. 5, we show there exist functions that require a logarithmic number of steps when restricted to constant reaction size, as well as the existence of $O(1)$-depth threshold circuits of fan-out f that require $\Omega(\log f)$ steps, which matches the $O(D \log f)$ upper bound for $(3,0)$ circuits. Finally, we show that it is coNP-complete to know whether a function can be strictly simulated by a step CRN system.

1.1   Previous Work

Computation in Chemical Reaction Networks. Stochastic Chemical Reaction Networks are only Turing-complete with the possibility for error [25] while

Table 1. Summary of n-bit circuit simulation results. D is the depth of the circuit, W is the width, G is the number of gates in a circuit or number of operators in a formula, F_{out} is the max fan-out, F_{maj} is the max fan-in of majority gates, and **TC** is Threshold Circuits. The k-CNOT is a k fan-in generalization of a Controlled NOT gate. Rule $(c, 0)$ means any size with integer constant $c > 0$.

Function Computation					
Rules	Species	Steps	Simulation	Family	Ref
$(3,0)$	$O(\min(W^2, GF_{out}))$	$O(D \log F_{out})$	Strict	**TC** Circuits	Theorem 1
$(2,0)(2,1)$	$O(G)$	$O(D)$	Strict	**TC** Circuits	Theorem 2
$(2,1)$	$O(G)$	$O(D \log F_{maj})$	Strict	**TC** Circuits	Corollary 1
$(c,0)$	any	$\Omega(\log k)$	Strict	k-CNOT	Theorem 3

Strict Function Verification			
Rules	Steps	Complexity	Ref
$(3,0)$	$O(1)$	coNP-complete	Theorem 6

error-free stochastic Chemical Reaction Networks can compute precisely the set of semilinear functions [5, 12]. CRNs have also recently been shown to be experimentally viable through DNA Strand Displacement (DSD) systems [26] with several CRN to DSD compilers now existing.

Boolean Circuits. Using molecules for information storage and Boolean logic is a deep field of study. Here, we show a few highlights, starting with one of the first discussions in 1988 [9] and an initial presentation of circuits with CRNs in 1991 [17]. Since then, the area has been extensively studied in CRNs and related models [8, 10, 13, 18, 22, 23]. Numerous gates have been built experimentally and proposed theoretically such as the AND [23, 30], OR [14, 23], NOT [10], XOR [10, 30], NAND [13, 29], NOR [10], Parity [16], and Majority [4, 20]. Symmetric boolean functions of n variables such as Majority have been found to have a circuit depth of $O(\log n)$ when implemented by AND, OR and NOT gates [24].

Void Rules. The reachability problem, with systems of only void rules in proper CRNs, was studied in [1]. Previous studies had included void rules as a part of their systems, but were never studied exclusively. They can also be considered a subcategory of the broader concept of the extinction of rules and species in a system as referred to in [29].

Mixing Systems. Another generalization of CRNs that is closely related to the step model is I/O CRNs [15], where additional inputs can be added at timed intervals. Still, those inputs are read-only in the system (used exclusively as catalysts). Step CRNs generalize I/O CRNs as the inputs are not read-only and are rate-independent, unlike I/O CRNs.

2   Preliminaries

Basics. Let $\Lambda = \{\lambda_1, \lambda_2, \cdots, \lambda_{|\Lambda|}\}$ denote some ordered alphabet of *species*. A configuration C over Λ is a length-$|\Lambda|$ vector of integers where the ith entry $C[i]$ denotes the number of copies of species λ_i. A *rule* or *reaction* is represented as an ordered pair of configuration vectors $R = (R_r, R_p)$. The *application* vector of R is $R_a = R_p - R_r$, which shows the net change in species counts after applying rule R once. For a configuration C and rule R, we say R is applicable to C if $C[i] \geq R_r[i]$ for all $1 \leq i \leq |\Lambda|$, and we define the *application* of R to C as the configuration $C' = C + R_a$. For a set of rules Γ, a configuration C, and rule $R \in \Gamma$ applicable to C that produces $C' = C + R_a$, we say $C \to_{\Gamma}^{1} C'$, a relation denoting that C can transition to C' by way of a single rule application from Γ. We further use the notation $C \to_{\Gamma}^{*} C'$ to signify the transitive closure of $\to_{\Gamma}^{1}$ and say C' is *reachable* from C under Γ, i.e., C' can be reached by applying a sequence of applicable rules from Γ to initial configuration C. Here, we use the following notation to depict a rule $R = (R_r, R_p)$: $R_r[1]\lambda_1 + \cdots + R_r[|\Lambda|]\lambda_{|\Lambda|} \to R_p[1]\lambda_1 + \cdots + R_p[|\Lambda|]\lambda_{|\Lambda|}$. For example, a rule turning two copies of species H and one copy of species O into one copy of species W would be written as $2H + O \to W$.

Definition 1 (Discrete Chemical Reaction Network). *A discrete chemical reaction network (CRN) is an ordered pair* (Λ, Γ) *where* Λ *is an ordered alphabet of species, and* Γ *is a set of rules over* Λ.

An initial configuration I and CRN (Λ, Γ) are together said to be *bounded* if a terminal configuration is guaranteed to be reached within some finite number of rule applications starting from configuration I. We denote the set of reachable configurations of a CRN as $REACH_{I,\Lambda,\Gamma}$. A configuration is called *terminal* with respect to a CRN (Λ, Γ) if no rule R can be applied to it. We define the subset of reachable configurations that are terminal as $TERM_{I,\Lambda,\Gamma}$.

Definition 2 (Void rules). *A rule* $R = (R_r, R_p)$ *is a* void *rule if the application vector* $R_p - R_r$ *has no positive entries and at least one negative entry. We say its a* true void *rule if the* R_p *vector is the* 0 *vector, and* catalytic *otherwise.*

Definition 3 (Volume and Rule Size). *The size/volume of a configuration vector* C *is* $\text{volume}(C) = \sum_{i=1}^{|\Lambda|} C[i]$. *A rule* $R = (R_r, R_p)$ *is said to be a size-* (i, j) *rule if* $(i, j) = (\text{volume}(R_r), \text{volume}(R_p))$. *A reaction is* trimolecular *if* $i = 3$ *and* bimolecular *if* $i = 2$.

2.1 Step CRNs

A step CRN is an augmentation of a basic CRN in which a sequence of additional copies of some system species are added after a terminal configuration is reached. Formally, a step CRN of k steps is an ordered pair $((\Lambda, \Gamma), (s_0, s_1, s_2, \cdots, s_{k-1}))$, where the first element of the pair is a normal CRN (Λ, Γ), and the second is a sequence of length-$|\Lambda|$ vectors of non-negative integers denoting how many copies of each species to add at each step. Figure 1 shows an example system.

Given a step CRN, we define the set of reachable configurations after each sequential step. To start off, let REACH_1 be the set of reachable configurations of (Λ, Γ) with initial configuration s_0, which we refer to as the set of configurations reachable *after step 1*. Let TERM_1 be the subset of configurations in REACH_1 that are terminal. Note that after a single step we have a normal CRN, i.e., 1-step

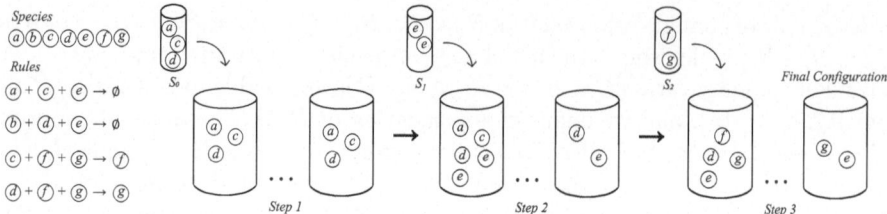

Fig. 1. An example step CRN system. The test tubes show the species added at each step and the system with those elements added. The CRN species and void rule-set are shown on the left.

CRNs are just normal CRNs with initial configuration s_0. For the second step, we consider any configuration in $TERM_1$ combined with s_1 as a possible starting configuration and define $REACH_2$ to be the union of all reachable configurations from each possible starting configuration attained by adding s_1 to a configuration in $TERM_1$. We then define $TERM_2$ as the subset of configurations in $REACH_2$ that are terminal. Similarly, define $REACH_i$ to be the union of all reachable sets attained by using initial configuration s_{i-1} plus any element of $TERM_{i-1}$, and let $TERM_i$ denote the subset of these configurations that are terminal. The set of reachable configurations for a k-step CRN is the set $REACH_k$, and the set of terminal configurations is $TERM_k$. A classical CRN can be represented as a step CRN with $k = 1$ steps and an initial configuration of $I = s_0$.

Our definitions assume only the terminal configurations of a given step are passed on to seed the subsequent step. This makes sense if we assume we are dealing with *bounded* systems, as this represents simply waiting long enough for all configurations to reach a terminal state before proceeding to the next step. In this paper we only consider bounded void-rule systems.

2.2   Computing Functions in Step CRNs

Here, we define what it means for a step CRN to compute a function $f(x_1, \cdots, x_n) = (y_1, \cdots, y_m)$ that maps n-bit strings to m-bit strings. For each input bit, we denote two separate species types, one representing bit 0, and the other bit 1. We add one copy for each bit to encode an input n-bit string. Similarly, each output bit has two representatives (for 0 and 1), and we say the step CRN computes function f if for any given n-bit input $x_1, \cdots, x_n$, the system results in a final terminal configuration whose output species encode the string $f(x_1, \cdots, x_n)$. For a fixed function f, the set of species s_i added at each step is fixed for all inputs to prevent encoding the output of the function within the configurations s_i.

Input-Strict Step CRN Computing. Given a Boolean function $f(x_1, \cdots, x_n) = (y_1, \cdots, y_m)$ that maps a string of n bits to a string of m bits, we define the computation of f with a step CRN. An input-strict step CRN computer is a tuple $C_s = (S, X, Y)$ where $S = ((\Lambda, \Gamma), (s_0, s_1, \cdots, s_{k-1}))$ is a step CRN, and $X = ((x_1^F, x_1^T), \cdots, (x_n^F, x_n^T))$ and $Y = ((y_1^F, y_1^T), \cdots, (y_m^F, y_m^T))$

are sequences of ordered-pairs with each $x_i^F, x_i^T, y_j^F, y_j^T \in \Lambda$. Given an n-input bit string $b = b_1, \cdots, b_n$, configuration $X(b)$ is defined as the configuration over Λ obtained by including one copy of x_i^F only if $b_i = 0$ and one copy of x_i^T only if $b_i = 1$ for each bit b_i. We consider this input to be strict, as opposed to allowing multiple copies of each input bit species. The corresponding step CRN $(\Lambda, \Gamma, (s_0 + X(b), \cdots, s_{k-1}))$ is obtained by adding $X(b)$ to s_0 in the first step, which conceptually represents the system programmed with specific input b.

An input-strict step CRN computer *computes* function f if, for all n-bit strings b and for all terminal configurations of $(\Lambda, \Gamma, (s_0 + X(b), \cdots, s_{k-1}))$, the terminal configuration contains at least 1 copy of y_j^F and 0 copies of y_j^T if the jth bit of $f(b)$ is 0, and at least 1 copy of y_j^T and 0 copies of y_j^F if the jth bit of $f(b)$ is 1, for all j from 1 to m.

We use the term *strict* to denote requiring exactly one copy of each bit species. See [2] for a recent consideration of non-strict computation that utilizes bimolecular reactions. Here, we only consider input-strict computation, so we use input-strict and strict interchangeably.

Relation to CRN Computers. Previous models of CRN computers considered functions over large domains such as the positive integers. Due to the infinite domain, the input to such systems cannot be bounded. As such, the CRN computers shown in [12] define the input in terms of the volume of some input species. In these scenarios, CRN computers are limited to computing semi-linear functions. Here, we instead focus on computing n-bit functions, and instead encode the input per bit with potentially unique species. This is a model more similar to the PSPACE computer shown in [27].

2.3   Boolean and Threshold Circuits

A Boolean circuit on n variables $x_1, x_2, \cdots, x_n$ is a directed, acyclic multi-graph. The vertices of the graph are generally referred to as *gates*. The in-degree and out-degree of a gate are called the *fan-in* and *fan-out* of the gate respectively. The fan-in 0 gates (*source* gates) are labeled from $x_1, x_2, \cdots, x_n$, or labeled by constants 0 or 1. Each non-source gate is labeled with a function name, such as AND, OR, or NOT. Given an assignment of Boolean values to variables $x_1, x_2, \cdots, x_n$, each gate in the circuit can be assigned a value by first assigning all source vertices the value matching the labeled constant or labeled variable value and subsequently assigning each gate the value computed by its labeled function on the values of its children. Given a fixed ordering on the output gates, the sequence of bits assigned to the output gates denotes the value computed by the circuit on the given input.

The *depth* of a circuit is the longest path from a source vertex to an output vertex. Here, we focus on circuits that consist of AND, OR, NOT, and MAJORITY gates with arbitrary fan-in. We refer to circuits that use these gates as *threshold circuits* (TC).

Notation. When discussing a Boolean circuit, we use the following variables to denote the properties of the circuit: Let D denote the circuit's depth, G the number of gates in the circuit, W the circuit's width, F_{out} the maximum fan-out of any gate in the circuit, F_{in} the maximum fan-in, and F_{maj} the maximum fan-in of any majority gate within the circuit.

3   Computation of Threshold Circuits with (3, 0) Rules

Here, we introduce a step CRN system construction with only true void rules that can compute TCs. In other words, given any TC and some truth assignment to the input variables, we can construct a step CRN with only true void rules that computes the same output as the circuit.

This section focuses on step CRNs consisting of $(3,0)$ rules. Section 3.1 shows how to compute individual logic gates, and we give an example construction of a circuit in Sect. 3.2. We then present the general construction of computing TCs by two different methods, differing in the number of species needed based on the fan-out and width of the circuit. This results in Theorem 1, which states that TCs can be strictly computed, even with unbounded fan-out, with $O(\min(W^2, GF_{out}))$ species, $O(D \log F_{out})$ steps, and $O(W)$ volume.

3.1   Computing Logic Gates

Indexing. The number of steps to compute an individual depth level of a circuit varies between 2–8 steps depending on the gates and wiring of the specified circuit. To convert a circuit into a $(3,0)$ step CRN system, we *index* the wires (input and output) at each level of the circuit in order to ensure the species is input to the correct gate. An example circuit with bit/wire indexing is shown in Fig. 3c. At each level, we call the indices of the inputs of gates the *input indices*, and the indices of the output of each gate the *gate indices*. Note that the index numbers may need to change along the wire, or change due to fan-out/fan-in (see Fig. 3c). This is assisted by species of the form $t_{j \to i}$ that map an input index of j to a gate index of i.

Bit Representation. The input bits of a binary gate are represented in a step CRN with $(3,0)$ rules by the species x_n^b, where $n \in \mathbb{N}$ and $b \in \{T, F\}$. n represents the bit's index (based on the ordering of all bits into the gates) and b represents its truth value. Let f_i^{in} be the set of all the indices of input bits fanning into a gate at index i (gate indices). Let f_i^{out} be the set of all indices of the output bits fanning out of a gate at index i.

The output bits of a gate are represented by the species $y_{n,g}^b$, where n is the output bit's index (input index of the next level) and g denotes the gate type $g \in \{B, A, O, N, M\}$ (BUFFER, AND, OR, NOT, and MAJORITY). For example, the outputs of an AND gate, an OR gate, and a NOT gate at index n are represented by the species $y_{n,A}^b$, $y_{n,O}^b$, and $y_{n,N}^b$, respectively.

AND/OR Gate. The general process to compute an AND gate (an OR gate is similar) is given in Table 2. First, all input species are converted into a new species $a_{i,g}^b$ (step 1). The species retains truth value b as the original input and

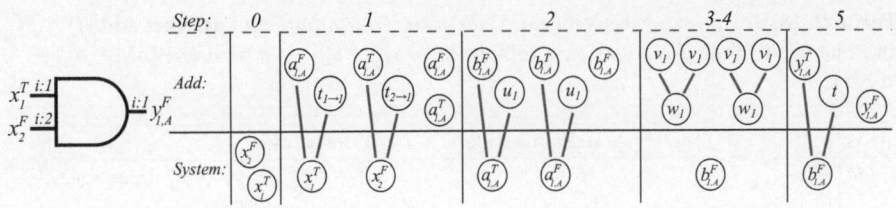

Fig. 2. Example AND gate and steps to compute using $(3,0)$ rules. Note the gate indexing of the wires ($i:1$ and $i:2$) and the input indexing for the next level ($i:1$ since there is only one gate). The process of computing the gate is shown on the right in steps. The new species added at each step are above and the remaining ones are below. The lines show the rules that would be executed during each step. To see the added species and rules in detail, see Table 2.

includes the gate's index and type i and g, respectively. The species $b_{i,g}^b$ is then introduced (step 2), which computes the operation of gate g across all existing species. Any species that do not share the same truth value as the gate's intended output are deleted (step 3–4). The species remaining after the operation are then converted into the correct output species (step 5).

The species u_i, v_i, w_i, and $t_{j\rightarrow i}$, where j is the input index and i is the gate index, are used to assist in removing excess species in certain steps.

AND Example. Consider an AND gate whose gate index is 1 with input bits 1 and 0 as shown in Fig. 2. Here, $|f_i^{in}| = 2$ and the initial configuration consists of the species x_1^T and x_2^F. By Table 2, this gate can be computed in five steps.

1. Two $a_{1,A}^T$, two $a_{1,A}^F$, one $t_{1\rightarrow 1}$, and one $t_{2\rightarrow 1}$ species are added to the system. This converts the two input species of the gate into $a_{1,A}^T$ and $a_{1,A}^F$ (causes all species except $a_{1,A}^T$ and $a_{1,A}^F$ to be deleted).
2. One $b_{1,A}^T$, two $b_{1,A}^F$, and two u_1 species are added. All species except a single $b_{1,A}^F$ are deleted by reactions.
3. Four v_1 species are added to remove excess species. There are none, so no reactions occur.
4. Two w_1 are added to delete excess species. Now, only a $b_{1,A}^F$ species remains.
5. One $y_{1,A}^T$, one $y_{1,A}^F$ and one t species are added. The $b_{1,A}^F$ species cause the $y_{1,A}^T$ and t species to be deleted. The $y_{1,A}^F$ species is the only species remaining, which represents the intended "false" output of the AND gate.

NOT Gate. Table 3 shows the general process to computing NOT gates. To compute a NOT gate, only the output species and species t are added in. In NOT gates specifically, the input species and the output species that share the same truth value b remove each other, leaving the complement of the input species as the remaining and correct output species.

Majority Gate. The majority gate outputs 1 if and only if more than half of its inputs are 1. Otherwise, it returns 0. The general step process is overviewed

Table 2. $(3, 0)$ rules and steps for an AND gate. To compute an OR gate, add $|f_i^{in}| \cdot b_{i,g}^T$ and one $b_{i,g}^F$ in Step 2 instead, and replace $w_i + a_{i,g}^F + b_{i,g}^F \to \emptyset$ with $w_i + a_{i,g}^T + b_{i,g}^T \to \emptyset$ in Step 4.

Steps	Relevant Rules	Description
1 $Add\ \|f_i^{in}\| \cdot a_{i,g}^T$ $\|f_i^{in}\| \cdot a_{i,g}^F$ $\forall j \in f_i^{in} : t_{j \to i}$	$\forall j \in f_i^{in} :$ $x_j^T + a_{i,g}^F + t_{j \to i} \to \emptyset$ $x_j^F + a_{i,g}^T + t_{j \to i} \to \emptyset$	$\forall j \in f_i^{in}$, convert x_j^b input species into $a_{i,g}^b$ species
2 $Add\ b_{i,g}^T$ $\|f_i^{in}\| \cdot b_{i,g}^F$ $\|f_i^{in}\| \cdot u_i$	$u_i + a_{i,g}^T + b_{i,g}^F \to \emptyset$ $u_i + a_{i,g}^F + b_{i,g}^T \to \emptyset$	Keep at least one of the correct output species and delete all incorrect species
3 $Add\ 2\|f_i^{in}\| \cdot v_i$	$u_i + v_i + v_i \to \emptyset$	Delete extra/unwanted species
4 $Add\ \|f_i^{in}\| \cdot w_i$	$w_i + v_i + v_i \to \emptyset$ $w_i + a_{i,g}^F + b_{i,g}^F \to \emptyset$	Delete extra/unwanted species
5 $Add\ y_{i,g}^T,\ y_{i,g}^F,\ t$	$b_{i,g}^T + y_{i,g}^F + t \to \emptyset$ $b_{i,g}^F + y_{i,g}^T + t \to \emptyset$	Convert $b_{i,g}^b$ into the proper output species $y_{i,g}^b$

Table 3. $(3, 0)$ rules and steps for a NOT gate.

Steps	Relevant Rules	Description
1 $Add\ y_{i,N}^T$ $y_{i,N}^F$ $t_{j \to i}$	$y_{i,N}^T + x_j^T + t_{j \to i} \to \emptyset$ $y_{i,N}^F + x_j^F + t_{j \to i} \to \emptyset$	The output species $(y_{i,N}^b)$ that is the complement of the input species (x_j^b) will be the only species remaining

in Table 4. To compute a majority gate, all input species are converted into a new species $a_{i,M}^b$ (step 1). The species retains the same index i and truth value b as the original input. If the fan-in of the majority gate is even, an extra *false* input species is added in. The species $b_{i,M}^b$ is then introduced, which computes the majority operation across all existing species. Any species that represent the minority inputs are deleted (step 2). The species remaining after the operation are converted into the correct output (gate index) species (step 5). The species u_i, v_i, w_i, and $t_{j \to i}$, where j is the input index and i is the gate index, are used to assist in removing excess species in certain steps.

3.2 (3,0) Circuit Example

With the computation of individual gates demonstrated in our system, we now expand these features to computing entire circuits. We begin with a simple example (Fig. 3c) to show the concepts before giving the general construction. The circuit has four inputs: x_1, x_2, x_3, and x_4. At the first depth layer, x_1 fans into a NOT gate and x_2 and x_3 are both fanned into an OR gate. At the next depth level, the output of the OR gate is fanned out twice. One of these outputs, along with the output of the NOT gate, is fanned into an AND gate, while the other and x_4 fans into another AND gate. At the last depth level, both AND gate outputs fan into an OR gate, which computes the final output of the circuit.

Table 4. (3, 0) rules and steps for a majority gate.

Steps	Relevant Rules	Description
1 $Add \mid f_i^{in} \mid \cdot a_{i,M}^T$ $\mid f_i^{in} \mid \cdot a_{i,M}^F$ $\forall j \in f_i^{in} : t_{j \to i}$	$\forall j \in f_i^{in} :$ $x_j^T + a_{i,M}^F + t_{j \to i} \to \emptyset$ $x_j^F + a_{i,M}^T + t_{j \to i} \to \emptyset$	$\forall j \in f_i^{in}$, convert x_j^b input species into $a_{i,M}^b$ species.
2 $Add \lfloor \mid f_i^{in} \mid /2 \rfloor \cdot b_{i,M}^T$ $\lfloor \mid f_i^{in} \mid /2 \rfloor \cdot b_{i,M}^F$ $(\mid f_i^{in} \mid - 1) \cdot u_i$	$u_i + a_{i,M}^T + b_{i,M}^F \to \emptyset$ $u_i + a_{i,M}^F + b_{i,M}^T \to \emptyset$	Adding $\lfloor \mid f_i^{in} \mid /2 \rfloor$ amounts of $b_{i,M}^T$ and $b_{i,M}^F$ species will delete all of the minority species, leaving some amount of the majority species remaining
3 $Add\, 2(\mid f_i^{in} \mid - 1) \cdot v_i$	$u_i + 2v_i \to \emptyset$	Delete extra/unwanted species
4 $Add\, (\mid f_i^{in} \mid - 1) \cdot w_i$	$w_i + 2v_i \to \emptyset$ $w_i + a_{i,M}^T + b_{i,M}^T \to \emptyset$ $w_i + a_{i,M}^F + b_{i,M}^F \to \emptyset$	Delete extra/unwanted species
5 $Add\, y_{i,M}^T$ $y_{i,M}^F$ t	$a_{i,M}^T + y_{i,M}^F + t \to \emptyset$ $a_{i,M}^F + y_{i,M}^T + t \to \emptyset$	Convert $a_{i,M}^b$ into the proper output species $(y_{i,M}^b)$

Table 5 shows how to compute the circuit in Fig. 3c. The primary inputs of the circuit in Fig. 3c are represented by the species in the initial configuration. Step 1 converts the primary inputs into input species. If there was any fan out of the primary inputs, it would be done in this step. Steps 2–6 compute the gates at the first depth level. Steps 7–8 compute the fan out between the first and second depth level. Step 9 converts the outputs of the gates at the first depth level into input species. Steps 10–14 use those inputs to compute the gates at the second depth level. Step 15 converts the outputs of these gates into inputs. Steps 16–20 compute the final gate. Step 21 converts the output of that gate into an input species that represents the solution to the circuit (x_1^F).

3.3 Computing Circuits

For TC circuits with a max fan-out of 2, we show two methods of encoding the gates into the species that yield different results. The method in Lemma 1 reuses the gate species at each level of the circuit, and the method in Lemma 2 assigns unique species for each gate. Theorem 1 is generalized for TC circuits with arbitrary fan-out and combines the results from the Lemmas.

Lemma 1. *Threshold circuits (TC) with a max fan-out of 2 can be strictly computed by a step CRN with only (3,0) rules, $O(W^2)$ species, $O(D)$ steps, and $O(W)$ volume.*

Proof. The initial configuration of the step CRN should consist of one $y_{n,B}^b$ species for each primary input with the appropriate indices and truth values. Section 3.1 explains how to compute TC gates. In order to apply a gate, we convert the outputs at an index i into the inputs for the next gate at index j. To simulate circuits with $O(W^2)$ species, we also must be able to reuse these input,

62   R. Anderson et al.

Table 5. (3,0) rules and steps to compute the circuit in Fig. 3c based on the indexing shown in Fig. 3a. Note that the 'Steps' column shows the number and types of species being added at the beginning of that step.

Initial Configuration: $y_{1,B}^T$ $y_{2,B}^T$ $y_{3,B}^T$ $y_{4,B}^F$

#	Steps	Relevant Rules	#	Steps	Relevant Rules
1	$x_1^T, x_2^T, x_3^T, x_4^T$ $t_{1\to1}, t_{3\to3}$ $x_1^F, x_2^F, x_3^F, x_4^F$ $t_{2\to2}, t_{4\to4}$	$y_{1,B}^T + x_1^F + t_{1\to1} \to \emptyset$ $y_{2,B}^T + x_2^F + t_{2\to2} \to \emptyset$ $y_{3,B}^T + x_3^F + t_{3\to3} \to \emptyset$ $y_{4,B}^F + x_4^T + t_{4\to4} \to \emptyset$	10	$2a_{1,A}^T, 2a_{2,A}^T$ $2a_{1,A}^F, 2a_{2,A}^F$ $t_{2\to1}, t_{4\to2}$ $t_{1\to1}, t_{3\to2}$	$x_1^F + a_{1,A}^T + t_{1\to1} \to \emptyset$ $x_2^T + a_{1,A}^F + t_{2\to1} \to \emptyset$ $x_3^T + a_{2,A}^F + t_{3\to2} \to \emptyset$ $x_4^T + a_{2,A}^F + t_{4\to2} \to \emptyset$
2	$y_{1,N}^T, 2a_{2,O}^T, y_{3,B}^T$ $t_{1\to1}, t_{3\to2}$ $y_{1,N}^F, 2a_{2,O}^F, y_{3,B}^F$ $t_{2\to2}, t_{4\to3}$	$x_1^T + y_{1,N}^T + t_{1\to1} \to \emptyset$ $x_2^T + a_{2,O}^F + t_{2\to2} \to \emptyset$ $x_3^T + a_{2,O}^T + t_{3\to2} \to \emptyset$ $x_4^T + y_{3,B}^T + t_{4\to3} \to \emptyset$	11	$b_{1,A}^T, b_{2,A}^T$ $2u_1, 2b_{1,A}^F$ $2b_{2,A}^F, 2u_2$	$a_{1,A}^T + b_{1,A}^F + u_1 \to \emptyset$ $a_{1,A}^F + b_{1,A}^T + u_1 \to \emptyset$ $a_{2,A}^T + b_{2,A}^F + u_2 \to \emptyset$ $a_{2,A}^F + b_{2,A}^T + u_2 \to \emptyset$
3	$2b_{2,O}^T, 2u_2, b_{2,O}^F$	$a_{2,O}^T + b_{2,O}^F + u_2 \to \emptyset$	12	$4v_1, 4v_2$	No Rules Apply
4	$4v_2$	$u_2 + v_2 + v_2 \to \emptyset$	13	$2w_1, 2w_2$	$w_1 + v_1 + v_1 \to \emptyset$ $w_2 + v_2 + v_2 \to \emptyset$
5	$2w_2$	$w_2 + v_2 + v_2 \to \emptyset$ $w_2 + a_{2,O}^T + b_{2,O}^F \to \emptyset$	14	$y_{1,A}^T, y_{2,A}^T, 2t$ $y_{1,A}^F, y_{2,A}^F$	$b_{1,A}^F + y_{1,A}^T + t \to \emptyset$ $b_{2,A}^F + y_{2,A}^T + t \to \emptyset$
6	$y_{2,O}^T, t, y_{2,O}^F$	$b_{2,O}^T + y_{2,O}^F + t \to \emptyset$	15	$x_1^T, x_2^T, t_{1\to1}$ $x_1^F, x_2^F, t_{2\to2}$	$y_{1,A}^F + x_1^T + t_{1\to1} \to \emptyset$ $y_{2,A}^F + x_2^T + t_{2\to2} \to \emptyset$
7	$y_{2,O}^T, r, y_{2,O}^F$	$y_{2,O}^T + y_{2,O}^F + r \to \emptyset$	16	$2a_{1,O}^T, t_{1\to1}$ $2a_{1,O}^F, t_{2\to1}$	$x_1^F + a_{1,O}^T + t_{1\to1} \to \emptyset$ $x_2^T + a_{1,O}^F + t_{2\to1} \to \emptyset$
8	$2y_{2,O}^T, 2y_{2,O}^F$	$y_{2,O}^F + y_{2,O}^T + y_{2,O}^F \to \emptyset$	17	$2b_{1,O}^T, 2u_1, b_{1,O}^F$	$a_{1,O}^F + b_{1,O}^T + u_1 \to \emptyset$
9	$x_1^T, x_2^T, x_3^T, x_4^T$ $t_{1\to1}, t_{2\to3}$ $x_1^F, x_2^F, x_3^F, x_4^F$ $t_{2\to2}, t_{3\to4}$	$y_{1,N}^F + x_1^T + t_{1\to1} \to \emptyset$ $y_{2,O}^T + x_2^F + t_{2\to2} \to \emptyset$ $y_{2,O}^T + x_3^F + t_{2\to3} \to \emptyset$ $y_{3,B}^F + x_4^T + t_{3\to4} \to \emptyset$	18	$4v_1$	No Rules Apply
			19	$2w_1$	$w_1 + v_1 + v_1 \to \emptyset$
			20	$y_{1,O}^T, t, y_{1,O}^F$	$b_{1,O}^F + y_{1,O}^T + t \to \emptyset$
			21	$x_1^T, t_{1\to1}\ x_1^F$	$y_{1,O}^F + x_1^T + t_{1\to1} \to \emptyset$

Table 6. (3, 0) rules for converting outputs into inputs per circuit level.

Steps	Relevant Rules	Description
1 Add $\forall j \in f_i^{out}$: $x_j^T, x_j^F, t_{i\to j}$	$\forall j \in f_i^{out}$: $y_{i,g}^T + x_j^F + t_{i\to j} \to \emptyset$ $y_{i,g}^F + x_j^T + t_{i\to j} \to \emptyset$	$\forall j \in f_i^{out}$, convert $y_{i,g}^b$ output species into x_j^b input species

output, and helper species. This is accomplished by having unique species for each gate at a given depth level. Figure 3a shows an example indexing.

When reusing species, we add a unique $t_{i\to j}$ species (different from $t_{j\to i}$ used in computing gates) for each gate at index i that converts the output species

Table 7. $(3,0)$ rules and steps for 2-fan out.

Steps	Relevant Rules	Description
1 Add $y_{i,g}^T, y_{i,g}^F, r$	$y_{i,g}^T + y_{i,g}^T + r \rightarrow \emptyset$ $y_{i,g}^T + y_{i,g}^F + r \rightarrow \emptyset$	Flip output's bit (e.g. if species $y_{i,g}^T$ is present, then delete it and preserve $y_{i,g}^F$)
2 Add $2y_{i,g}^T, 2y_{i,g}^F$	$y_{i,g}^T + y_{i,g}^T + y_{i,g}^T \rightarrow \emptyset$ $y_{i,g}^F + y_{i,g}^F + y_{i,g}^F \rightarrow \emptyset$	Delete all copies of the negation of the initial input, and preserve the two copies of the input that were just added

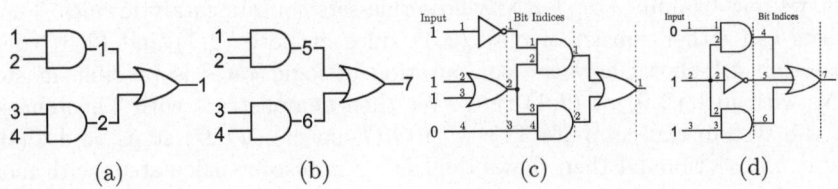

(a)   (b)   (c)   (d)

Fig. 3. (a) Example indexing pattern of wires for the step CRN method using $O(W^2)$ species. (b) Example indexing pattern of wires for the step CRN method using $O(G)$ species. (c) Example circuit (with indexing) for Table 5. (d) Example circuit (with indexing) for Table 10.

into an input species with index j. Converting outputs into inputs is done for all gates at the same depth level. Table 6 shows the steps and rules for this process.

Fan Out. In order to perform a 2-fan out, we create a second copy of the output species that is fanning out. Table 7 shows the steps and rules needed for this duplication. After duplication, the simulation continues as usual. All outputs at the same depth level can be fanned out at the same time using these two steps.

Complexity. The $t_{i \rightarrow j}$ approach uses at most W^2 unique species since $1 \leq i, j \leq W$. All other types of species either have $O(1)$ or $O(W)$ unique species. Thus, a simulation of a circuit with a max fan-out of 2 requires $O(W^2)$ species.

All gates at a given depth level are evaluated at the same time, so a simulation of a circuit with a max fan-out of 2 requires $O(D)$ steps. Additionally, circuits are evaluated one depth level at a time. Thus, at most, a max width amount of input, output, and helper species are added at the same time. All of the input, output, and helper species from previous depth levels get deleted when progressing to the next depth level, so the simulation requires $O(W)$ volume. A constant number of species, steps, and volume are needed to perform a 2-fan out, so a 2-fan out operation does not affect the complexity.

Lemma 2. *Threshold circuits (TC) with a max fan-out of 2 can be strictly computed by a step CRN with only $(3, 0)$ rules, $O(G)$ species, $O(D)$ steps, and $O(W)$ volume.*

Theorem 1. *Threshold circuits (TC) can be strictly computed by a step CRN with only* $(3,0)$ *rules,* $O(\min(W^2, G \cdot F_{out}))$ *species,* $O(D \log F_{out})$ *steps, and* $O(W)$ *volume.*

Proof. This follows by expanding a given TC circuit to a fan-out 2 circuit and by applying the methods of Lemmas 1 and 2.

4   TCs with $(2, 0)$ and $(2, 1)$ Catalyst Rules

Having established computation results with step CRNs using only true void rules, we now examine step CRNs whose rule-sets contain catalytic rules. These rulesets can either consist of only $(2,1)$ rules or both $(2,1)$ and $(2,0)$ rules. Subsection 4.1 shows how the computation of logic gates is possible in step CRNs with just $(2,0)$ or $(2,1)$ rules. We then demonstrate with Theorem 4.3 how the system can compute TCs with $O(G)$ species, $O(D)$ steps, and $O(W)$ volume. Subsection 4.4 then shows that TCs can also be calculated (with more steps) with only the $(2,1)$ catalyst rules.

4.1   Computing Logic Gates

Bit Representation and Indexing. The inputs of a binary gate are constructed as in Sect. 3.1. However, with catalysts, we modify our indexing scheme. When fanning out, we do not split the output of the gate into input species with different indices because the catalyst rules remove the need to differentiate the input species. Let f_i^{in} be the set of all indices of the inputs fanning into a gate at index i. Let f_i^{out} be the set of all the indices of the inputs fanning out of a gate at index i. The output of a gate is represented by the species y_i^b or $y_{j \to i}^b$, where j is the index of the input bit and i is the index of the gate.

AND/OR/NOT Gate. Table 8 shows the general process to computing AND, OR, and NOT gates. To compute an AND gate, we add a single copy of the species representing a true output (y_i^T) and a species representing a false output for each input $(\forall j \in f_i^{in} : y_{j \to i}^F)$. To compute an OR gate instead, we add a species representing a true output $(y_{j \to i}^T)$ for each input and a single y_i^F species. To compute NOT gates, we add one copy of each output species (y_i^b). For every input into an AND/OR/NOT gate, a corresponding rule should be created to remove the output species of the gate with the opposite truth value to the input. If the output species has a unique $j \to i$ index, then only the input with the corresponding i can delete that output species.

These gates can also be computed with $(2,1)$ catalyst rules by making the x_j^b species a catalyst. For example, the rule $x_j^T + y_i^T \to \emptyset$ would be replaced by the rule $x_j^T + y_i^T \to x_j^T$.

OR Example. Consider an OR gate whose gate index is 1 with input bits 0 and 1. Here, $|f_i^{in}| = 2$, and the initial configuration consists of the species x_1^F and a x_2^T. This gate can be computed in one step, following Table 8, by adding

Table 8. *(2, 0) rules for AND, OR, and NOT gates.*

Gate Type	Step	Relevant Rules	Description
AND	$Add\, y_i^T$ $\forall j \in f_i^{in} : y_{j \to i}^F$	$x_j^T + y_{j \to i}^F \to \emptyset$ $x_j^F + y_i^T \to \emptyset$	An input species with a certain truth value deletes the complement output species
OR	$Add\, y_i^F$ $\forall j \in f_i^{in} : y_{j \to i}^T$	$x_j^T + y_i^F \to \emptyset$ $x_j^F + y_{j \to i}^T \to \emptyset$	An input species with a certain truth value deletes the complement output species
NOT	$Add\, y_i^T$ y_i^F	$x_j^T + y_i^T \to \emptyset$ $x_j^F + y_i^F \to \emptyset$	The input and output species that share the same truth value delete each other

Table 9. *(2, 0) rules for majority gates.*

Steps	Relevant Rules	Description
1	$Add\, |f_i^{in}| \cdot a_i^T$ $|f_i^{in}| \cdot a_i^F$	$\forall j \in f_i^{in} :$ $x_j^T + a_i^F \to \emptyset$ $x_j^F + a_i^T \to \emptyset$	$\forall j \in f_i^{in}$, convert x_j^b input species into a_i^b species
2	$Add\, \lfloor |f_i^{in}|/2 \rfloor \cdot b_i^T$ $\lfloor |f_i^{in}|/2 \rfloor \cdot b_i^F$	$a_i^T + b_i^F \to \emptyset$ $a_i^F + b_i^T \to \emptyset$	Adding $\lfloor |f_i^{in}|/2 \rfloor$ amounts of b_i^T and b_i^F species will delete all of the minority species, leaving some amount of the majority species remaining
3	$Add\, y_i^T$ y_i^F	$a_i^T + y_i^F \to \emptyset$ $a_i^F + y_i^T \to \emptyset$	Convert a_i^b into the proper output species (y_i^b)

one $y_{1 \to 1}^T$, one $y_{2 \to 1}^T$, and one y_1^F species to the system. The species x_2^T and y_1^F delete each other. x_1^F and $y_{1 \to 1}^T$ are also removed together. Only the species $y_{2 \to 1}^T$ remains, which represents the intended "true" output of the OR gate.

Majority Gate. The general process of computing a majority gate is shown at Table 9. To compute a majority gate, all input species are converted into a new species a_i^b (Step 1). The species retain the same truth value b as the original input and has gate index i. If the number of species fanning into the majority gate is even, an extra *false* input species is added. The species b_i^b is then introduced, which computes the majority operation across all existing species. Any species that represent the minority inputs are deleted (Step 2). The species remaining afterwards are then converted into the correct output species (Step 3).

4.2   Examples

With the computation of individual gates demonstrated in our system, we now expand these features to computing entire circuits. We begin with a simple example in Fig. 3d to show the concepts before giving the general construction.

Table 10. *(2, 0) and (2, 1) rules and steps to compute the circuit in Fig. 3d with Fig. 3b's indexing.*

Initial Configuration: y_1^F y_2^T y_3^T			
Steps	**Relevant Rules**	**Steps**	**Relevant Rules**
1 $Add\,d_x$	No Rules Apply	8 $Add\,d_x$	$d_x + d_x \to \emptyset$
2 $Add\,d_x$	$d_x + d_x \to \emptyset$	$x_4^T,\, x_4^F$	$y_{1\to4}^F + x_4^T \to y_{1\to4}^F$
$x_1^T,\, x_1^F$	$y_1^F + x_1^T \to y_1^F$	9 $Add\,x_5^T,\, x_5^F$	$y_5^F + x_5^T \to y_5^F$
3 $Add\,3x_2^T,\, 3x_2^F$	$y_2^F + x_2^F \to y_2^F$	$x_6^T,\, x_6^F$	$y_6^T + x_6^F \to y_6^T$
$x_3^T,\, x_3^F$	$y_3^T + x_3^F \to y_3^T$		$y_{1\to4}^F + d_y \to d_y$
	$y_1^F + d_y \to d_y$	10 $Add\,d_y$	$y_5^F + d_y \to d_y$
4 $Add\,d_y$	$y_2^T + d_y \to d_y$		$y_6^T + d_y \to d_y$
	$y_3^T + d_y \to d_y$	11 $Add\,d_y$	$d_y + d_y \to \emptyset$
5 $Add\,d_y$	$d_y + d_y \to \emptyset$		$x_4^F + y_{4\to7}^T \to \emptyset$
		12 $Add\,\begin{matrix}y_{4\to7}^T,\, y_{5\to7}^T\\ y_{6\to7}^T,\, y_7^F\end{matrix}$	$x_5^F + y_{5\to7}^T \to \emptyset$
$y_4^T,\, y_{1\to4}^F$	$x_1^F + y_4^T \to \emptyset$		$x_6^F + y_7^F \to \emptyset$
6 $Add\,\begin{matrix}y_5^T,\, y_{2\to4}^F\\ y_5^F,\, y_{2\to6}^F\\ y_6^T,\, y_{3\to6}^F\end{matrix}$	$x_2^T + y_{2\to4}^F \to \emptyset$	13 $Add\,d_x$	No Rules Apply
	$x_2^T + y_5^F \to \emptyset$	14 $Add\,d_x$	$d_x + d_x \to \emptyset$
	$x_2^T + y_{2\to6}^F \to \emptyset$	15 $Add\,x_7^T,\, x_7^F$	$y_{6\to7}^T + x_7^F \to y_{6\to7}^T$
	$x_3^T + y_{3\to6}^F \to \emptyset$	16 $Add\,d_y$	$y_{6\to7}^T + d_y \to d_y$
7 $Add\,d_x$	No Rules Apply	17 $Add\,d_y$	$d_y + d_y \to \emptyset$

Our example circuit has three inputs: x_1, x_2, and x_3. In the first layer, x_2 is fanned out three times. One is fanned into an AND gate with x_1, another fanned into a NOT gate, and the other fanned into an AND gate with x_3. Finally, at the next depth level, the output of all three gates are fanned into an OR gate, whose output is the final circuit output.

Table 10 shows how to compute the circuit in Fig. 3d. The primary inputs of the circuit in Fig. 3d are represented by the species in the initial configuration. Steps 1–5 fan out the second primary input, convert the output species (y_n^b) into input species (x_n^b), and delete excess species. Step 6 computes the gates at the first depth level. Steps 7–11 convert the output species into input species and deletes excess species. Step 12 computes the final gate. Steps 13–17 delete excess species and converts the output of the final gate into an input species that represents the solution to the circuit (x_7^T).

4.3   Computing Circuits with (2,0) Void and (2,1) Catalyst Rules

Theorem 2. *Threshold circuits (TC) can be strictly computed with $(2,0)$ void rules and $(2,1)$ catalyst rules, $O(G)$ species, $O(D)$ steps, and $O(W)$ volume.*

Due to space constraints, the proof is omitted.

Table 11. *(2, 0) and (2, 1) rules and steps for a gate with arbitrary fan out.*

Steps	Relevant Rules	Description
1 $Add\, d_x$	$\forall n \in \{1, \cdots, G\}:$ $\forall b \in \{T, F\}$ $d_x + x_n^b \to d_x$ $d_x + a_n^b \to d_x$ $d_x + b_n^b \to d_x$	Delete all input species (x_n^b) and helper species that are no longer needed
2 $Add\, d_x$	$d_x + d_x \to \emptyset$	Remove deleting species d_x
3 $Add\, \lvert f_i^{out} \rvert \cdot x_i^T$ $\lvert f_i^{out} \rvert \cdot x_i^F$	$y_i^T + x_i^F \to y_i^T$ $y_i^F + x_i^T \to y_i^F$ $\forall j \in f_i^{in}:$ $y_{j \to i}^T + x_i^F \to y_{j \to i}^T$ $y_{j \to i}^F + x_i^T \to y_{j \to i}^F$	Add species representing true and false inputs and delete the species that are the complement of the output. A single output species can assign the truth value for as many input species as needed
4 $Add\, d_y$	$\forall n \in \{1, \cdots, G\}:$ $d_y + y_n^T \to d_y$ $d_y + y_n^F \to d_y$ $\forall j \in f_i^{in}:$ $d_y + y_{j \to i}^T \to d_y$ $d_y + y_{j \to i}^F \to d_y$	Delete all output species (y_n^b) that no longer needed
5 $Add\, d_y$	$d_y + d_y \to \emptyset$	Remove deleting species d_y

4.4   Computing Circuits with (2,1) Catalyst Rules

Note that $(2,1)$ catalyst rules are able to compute TCs alone. However, there is no known way to directly compute majority gates with $(2,1)$ void rules, only $(2,0)$. Thus, any majority gate is computed using AND, OR, and NOT gates when using only catalyst rules. Furthermore, deleting species that are no longer needed is slightly more convoluted with $(2,1)$ rules compared to pure void rules (Table 11).

Corollary 1. *Threshold circuits (TC) can be strictly computed with only $(2, 1)$ catalyst rules, $O(G)$ species, $O(D \log F_{maj})$ steps, and $O(W)$ volume.*

Due to space constraints, the proof is omitted. The basic idea, however, is simply that it takes an additional log steps to handle the fan-in of the majority gates, which we can easily do with $(2, 1)$ catalyst rules (Table 12).

5   Lower Bounds and Hardness

In this section, we prove negative results for computing with step CRNs. First, we show there exists a family of functions that require a logarithmic number of steps to compute. Then, we show hardness of verifying whether a step CRN properly computes a given function.

Table 12. *(2, 1) rules and steps for a gate with arbitrary fan out.*

Steps	Relevant Rules	Description
1 Add d'_x	$d'_x + d''_x \to d'_x$	Deleting species d''_x makes it possible for species d_x to exist in the next step without complications
2 Add d_x	$d_x + d'_x \to d_x$ $\forall n \in \{1, \cdots, G\}:$ $\forall b \in \{T, F\}$ $d_x + x^b_n \to d_x$ $d_x + a^b_n \to d_x$ $d_x + b^b_n \to d_x$	Deleting species d'_x makes it possible for species d''_x to exist in the next step without complications. Delete all input species (x^b_n) and helper species that are no longer needed
3 Add d''_x	$d_x + d''_x \to d''_x$	Removes deleting species d_x
4 Add d'_y	$d'_y + d''_y \to d'_y$	Deleting species d''_y makes it possible for species d_y to exist in the next step without complications
5 Add x^T_i x^F_i	$y^T_i + x^F_i \to y^T_i$ $y^F_i + x^T_i \to y^F_i$ $\forall j \in f^{in}_i:$ $y^T_{j\to i} + x^F_i \to y^T_{j\to i}$ $y^F_{j\to i} + x^T_i \to y^F_{j\to i}$	Add species representing true and false inputs and delete the species that are the complement of the output. A single output species can assign the truth value for as many input species as needed
6 Add d_y	$d_y + d'_y \to d_y$ $\forall n \in \{1, \cdots, G\}:$ $d_y + y^T_n \to d_y$ $d_y + y^F_n \to d_y$ $\forall j \in f^{in}_i:$ $d_y + y^T_{j\to i} \to d_y$ $d_y + y^F_{j\to i} \to d_y$	Deleting species d'_y makes it possible for species d''_y to exist in the next step without complications. Delete all output species (y^b_n) that are no longer needed
7 Add d''_y	$d_y + d''_y \to d''_y$	Remove deleting species d_y

5.1 Step Lower Bound for Controlled NOT

CNOT. The Controlled NOT gate is a 2-bit input and 2-bit output gate taking inputs X and Y, and outputting X and $X \oplus Y$, i.e., the gate flips Y if X is true.

k-CNOT. We generalize this to a Controlled k-NOT gate. This is a $(k+1)$-bit gate with inputs $X, Y_1, \cdots, Y_k$. The Y bits all flip if X is true. We choose this function since it has the property that changing 1 bit of the input changes a large number of output bits.

Configuration Distance. Recall configurations are defined as vectors. For two configurations c_0, c_1, we say the distance between them is $||c_0 - c_1||_1$, i.e., the sum of the absolute value of each entry in $c_0 - c_1$ (For two vectors $X = (x_1, \cdots, x_n)$ and $Y = (y_1, \cdots, y_n)$, $||X - Y||_1 = \sum_{i=1}^{n} |x_i - y_i|$).

Lemma 3. *Let r be a positive integer parameter. For all step CRNs Γ with void rules of size $(r_1, 0)$ with $r_1 \leq r$ and pairs of initial configurations c_T and c_F with distance 2 and equal volume, for any configuration c_{Ts} terminal in the step s from c_T, there exists a configuration c_{Fs} terminal in step s from c_F such that the distance between c_{Ts} and c_{Fs} is at most $2r^s$.*

Due to space constraints, the proof is omitted. The configuration distance between two output configurations is related to the Hamming distance of the output strings they represent. Lemma 3 can be used to get a logarithmic lower bound for the number of steps required when we fix our rule size to be a constant.

Theorem 3. *For all constants r, any CRN that strictly computes a k-CNOT gate with rules of size $(r_1, 0)$ satisfying $r_1 \leq r$ requires $\Omega(\log k)$ steps.*

Due to space constraints, the proof is omitted. We also note the k-CNOT can be computed by k XOR gates in parallel. This implies this lower bound does not hold with catalytic reactions either as Theorem 2 shows this can be computed in $O(1)$ steps or without the input-strict requirement. This is because increasing the fan-out of the X bit does not incur a cost in the number of steps in both of these generalizations. Plugging this XOR circuit into Theorem 1 gives a bound of $\Theta(\log k)$ steps showing the construction is optimal for some circuits.

5.2   Function Verification Hardness

We have established that void step CRNs can simulate Boolean circuits. We now discuss the complexity of determining if a given (void) step CRN does compute a given function. Specifically, we consider the following decision problem, and show that with void rules it is coNP-hard (Theorem 4), and has coNP membership (Theorem 5). Due to space, the proofs are omitted.

Definition 4 ((Strict Function Verification)). *Given a step CRN $C_S = (S, X, Y)$ and a Boolean function $f(\cdot)$[1] where $f(x_1, \cdots, x_n) = y_1 : \{0,1\}^n \to \{0,1\}$, decide if C_S computes Boolean function $f(\cdot)$. In particular, let $f_0(x_1, \cdots, x_n) = false$, which is false for all inputs.*

Theorem 4. *It is coNP-hard to determine if a given $O(1)$-step CRN $C_S = (S, X, Y)$ with $(3, 0)$ rules computes the Boolean function $f_0(x_1, \cdots, x_n)$.*

Theorem 5. *Determining if a given s-step CRN $C_S = (S, X, Y)$ with $(r, 0)$ rules computes the Boolean function $f_0(x_1, \cdots, x_n)$ is in coNP.*

Theorem 6. *It is coNP-complete to determine if a given $O(1)$-step CRN $C_S = (S, X, Y)$ with $(3, 0)$ rules computes the Boolean function $f_0(x_1, \cdots, x_n)$.*

---

[1] We assume that $f(\cdot)$ is given in the form of a circuit c_f. We leave as future work the complexity of other representations such as a truth table.

References

1. Alaniz, R.M., et al.: Reachability in restricted chemical reaction networks (2022). arXiv:2211.12603
2. Anderson, R., et al.: Computing threshold circuits with bimolecular void reactions in step chemical reaction networks. In: Proceedings of the 21st International Conference on Unconventional Computation and Natural Computation, UCNC 2024 (2024, to appear)
3. Angluin, D., Aspnes, J., Diamadi, Z., Fischer, M.J., Peralta, R.: Computation in networks of passively mobile finite-state sensors. Disturb. Comput. **18**(4), 235–253 (2006). https://doi.org/10.1007/s00446-005-0138-3
4. Angluin, D., Aspnes, J., Eisenstat, D.: A simple population protocol for fast robust approximate majority. Distrib. Comput. **21**, 87–102 (2008)
5. Angluin, D., Aspnes, J., Eisenstat, D., Ruppert, E.: The computational power of population protocols. Distrib. Comput. (2007)
6. Aris, R.: Prolegomena to the rational analysis of systems of chemical reactions. Arch. Ration. Mech. Anal. **19**(2), 81–99 (1965)
7. Aris, R.: Prolegomena to the rational analysis of systems of chemical reactions II. Some addenda. Arch. Ration. Mech. Anal. **27**(5), 356–364 (1968)
8. Arkin, A., Ross, J.: Computational functions in biochemical reaction networks. Biophys. J . **67**(2), 560–578 (1994)
9. Aviram, A.: Molecules for memory, logic, and amplification. J. Am. Chem. Soc. **110**(17), 5687–5692 (1988)
10. Cardelli, L., Kwiatkowska, M., Whitby, M.: Chemical reaction network designs for asynchronous logic circuits. Nat. Comput. **17**, 109–130 (2018)
11. Cardelli, L., Tribastone, M., Tschaikowski, M.: From electric circuits to chemical networks. Nat. Comput. **19**, 237–248 (2020)
12. Chen, H.L., Doty, D., Soloveichik, D.: Deterministic function computation with chemical reaction networks. Nat. Comput. **13**(4), 517–534 (2014)
13. Cook, M., Soloveichik, D., Winfree, E., Bruck, J.: Programmability of chemical reaction networks. In: Algorithmic Bioprocesses, pp. 543–584. Springer, Cham (2009)
14. Dalchau, N., Chandran, H., Gopalkrishnan, N., Phillips, A., Reif, J.: Probabilistic analysis of localized DNA hybridization circuits. ACS Synth. Biol. **4**(8), 898–913 (2015)
15. Ellis, S.J., Klinge, T.H., Lathrop, J.I.: Robust chemical circuits. Biosystems **186**, 103983 (2019)
16. Fan, D., Wang, J., Han, J., Wang, E., Dong, S.: Engineering DNA logic systems with non-canonical DNA-nanostructures: basic principles, recent developments and bio-applications. Sci. China Chem. **65**(2), 284–297 (2022)
17. Hjelmfelt, A., Weinberger, E.D., Ross, J.: Chemical implementation of neural networks and turing machines. Proc. Natl. Acad. Sci. **88**(24), 10983–10987 (1991)
18. Jiang, H., Riedel, M.D., Parhi, K.K.: Digital logic with molecular reactions. In: International Conference on Computer-Aided Design, ICCAD 2013, pp. 721–727. IEEE (2013)
19. Karp, R.M., Miller, R.E.: Parallel program schemata. J. Comput. Syst. Sci. **3**(2), 147–195 (1969)
20. Mailloux, S., Guz, N., Zakharchenko, A., Minko, S., Katz, E.: Majority and minority gates realized in enzyme-biocatalyzed systems integrated with logic networks and interfaced with bioelectronic systems. J. Phys. Chem. B **118**(24), 6775–6784 (2014)

21. Petri, C.A.: Kommunikation mit Automaten. Ph.D. thesis, Rheinisch-Westfälischen Institutes für Instrumentelle Mathematik an der Universität Bonn (1962)
22. Qian, L., Winfree, E.: Scaling up digital circuit computation with DNA strand displacement cascades. Science **332**(6034), 1196–1201 (2011)
23. Qian, L., Winfree, E.: A simple DNA gate motif for synthesizing large-scale circuits. J. R. Soc. Interface **8**(62), 1281–1297 (2011)
24. Sergeev, I.S.: Upper bounds for the formula size of symmetric Boolean functions. Russ. Math. **58**, 30–42 (2014)
25. Soloveichik, D., Cook, M., Winfree, E., Bruck, J.: Computation with finite stochastic chemical reaction networks. Nat. Comput. **7**(4), 615–633 (2008)
26. Soloveichik, D., Seelig, G., Winfree, E.: DNA as a universal substrate for chemical kinetics. Proc. Natl. Acad. Sci. **107**(12), 5393–5398 (2010)
27. Thachuk, C., Condon, A.: Space and energy efficient computation with DNA strand displacement systems. In: International Workshop on DNA-Based Computers (2012)
28. Wang, B., Thachuk, C., Ellington, A.D., Winfree, E., Soloveichik, D.: Effective design principles for leakless strand displacement systems. Proc. Natl. Acad. Sci. **115**(52), E12182–E12191 (2018)
29. Winfree, E.: Chemical reaction networks and stochastic local search. In: DNA Computing and Molecular Programming, DNA 2019. Springer (2019)
30. Xiao, W., Zhang, X., Zhang, Z., Chen, C., Shi, X.: Molecular full adder based on DNA strand displacement. IEEE Access **8**, 189796–189801 (2020)

Universality of Turing Tumble of Finite Size

Artiom Alhazov[1] , Rudolf Freund[2] , Sergiu Ivanov[3] ,
and Sergey Verlan[4(✉)]

[1] Vladimir Andrunachievici Institute of Mathematics and Computer Science,
Academiei 5, Chişinău 2028, Moldova
artiom@math.md
[2] Faculty of Informatics, TU Wien, Favoritenstraße 9–11, 1040 Wien, Austria
rudi@emcc.at
[3] Université Paris-Saclay, Université Évry, IBISC, 91020 Évry-Courcouronnes, France
sergiu.ivanov@ibisc.univ-evry.fr
[4] Univ. Paris Est Creteil, LACL, 94010 Creteil, France
verlan@u-pec.fr

Abstract. The Turing Tumble is a mechanical puzzle game that simulates the operations of a computer processor using marbles and various mechanical components. The game allows for a visual representation of the computation and is widely used in the educational context. It was shown to be Turing-complete providing that an appropriate infinite configuration of the board, an infinite marble supply and the possibility to construct arbitrarily long frictionless gear chains are available. In this paper we show the computational universality of the game for a finite configuration and no unbounded gear chains. The only source of infinity is the supply of marbles and the unbounded drop capacity. We also provide a thoughtful analysis of the computation representation in Turing Tumble and discuss the possible input and output types.

Keywords: Turing Tumble · Universality · Mechanical computer

1 Introduction

In recent years, there has been a growing interest in educational tools that promote computational thinking and introduce fundamental concepts of computer science in a tangible and intuitive manner [7]. One such tool that has garnered attention is the Turing Tumble puzzle. Developed by Paul Boswell, the Turing Tumble is a mechanical puzzle game that offers a hands-on approach to learning binary logic, algorithms, and machine learning principles. Its unique design allows players to construct and manipulate mechanical circuits using marbles and various mechanical components, simulating the operations of a computer processor [18]. Figure 1 shows a Turing Tumble in use.

The Turing Tumble has noteworthy educational value. Via its hands-on learning approach, it provides a tactile experience of computer logic—the player

E. Formenti and J. Durand-Lose (Eds.): MCU 2024, LNCS 15270, pp. 72–88, 2025.
https://doi.org/10.1007/978-3-031-81202-6_5

Fig. 1. A picture of the Turing Tumble in use [18], showing the inclined board with two sets of blue and red marbles near the top, the elements for performing computation (see Sect. 2.2 for an overview), the black levers for triggering the corresponding marbles near the bottom of the board, as well as the set of additional pieces on the table.

physically builds and observes the behavior of circuits. This facilitates intuitive understanding and helps demystify abstract concepts like the binary number system, logic gates, algorithms, etc. Finally, the process of designing a Turing Tumble program develops problem-solving skills, and allows for discussing different aspects of complexity and efficiency of algorithms and implementations.

While the Turing Tumble was initially conceived as an educational tool for teaching computer science concepts, its potential for exploring more complex computations has become increasingly apparent. The puzzle's versatility in representing a wide range of computational tasks and its ability to simulate complex algorithms suggest that the Turing Tumble may possess the capacity to compute any computable function, given the appropriate configuration, which means that it is universal. It was shown in [10,14] that the Turing Tumble has the computational power of a Turing machine, hence, it is Turing-universal.

The concept of (Turing) universality is one of the fundamental notions in the theory of computation. For an arbitrary class $\mathfrak{C}$ of computing devices, the universality problem consists in finding a fixed element $\mathcal{M}_0$ able to simulate any other element $\mathcal{M} \in \mathfrak{C}$, i.e., if the result of running $\mathcal{M}$ with the input x is y (usually written as $\mathcal{M}(x) = y$), then $y = f(\mathcal{M}_0(g(\mathcal{M}), h(x))$, where g is the function enumerating $\mathfrak{C}$, and f and h are the decoding and encoding functions, respectively. Remark that $\mathcal{M}_0$ has two inputs: the code of the machine and the encoding of the input. It is possible to consider that it has a single input by using a coding function for couples, for example, the Cantor pairing function. Usually we consider that $\mathcal{M}_0 \in \mathfrak{C}$, however this is not mandatory, e.g., the universal function for primitive recursive functions is general recursive. A Turing universal computing device is the solution to the universality problem for the class $\mathcal{NRE}$ of recursively enumerable sets of numbers and it is traditionally referred to as just universal. It is generally agreed that f and h should not be "too" complicated in order not to carry the computation, e.g., $f(x) = \log_a(x)$ and $h(x) = b^x$, for some $a, b \in \mathbb{N}$ (cf. [9,15]).

In this paper, we follow [8] and call the element $\mathcal{M}_0$ defined as above *weakly universal* (or just universal). If functions f and h are additionally required to be identities, $\mathcal{M}_0$ will be referred to as *strongly* universal. Hence, the strong universality permits to capture the situations when the encoding does not alter the power of the device. For example, 2-register machines are weakly universal [9], but they cannot be strongly universal as they cannot compute even the square function [3,12].

We would like to stress that the above discussion concerns devices with a finite description and capable of performing finite computations of unbounded length, i.e., computing devices having halting configurations. For devices without halting configurations, e.g. cellular automata, the notion of universality is more complex (generally it corresponds to a weak universality) and we refer to [11] for a detailed discussion.

The existing results on the universality of the Turing Tumble are based on the simulation of cellular automata [4,13], reversible logic elements [14], register machines [16], and Turing machines [10]. However, all these results require using a board with a predefined infinite configuration (like in the case of cellular automata).

In this paper we consider another way of representing a computation in the Turing Tumble using marble number encoding that was not considered before. This allows for reducing the sources of infinity to unlimited marbles and unbounded drops only. We show that under this setup the Turing Tumble is capable of universal computations on a finite board. We also investigate different representations of the input and the output of the computations in the Turing Tumble, resulting in different ways of achieving the computational universality.

The paper is organized as follows. Section 2 introduces the basic definitions and provides a concise description of the Turing Tumble game and its elements. Section 3 discusses different ways to represent the input and output. Section 4 presents the construction of the universality of the Turing Tumble of finite size. Finally, Sect. 5 concludes the paper.

2   Preliminaries

2.1   Register Machine

A (deterministic) register machine [9] is a 5-tuple $M = (Q, R, q_0, q_f, P)$, where

- Q is a finite non-empty set, called the set of states,
- $R = \{R_1, \ldots, R_m\}$, $m \geq 1$, is a set of registers,
- $q_0 \in Q$ is the initial state,
- $q_f \in Q$ is the final state.
- P is a set of instructions of the following forms:
  - $(p, A+, q)$, with $p, q \in Q, p \neq q_f, A \in R$, called an *increment* instruction,

- $(p, A-, q, s)$, with $p, q, s \in Q, p \neq q_f, A \in R$, called a *decrement* instruction.

For every $p \in Q$, $(p \neq q_f)$, there is exactly one instruction of the form either $(p, A+, q)$ or $(p, A-, q, s)$.

A configuration of a register machine M, as defined above, is an $(m+1)$-tuple $(q, v_1, \ldots, v_m)$, where $q \in Q$ and $v_1, \ldots, v_m$ are non-negative integers; q is the current state of M and $v_1, \ldots, v_m$ are the current numbers stored in the registers (the current contents of the registers or the values of the registers) $R_1, \ldots, R_m$, respectively.

A transition of the register machine consists in executing an instruction. An increment instruction $(p, A+, q) \in P$ is performed if M is in state p, the number stored in register A is increased by 1, and after that M enters in state q. A decrement instruction $(p, A-, q, s) \in P$ is performed if M is in state p, and if the number stored in register A is positive, then it is decreased by 1, and then M enters state q, and if the number stored in A is 0, then the contents of A remains unchanged and M enters state s.

A register machine $M = (Q, R, q_0, q_f, P)$ computes y on the input $x_1, \ldots, x_k$ if starting from the initial configuration $(q_0, 0, x_1, \ldots, x_k, 0, \ldots, 0)$ it enters the final configuration $(q_f, y, 0, \ldots, 0)$. We also say that M accepts a non-negative integer n if starting from the initial configuration $(q_0, n, 0, \ldots, 0)$ it enters the final configuration $(q_f, 0, 0, \ldots, 0)$.

It is known that register machines with 3 registers accept the family of all recursively enumerable sets of integers [9]. In [8] several universal and weakly universal register machines (with different types of instructions) are constructed with the aim of minimizing the number of states. It features a universal register machine with 8 registers as well as 9 increment and 13 decrement instructions as defined above.

2.2 The Turing Tumble

In this section we give a concise description of the puzzle elements (sometimes called "gadgets") of the Turing Tumble, as well as of how it functions. We rely on the Turing Tumble simulator [5] for the images.

Game Elements:

Board: The Turing Tumble board consists of a grid with pegs arranged in rows and columns (Fig. 2). Roughly half of the positions have an additional semi-circular cut in the board. All elements except gears are placed at the positions with the cut, which makes them positioned on a rectangular grid rotated by 45°. Marbles are released from the top, and they interact with various components as they fall. Because of the placement of the elements, the marbles fall either left or right at 45° to the next element of the grid.

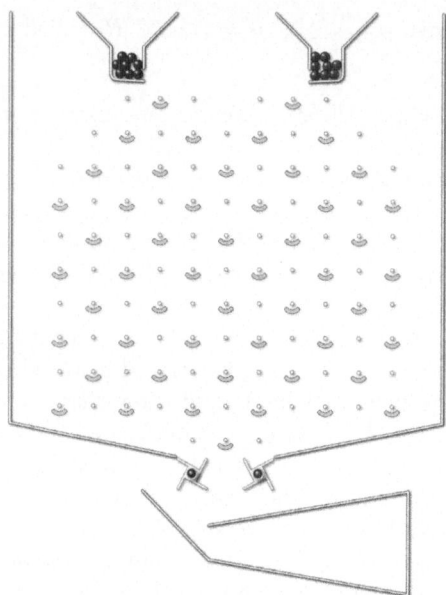

Fig. 2. The basic setup of the Turing Tumble implemented in the Turing Tumble simulator [5].

Drop: Contains a supply of marbles and releases marbles one by one when acted upon by a turnstile.

Turnstile: When a ball hits a turnstile (also called trigger in some places), it releases a marble from the corresponding drop.

Ramp: Routes the marble to the left if oriented as shown in the figure, or to the right if flipped around the vertical axis. This corresponds to the movement of the ball down left or down right at 45° angle.

Crossover: Routes the marbles arriving from its left to the right, and the marbles arriving from the right to its left.

Interceptor: Intercepts all marbles and prevents them from reaching the bottom of the board.

Bit: A two-state memory element, may point to the left or to the right. If the bit points to the left, it directs the marble coming from any direction to the right and changes the state to point to the right. If the bit points to the right, it directs the marble coming from any direction to the left and changes the state to point to the left.

Gear bit: Similar to the bit: may point to the left or to the right, directs  the marble to the right or the left respectively, and changes its state. Gear bits can be connected using gears that allow for synchronously changing the state of all connected gear bits.

Gear: Allows for connecting two or more gear bits to synchronize their state changes.

From the computer science standpoint, the bit and the gear bit both play the important role of binary memory elements. More concretely, we can assign a binary value to the orientation—e.g., 0 if the (gear) bit points to the left and 1 if it points to the right—and interpret the marble falling through the element as reading and/or modifying the memory state. Gear bits bring in the additional capability of being connected in chains via gears, as shown for example in Fig. 5. Connecting two or more gear bits via gears synchronizes the direction change: when one gear bit changes direction, all connected gear bits do as well. This introduces another way of propagating a signal across the board, besides the falling marble. Furthermore, if two gear bits are arranged and oriented in such a way that the marble passes through both of them—as the two leftmost gear bits in Fig. 5—then both gear bits will change their direction twice, i.e., return into the state they were in before the marble touched them at all. This effect allows for implementing read-only memory, as explained in Fig. 6.

Gameplay: Figures 1 and 2 show the basic setup of the Turing Tumble: two marble containers (drops in the simulator) with red and blue marbles at the top of the board, two levers (turnstiles in the simulator) at the bottom of the board releasing the marbles from the corresponding container, as well as various elements on the board itself, forming the program. The Turing Tumble is typically operated by a single player, releasing one blue or one red marble to start the execution of the program routing the marble to the turnstile corresponding to the color of the marble which should be released next.

As the falling marbles traverse the program, they may hit memory elements—bits and gear bits—changing their state and modifying their trajectories accordingly. The goal of the player is to design an arrangement of the elements such that it performs a specific task: producing a given color sequence in the marble container at the bottom of the board, counting, or adding numbers in binary using the bit elements on the board itself. Strategical arrangements of these elements allow for implementing logic gates [14], cells of cellular automata [13], or even more complex ensembles simulating Turing machines or entire simple CPUs [6,10,16], implying in particular that the Turing Tumble is computationally complete under certain assumptions: e.g., an unbounded board and some elements available in unlimited amounts, infinite marble supply in some drops, no friction in gear chains, etc.

Figure 3 shows an example of a 3-bit counter built using Turing Tumble components. In the initial configuration all bits point to the left, which corresponds

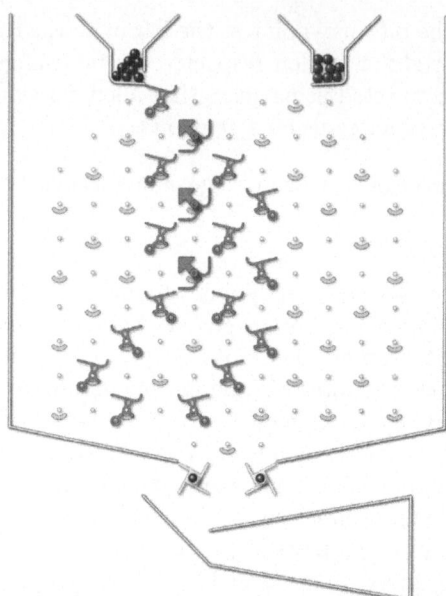

Fig. 3. The Turing Tumble configuration implementing a 3-bit binary counter. The initial configuration corresponds to the zero value as all bits are turned to the left.

to the zero value of the counter. When a blue marble is released it switches the position of the first bit and falls down using ramps until it hits the blue turnstile. This releases a new blue marble that switches the position of the first bit to zero and that of the second bit to one. By continuing this process, all values from 0 to 7 will be represented by the three bits of the counter. When the counter reaches the value 111, it moves on to 000.

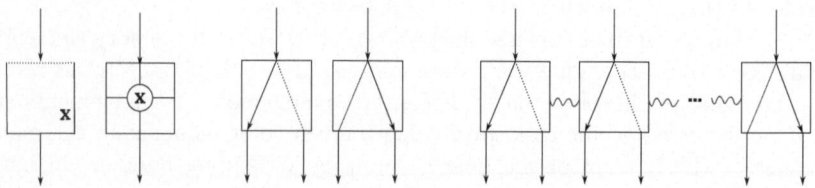

Fig. 4. Abstract representation of the Turing Tumble elements. From left to right: drop labelled by x, turnstile actioning the drop x, bit positioned to the left, bit positioned to the right, a gear line connecting several bits that can be in different positions and which flip synchronously.

To better abstract the functioning of the Turing Tumble, we introduce a simpler graphical notation for its elements, depicted in Fig. 4. Then, we will construct circuits out of these elements, using the convention that the marbles are released from the top of the board and they fall down by moving a fixed distance (usually corresponding to an element) per step. We will also use the letter X to denote the interceptors serving as marble sinks, i.e., the number of marbles they contain is irrelevant for the computation. We remark that gear lines can be of arbitrary length and also spread in different directions, so these chains resemble a graph.

2.3   The Flip-Flop Element

The key element of our universality construction is the flip-flop element. It is depicted in Fig. 5 reproduced from [17].

Fig. 5. The flip-flop element implementation taken from [17].

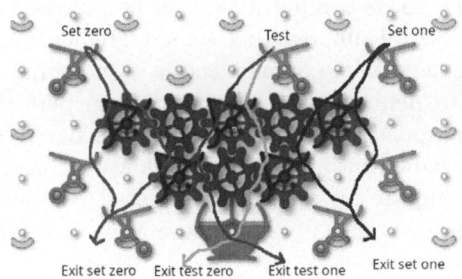

Fig. 6. The flip-flop element functioning. When a marble enters the "Set zero" path, it flips all bits to the left, disregarding the initial position of the bit (however taking a different path if the bit is zero or one). When a marble enters the "Set one" path, it flips all bits to the right. When a marble enters the "Test" path, it goes to "Exit test zero" if the bits are initially set to the left, and "Exit test one" otherwise.

The flip-flop element is composed of 5 gear bits that turn synchronously, so that they represent a single bit of information. It has three entry points, allowing for performing the following operations:

– Set zero: all gear bits are set to 0.
– Set one: all gear bits are set to 1.
– Test: the flip-flop is tested for zero and the marble continues on the path corresponding to the result of the test.

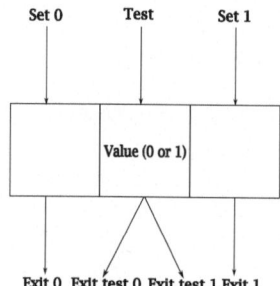

Fig. 7. The abstract representation of the flip-flop element.

The correspondence between the entry points and the operations is explained in Fig. 6. Similarly to Fig. 4, in Fig. 7 we introduce an abstract representation of the flip-flop, which we will use in the circuits in the rest of the paper.

3 Computations in the Turing Tumble

In the original Turing Tumble everything is finite (board size, number of elements, marble count), so its computations can be represented by a finite state automaton. However, if we suppose that some ingredients can be infinite, then the computation becomes more complex and is even Turing-complete.

It is important to define how a computation is performed, more exactly how the input is encoded and the output is decoded (the computational step obeys standard game rules). This would allow for considering Turing Tumble machines that compute an output value based on some input. We below consider the most natural types of input and output encodings.

Input Encodings:

Configuration (bit) input: The input is encoded in a finite portion of the initial configuration of the board (that can itself be infinite). It is a sequence of bit values (supposing each bit is numbered) that can be grouped into numbers, vectors or strings. This type of input is somewhat similar to cellular automata or Turing machine inputs.

Marble input: The input is encoded in the sequence of marbles, in one of the following ways:
  – Number input: the number of marbles dropped down from some particular drop.

- Vector input: a subset of drops is ordered and each drop is considered as a component of the input vector.
- String input: *each drop* from a designated subset of drops is associated to a letter of an alphabet. The input string is the sequence of letters corresponding to the drops, ordered by the times at which the drops release their marbles.
- Single string input: *each marble* is associated to a letter of an alphabet. The input string corresponds to the sequence of letters falling from a specially designated drop.

Hybrid input: The input is a combination of the above.

Output Encodings:

Configuration output: The output is encoded in a finite portion of the final configuration of the board. This may be implemented in several ways:
- Bit output: the output is a sequence of particular bit values (each bit is numbered). Since only the bits have a state, this is sufficient to fully describe the data stored in the configuration.
- Surface decision output: it is a particular variant of bit output, where the result is read on a single bit and it is interpreted as a "yes" or "no" answer to a decision problem.

Marble output: The output is the sequence of marbles. This can be implemented in one of the following ways:
- Decision output: the output is a single marble that is caught by one of two particular interceptors, corresponding to a "yes" or "no" answer to a decision problem. As a variation, there might be a single interceptor, but with marbles of different colors/labels.
- Number output: the number of marbles caught by some particular interceptor or located in an initially empty drop.
- Vector output: a subset of interceptors is ordered and each interceptor is considered as a component of the output vector.
- String output: each marble from a drop is associated to a letter of an alphabet. The output string corresponds to the sequence of letters caught by a particular interceptor arranged by the catch time.

Hybrid output: The output is a combination of the above.

We remark that the bottom line of the board can be considered as a special interceptor keeping track of the order of arrival of marbles. Furthermore, marbles need to be released in order for an action to be performed. In this way, a marble can be seen as the counterpart of energy, acting on the bits on the board. A marble can also be seen as carrying information down the board.

More generally, the information flow in the Turing Tumble can be represented in one of the following ways:

- the path of a marble from a drop to an interceptor,
- the propagation of a rotation among gear lines.

In the first case the flow goes from top to bottom, so in order to make loops it is necessary to trigger turnstiles dropping marbles from the top of the board. In the second case the flow can go in any direction. It is implicitly assumed that gears have zero friction, so lines of any length can be activated by a single marble, transmitting the information instantaneously across any distance along the line.

4   The Universality Construction

Our universality construction is based on several assumptions about the structure and functioning of the game. We list them below in order to make the construction clearer.

- The board is of finite size (although bigger than the original game).
- The number of elements on the board is finite.
- There might be several drops and associated turnstiles. The association is done in a one-to-many manner, i.e., one drop may be triggered by multiple turnstiles. We shall use the same label for a drop and all its associated turnstiles.
- A drop can be placed at any position on the board. It can receive marbles that are dropped from above. It may also contain an initial number of marbles. The number of marbles appearing in a drop is not bounded.
- The top drops have an infinite supply of marbles.
- An interceptor can hold an unbounded number of marbles.
- There is a notion of time: a marble needs a time step to go through an element of the board. For the needs of this paper we do not count the elapsed time, it is sufficient to assume that some paths are longer than the others, implying that some marbles will arrive faster to an element than others using shorter paths.
- Multiple marbles may run in parallel on the board. If there are several marbles that arrive at the same place at the same time, then this corresponds to an error condition and the computation is considered as failed.

Two main points are different in our formalization as compared to previous formalizations of the Turing Tumble. The first one is the arbitrary positioning of the drops, and the fact that they can *receive* marbles. This can be physically implemented by joining several boards and thus placing the drops in different positions. Also, it is not difficult to cut the upper part of the board to allow drops to receive marbles. The simulator [5] already implements these features, even though associating drops to turnstiles is not always easy to achieve. Of course, the unbounded capacity of drops (and interceptors) cannot be faithfully implemented in the physical world.

The second point is the notion of time. In previous formalizations only one marble runs on the board at any given moment. In our case, multiple marbles can run on different portions of the board. Our construction considers lines of

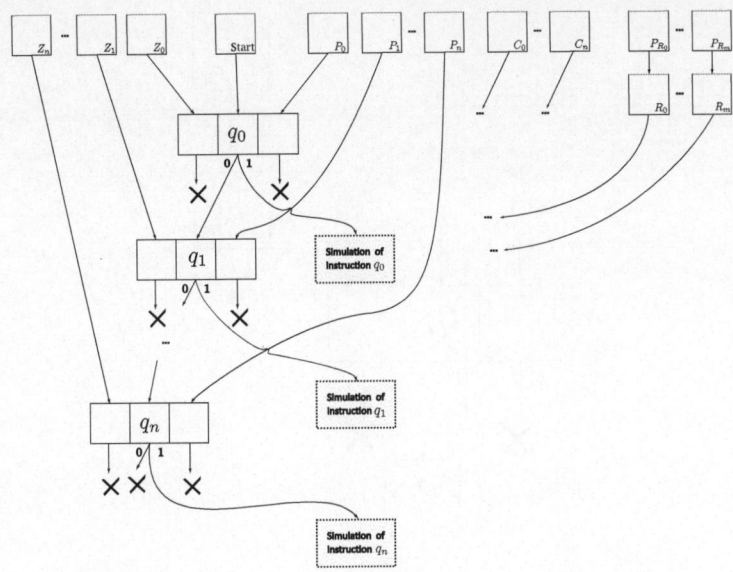

Fig. 8. The general schema of the universality construction. The drops at the top have an infinite supply of marbles. The drops $R_1, \ldots, R_m$ are of unbounded capacity and are situated higher than the position of the flip-flop q_0. Drops C_i, $1 \leq i \leq n$, and R_k, $1 \leq k \leq m$, are connected to the corresponding elements simulating each instruction via ramps.

different lengths, so the marbles arrive at some element at different times, thus avoiding competition for elements and subsequent race conditions.

We now show how any register machine can be simulated using the Turing Tumble (machine). Consider an arbitrary register machine $M = (Q, R, q_0, q_f, P)$ with m registers. The general schema of the construction is depicted on Fig. 8. Each state is represented by a flip-flop element q_i and only one of all these elements is in state "one". Each register R_k is a drop labelled by R_k. When a marble is released from the "Start" drop it will go through the test input of the first flip-flop (corresponding to state q_0) and if it is zero, it will follow through to the second flip-flop (corresponding to state q_1) and so on, until it reaches the (unique) flip-flop q_i that has the value 1. Then the simulation of the instruction q_i starts.

If q_i corresponds to the instruction (q_i, R_k+, q_j), then the corresponding simulation block is depicted on Fig. 9. The marble triggers the turnstile Z_i that updates the value of the flip-flop q_i to zero. Next, the marble triggers the turnstile P_{R_k} that releases a fresh marble going to the drop R_k, thus updating (i.e., incrementing) the register. Then the marble triggers the turnstile P_j that updates the value of the flip-flop q_j to one. Finally, the turnstile "Start" is triggered again, allowing the simulation of the next instruction to be started. We remark that since the turnstile "Start" is triggered *after* the previous three ones, the corresponding marble will reach the flip-flop q_j *after* it has been updated to one by

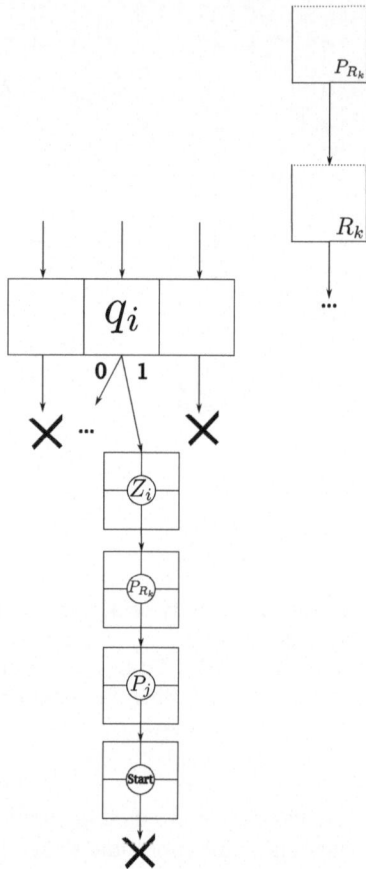

Fig. 9. The simulation of an instruction (q_i, R_k+, q_j). The register increment is done using a turnstile. All register drops should be located above all instructions.

the marble from the drop P_j. Moreover, if $i \neq j$, then the flip-flop q_i will have the value zero when the "Start" marble reaches it. For the register R_k, the marble will reach it before the "Start" marble reaches the flip-flop q_j because the path to R_k is shorter—it is placed higher than state flip-flops.

If q_i corresponds to the instruction (q_i, R_k-, q_j, q_s), then the corresponding simulation block is depicted in Fig. 10. We emphasize that the construction has to take into account all instructions q_t decrementing register R_k, although at the end a possible decrement will only result in setting to one the flip-flop corresponding to q_j. First, the marble resets the flip-flop v_i^k to zero. Then it triggers the turnstile R_k that releases a marble going from the drop R_k if R_k is not empty. Next, the marble triggers the turnstiles C_i and Z_i (the last one will reset to zero the state flip-flop q_i). In the meantime, if R_k has not been zero, the corresponding marble sets the value of all flip-flops v_t^k to one, for all instructions q_t that decrement register R_k (including v_i^k). If R_k is empty (hence corresponding register is zero), then no marble from the drop R_k will be released and the value of flip-flop v_i^k will remain zero. Finally, the marble from C_i (which is the topmost drop) reaches the flip-flop v_i^k (several steps *after* the R_k marble), and depending on its value (storing the information whether R_k is empty or not), either triggers the turnstile P_j (if $v_i^k = 1$) or P_s (if $v_i^k = 0$). Finally, this marble triggers the turnstile "Start" thus restarting the computation for the next state.

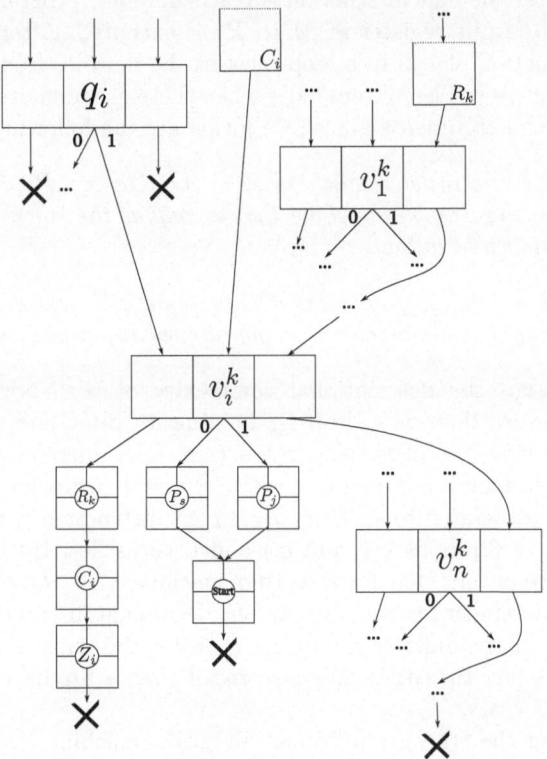

Fig. 10. The simulation of an instruction (q_i, R_k-, q_j, q_s). The drop R_k is lower than C_i but higher than q_i. The chain of flip-flops v_t^k contains a flip-flop for every instruction q_t such that q_t decrements register R_k. This diagram only shows the part of the machine containing all instructions which decrement register R_k, hence, all flip-flops v_t^k have the same superscript k. All the flip-flops v_t^k are to be connected to the corresponding flip-flops q_t and C_t, as well as the other elements below, as only depicted for v_i^k.

Finally, if q_i is the halt instruction q_f, then it can either be implemented by the "forget" element (X), or by not triggering the "Start" turnstile in the simulation of the preceding instruction.

In the initial configuration of the Turing Tumble the flip-flop q_0 is set to one, and all other flip-flops to zero. Next, the drops R_k are set to the initial values of the registers. The simulation of the machine starts by releasing a marble from the drop "Start". The simulation of the machine stops when the halt instruction is reached, so the "Start" turnstile is not triggered anymore. The output of the machine is read as the contents of the drops that corresponds to the output registers of the machine.

It is possible to modify the construction in order to have a number output in an interceptor. Here, we only provide a brief overview of the idea. First, the machine M should be extended by an additional register R_f, which will only be incremented. After the halt instruction is reached, a new program that transfers the value of the output register of M to R_f is executed. After that, a special decrement instruction placed in a loop releases the marbles from R_f directly to the output interceptor. The system halts when there are no more marbles in R_f.

Considering the arguments above, we formulate the following theorem.

Theorem 1. *For any register machine $M = (Q, R, q_0, q_f, P)$ with m registers, there exists a Turing Tumble machine that simulates the computation of M by using number input and output.*

Corollary 1. *The family of all recursively enumerable sets of integers can be accepted by Turing Tumble machines using number input and output.*

Now we discuss the descriptional complexity of the above construction. For each register R_k there is a drop R_k holding its value and a top drop P_{R_k} that refills R_k during the increment instruction. Each increment instruction q_i requires a flip-flop (corresponding to the state) and 4 turnstiles. Also, there are drops Z_i and P_i associated to q_i. Each decrement instruction q_i requires 3 drops (Z_i, P_i and C_i), 2 flip-flops (v_i^k and q_i) and 6 turnstiles. By summing up all these numbers we obtain that for a register machine $M = (Q, R, q_0, q_f, P)$ with m registers, n_1 increment instructions, and n_2 decrement instructions, the Turing Tumble machine that simulates it requires $n_1 + 2n_2$ flip-flops, $2n_1 + 3n_2 + m + 1$ drops and $4n_1 + 6n_2$ turnstiles. We also recall that a flip-flop is composed of 5 gear bits and 3 gears.

By simulating the strongly universal 8-register machine U_{22} from [8] using $n_1 = 9$ increment and $n_2 = 13$ decrement instructions, we obtain the following result.

Theorem 2. *There exists a strongly universal Turing Tumble machine composed of 35 flip-flops (175 gear bits and 105 gears), 66 drops, and 114 turnstiles.*

5   Conclusion

In this paper, we revisited the computational universality of the Turing Tumble game by considering a different representation of the input and the output based on the marble count. We showed that an arbitrary register machine can be simulated on a finite board, which implies the existence of a universal Turing Tumble machine of finite size.

There are several directions for future research. The first one is to consider different variants of register machines using different stronger types of instructions [1,8]. For example, one may merge the increment instructions into the preceding decrement instructions [2]. In this case only 13 instructions are needed, which significantly reduces the number of used ingredients, especially of flip-flops.

Another direction is to minimize the number of used drops and turnstiles. We conjecture that there is a trade-off between the number of flip-flops and the number of drops and turnstiles, and that it might be possible to decrease the number of drop/turnstile pairs below 10.

Finally, it would be interesting to consider number input/output Turing Tumble machines that do not use gears and gear bits at all. While these elements are essential for configuration input/output mechanisms, this might be different in the case of marble number input/output, especially if different marble colors are actively used.

References

1. Alhazov, A., Ivanov, S., Pelz, E., Verlan, S.: Small universal deterministic Petri nets with inhibitor arcs. J. Autom. Lang. Comb. **21**(1–2), 7–26 (2016)
2. Alhazov, A., Verlan, S.: Minimization strategies for maximally parallel multiset rewriting systems. Theoret. Comput. Sci. **412**(17), 1581–1591 (2011). https://doi.org/10.1016/j.tcs.2010.10.033
3. Barzdin, I.M.: Ob odnom klasse machin Turinga (machiny Minskogo), Russian. Algebra Logika **1**, 42–51 (1963)
4. Crossen, J.: Simulation of cellular automata using Turing Tumble (2018). https://community.turingtumble.com/t/proof-of-turing-completeness/372/23
5. Crossen, J.: A simulator for the Turing Tumble (2018). https://github.com/jessecrossen/ttsim/
6. Johnson, M.P.: Turing tumble is PSPACE)-complete. In: Heggernes, P. (ed.) CIAC 2019. LNCS, vol. 11485, pp. 274–285. Springer, Cham (2019). https://doi.org/10.1007/978-3-030-17402-6_23
7. Kong, S.-C., Abelson, H. (eds.): Computational Thinking Education. Springer, Singapore (2019). https://doi.org/10.1007/978-981-13-6528-7
8. Korec, I.: Small universal register machines. Theoret. Comput. Sci. **168**(2), 267–301 (1996)
9. Minsky, M.: Computations: Finite and Infinite Machines. Prentice Hall, Englewood Cliffts (1967)
10. Pitt, L.: Turing tumble is turing-complete. Theor. Comput. Sci. **948**, 113734 (2023). https://doi.org/j.tcs.2023.113734
11. Rozenberg, G., Bäck, T., Kok, J.N. (eds.): Handbook of Natural Computing. Springer, Cham (2012)
12. Schroeppel, R.: A two counter machine cannot calculate 2^N. In: AI Memos. MIT AI Lab (1972)
13. Tomita, T., Lee, J., Isokawa, T., Peper, F., Kamiura, N., Yumoto, T.: Cellular automaton model for Turing tumble mechanical computer. In: Sixth International Symposium on Computing and Networking, CANDAR Workshops 2018, Takayama, Japan, 27–30 November 2018, pp. 32–37. IEEE Computer Society (2018). https://doi.org/10.1109/CANDARW.2018.00014

14. Tomita, T., Lee, J., Isokawa, T., Peper, F., Yumoto, T., Kamiura, N.: Universal logic elements constructed on the Turing Tumble. Nat. Comput. **19**(4), 787–795 (2020). https://doi.org/10.1007/S11047-019-09760-8
15. Woods, D., Neary, T.: The complexity of small universal Turing machines: a survey. Theoret. Comput. Sci. **410**(4–5), 443–450 (2009)
16. Yama-chan: Turing Tumble CPU (2019). https://community.turingtumble.com/t/turing-tumble-cpu/750
17. Turing Tumble: Educator guide. https://upperstory.com/turingtumble/edu/resources/
18. Turing Tumble - Build marble-powered computers (2024). https://upperstory.com/turingtumble/

On the Power of Small Watson-Crick Automata and Variants of String Assembling Systems

András Murvai and György Vaszil[(✉)]

Department of Computer Science, Faculty of Informatics, University of Debrecen, Kassai út 26, Debrecen 4028, Hungary
murvai.andras98@gmail.com, vaszil.gyorgy@inf.unideb.hu

Abstract. We investigate the relationship of languages characterized by variants of string assembling systems and by Watson-Crick automata with a small number of states. Besides the general variant, we consider so-called free and pure string assembling systems, and compare their language generating power to Watson-Crick automata having one, two, or three states in their state sets. In some cases, restricted variants of the models describing unary languages are also considered.

1 Introduction

The double stranded structure of DNA molecules motivated the introduction and study of double stranded strings with the tools and techniques of formal language theory. The notion of double stranded string was accompanied by the definition of string operations intended to model the biochemical processes that the double stranded molecules corresponding to these types of strings can undergo. The idea is realized by the introduction of a complementarity relation on the elements of the alphabet (motivated by the complementary pairs of bases which make up the double stranded structure of the DNA). The complementarity relation on the alphabet determines how double stranded strings can be formed through the requirement that corresponding symbols on the upper and lower strands of the string must be complementary. More details on these developments and the computational models that can be derived on this basis can be found in the monograph [8] or in the handbook chapter [3]. In the following we only discuss two models related to the topic of our current investigations, these are sticker systems and Watson-Crick automata.

Sticker systems were introduced in [2], they use double stranded string "pieces" (possibly with single stranded "sticky ends") as building blocks to assemble longer double stranded strings by gluing together their single stranded sticky ends according to the Watson-Crick complementarity relation. Sticker systems are basically sets of such pieces (such building blocks), they describe formal languages (sets of double stranded strings) which can be "stick" together

Supported by the University of Debrecen Scientific Research Bridging Fund (DETKA).

E. Formenti and J. Durand-Lose (Eds.): MCU 2024, LNCS 15270, pp. 89–102, 2025.
https://doi.org/10.1007/978-3-031-81202-6_6

starting from the set of initial pieces. Depending on how we specify the details of the functioning of the system, simple languages (like regular languages which can be described by finite automata), or more complicated languages (like recursively enumerable languages which can be described by Turing machines) can be generated by sticker systems.

The other model we discuss (since it is a topic of our current investigations) is called a Watson-Crick automaton, and it was introduced in [1]. Watson-Crick automata are sometimes considered to be the automata counterparts of sticker systems. They are similar to ordinary finite automata in the sense that their internal control can be in one of a finite set of internal states, and they read strings written on their input tape, either accepting or rejecting them when the reading process is finished. Similarly to sticker systems, Watson-Crick automata work on double stranded strings, thus, they have a double stranded tape that contains two complementary strings which are read by two separate reading heads being able to move independently of each other, one on the upper and one on the lower strand of the tape, their languages consist of the set of strings that are accepted. Concerning their computational power, these types of automata can describe more complicated language classes than ordinary finite automata. Even in their most basic setup, they are able to accept non-context-free languages, such as, for example, the language made up of the strings of the form $a \ldots ab \ldots bc \ldots c$ where the lengths of the sequences of the different letters are equal.

Besides their apparent similarities, there are also obvious differences between the two models. One might argue that the most important one of these is the fact that the two heads of Watson-Crick automata can move independently of each other, while the building blocks that sticker systems use are fixed. This can be important because in Watson-Crick automata the length difference of the upper and lower parts of the input which is processed by the reading heads can be arbitrarily large, so it is possible to establish relationships between symbols of the input which are arbitrarily far away from each other. On the other hand, this does not seem to be possible in sticker systems (at least in the basic setting), as the length of the single stranded sticky ends of the building blocks are finitely bounded. (The intention to introduce a similar restriction in Watson-Crick automata motivated the study of Watson-Crick automata with delays in [11]).

The above described important restriction (a built-in feature of sticker systems) is lifted in the model called string assembling systems. String assembling systems were defined in [5], they also assemble double stranded strings from a finite set of building units, but these units are not considered as fixed double stranded blocks, but as string pairs: one string to join to the upper strand, and another to join to the lower strand of the double stranded string which is being built. This is a significant modification because this way that the length difference between the upper and lower strands during the assembly process can be arbitrarily high, similarly to the distance of the reading heads of Watson-Crick automata. The relationship of the two models, however, is more complicated than it might seem at first, since string assembling systems also introduce a feature distinct from Watson-Crick automata, namely that the prefix (the beginning) of the newly joined string must coincide with the suffix (the end) of the part that is already built.

In the following we continue the investigations started in [7] concerning the relationship of the two models. There we studied the relationship of languages generated by string assembling systems and Watson-Crick automata in general, and stateless Watson-Crick automata (automata having a single state) in particular. We will review some of these results in the first part of Sect. 3 after the necessary notions and notations are introduced in Sect. 2. In the rest of the paper we consider several variants of string assembling systems introduced in [6], and relate the languages they generate to Watson-Crick automata with one, two, or three states in their state sets. Besides the general variant, we consider so-called free and pure string assembling systems and compare their language generating power to Watson-Crick automata. In some cases, restricted variants of the models describing unary languages are also considered. We close the paper with conclusions and an open problem in Sect. 4.

2 Preliminaries

In the following, we briefly recall the mathematical notions and notations that we will use. See the monograph [10] or the handbook [9] for more on formal languages in general, and [8] or [3] for more details on notions related to DNA computing. Given a finite alphabet of symbols (or letters) V, let V^* denote the set of all strings over V and let $V^+ = V^* \setminus \{\lambda\}$ where λ denotes the empty string. A language $L \subseteq V^*$ is a set of strings (or words) over V, and two languages $L_1, L_2 \subseteq V^*$ are considered equal if they differ in at most the empty string, that is, if $L_1 \setminus \{\lambda\} = L_2 \setminus \{\lambda\}$. The length of a word $w \in V^*$ is denoted by $|w|$.

A double stranded string over V is a pair of strings $(w_1, w_2) \in V^* \times V^*$, which we also write as $\begin{pmatrix} w_1 \\ w_2 \end{pmatrix}$, and the set of pairs $V^* \times V^*$ is written as $\begin{pmatrix} V^* \\ V^* \end{pmatrix}$.

We denote the last and the first letters of a string pair $\begin{pmatrix} u \\ v \end{pmatrix}$ as $end\left(\begin{pmatrix} u \\ v \end{pmatrix} \right)$ and $bgn\left(\begin{pmatrix} u \\ v \end{pmatrix} \right)$, respectively, that is,

1. for $x_1, y_1 \in V$, $u', v' \in V^*$ and $u = u'x_1$, $v = v'y_1$, we have $end\left(\begin{pmatrix} u \\ v \end{pmatrix} \right) = end\left(\begin{pmatrix} u'x_1 \\ v'y_1 \end{pmatrix} \right) = \begin{pmatrix} x_1 \\ y_1 \end{pmatrix}$, and similarly, for $u = x_2u''$ and $v = y_2v''$, we have $bgn\left(\begin{pmatrix} u \\ v \end{pmatrix} \right) = bgn\left(\begin{pmatrix} x_2u'' \\ y_2v'' \end{pmatrix} \right) = \begin{pmatrix} x_2 \\ y_2 \end{pmatrix}$ where $x_2, y_2 \in V$, $u'', v'' \in V^*$.
   Otherwise,

2. if one of the strings is empty, we have $end\left(\begin{pmatrix}\lambda\\v\end{pmatrix}\right) = end\left(\begin{pmatrix}\lambda\\v'y_1\end{pmatrix}\right) = \begin{pmatrix}\lambda\\y_1\end{pmatrix}$, $end\left(\begin{pmatrix}u\\\lambda\end{pmatrix}\right) = end\left(\begin{pmatrix}u'x_1\\\lambda\end{pmatrix}\right) = \begin{pmatrix}x_1\\\lambda\end{pmatrix}$, $bgn\left(\begin{pmatrix}\lambda\\v\end{pmatrix}\right) = bgn\left(\begin{pmatrix}\lambda\\y_2v''\end{pmatrix}\right) = \begin{pmatrix}\lambda\\y_2\end{pmatrix}$, and $bgn\left(\begin{pmatrix}u\\\lambda\end{pmatrix}\right) = bgn\left(\begin{pmatrix}x_2u''\\\lambda\end{pmatrix}\right) = \begin{pmatrix}x_2\\\lambda\end{pmatrix}$ for $x_1, x_2, y_1, y_2 \in V$, $u', u'', v', v'' \in V^*$.

A *complementarity relation* $\rho \subseteq V \times V$ is a symmetric relation on the letters of the alphabet. The set of sequences of pairs of complementary symbols is called a *Watson-Crick domain*, denoted with $WK_\rho(V)$, that is,

$$WK_\rho(V) = \left\{ \begin{bmatrix}x\\y\end{bmatrix} \middle| x, y \in V, \ (x,y) \in \rho \right\}^*.$$

The string pair $\begin{bmatrix}x_1\\y_1\end{bmatrix}\begin{bmatrix}x_2\\y_2\end{bmatrix}\cdots\begin{bmatrix}x_n\\y_n\end{bmatrix} \in WK_\rho(V)$ can also be written as $\begin{bmatrix}w_1\\w_2\end{bmatrix}$ if $w_1 = x_1x_2\ldots x_n$ and $w_2 = y_1y_2\ldots y_n$.

Note the difference between the round and the square brackets: $\begin{pmatrix}w_1\\w_2\end{pmatrix}$ is only an alternative notation for (w_1, w_2), while $\begin{bmatrix}w_1\\w_2\end{bmatrix} \in WK_\rho(V)$ implies that $|w_1| = |w_2|$ and that w_2 is the complement of w_1, meaning that $w_2 = y_1y_2\ldots y_n$, $w_1 = x_1x_2\ldots x_n$, $x_i, y_i \in V$, and $(x_i, y_i) \in \rho$ for all $1 \leq i \leq n$.

The notion of Watson-Crick automata was introduced in [1]. A *Watson-Crick automaton* (WK automaton in short) is a construct $M = (V, \rho, Q, q_0, F, \delta)$, where

- V is the input alphabet,
- $\rho \subseteq V \times V$ is the complementarity relation,
- Q is the nonempty finite set of states,
- $q_0 \in Q$ is the initial state,
- $F \subseteq Q$ is the set of accepting states, and
- $\delta : Q \times \begin{pmatrix}V^*\\V^*\end{pmatrix} \to 2^Q$ is a finite relation, the state transition relation.

Remark 1. It is known from [4] that the computational power of WK automata is not influenced by the complementarity relation. For any WK automata M, we can construct an M', such that it uses the relation $\rho_{id} = \{(x, x) \mid x \in V\}$, and $L(M) = L(M')$. Moreover, M' has the same set of states as M. (This is important, as we will be concerned with languages accepted by WK automata with state sets of a fixed size.) Based on this result, we assume in the following that the complementarity relation is the identity relation.

Remark 2. We use WK as the abbreviation for "Watson-Crick" in the short name of the automaton and in the notation for related notions. In this respect, we follow [8] where the abbreviation WK was introduced by selecting the beginning and the ending symbols of the sequence W A T S O N C R I C K.

A *configuration* of such a WK automaton is denoted as $\begin{pmatrix} w_1 \\ w_2 \end{pmatrix} q \begin{pmatrix} w_3 \\ w_4 \end{pmatrix}$ where $\begin{pmatrix} w_1 \\ w_2 \end{pmatrix} \in \begin{pmatrix} V^* \\ V^* \end{pmatrix}$ is the part of the input which is already read, $q \in Q$ is the state of the WK automaton, and $\begin{pmatrix} w_3 \\ w_4 \end{pmatrix} \in \begin{pmatrix} V^* \\ V^* \end{pmatrix}$ is the part of the input which is not read yet.

The *transition* between two configurations is denoted by $\Rightarrow$ and defined as follows. If $\begin{pmatrix} u_1 \\ v_1 \end{pmatrix}, \begin{pmatrix} u_2 \\ v_2 \end{pmatrix}, \begin{pmatrix} u_3 \\ v_3 \end{pmatrix} \in \begin{pmatrix} V^* \\ V^* \end{pmatrix}, \begin{bmatrix} u_1 u_2 u_3 \\ v_1 v_2 v_3 \end{bmatrix} \in WK_\rho(V), q, q' \in Q,$ then

$$\begin{pmatrix} u_1 \\ v_1 \end{pmatrix} q \begin{pmatrix} u_2 u_3 \\ v_2 v_3 \end{pmatrix} \Rightarrow \begin{pmatrix} u_1 u_2 \\ v_1 v_2 \end{pmatrix} q' \begin{pmatrix} u_3 \\ v_3 \end{pmatrix}$$

if and only if, $q' \in \delta(q, \begin{pmatrix} u_2 \\ v_2 \end{pmatrix})$. In this case, we may also write

$$\begin{pmatrix} u_1 \\ v_1 \end{pmatrix} \Rightarrow \begin{pmatrix} u_1 u_2 \\ v_1 v_2 \end{pmatrix}$$

if we are not interested in the states of the automaton and in the rest of the input to be read.

If the reflexive and transitive closure of $\Rightarrow$ is denoted by $\Rightarrow^*$, then $L(M) \subseteq V^*$, the *language accepted by* M, is defined as

$$L(M) = \left\{ w \in V^* \middle| q_0 \begin{bmatrix} w \\ w' \end{bmatrix} \Rightarrow^* \begin{bmatrix} w \\ w' \end{bmatrix} q_f, \text{ where } \begin{bmatrix} w \\ w' \end{bmatrix} \in WK_\rho(V), q_f \in F \right\}.$$

We denote the class languages accepted by WK automata by $\mathcal{L}(\text{WK})$. To indicate the number of states of the class of automata in question, we add the subscript $|Q| = k$. Thus, for example, the class of languages accepted by stateless WK automata is denoted by $\mathcal{L}(\text{WK}_{|Q|=1})$.

Now we recall the notion of string assembling systems from [5]. Instead of accepting or rejecting inputs by reading a double stranded tape as WK automata do, they generate words by assembling double stranded strings from a finite set of given double stranded building units. They are able to append such a double stranded unit to an initial double stranded prefix (an axiom) by merging the last letters of the strands of the first unit and the first letters of the corresponding strands of the second unit if these letters coincide, and moreover, if the corresponding upper and lower letters of the resulting complex are identical (thus, the upper and lower strands satisfy the complementarity relation which is the identity relation in this case).

A *string assembling system* (SAS in short) is a construct $S = (\Sigma, A, T, E)$, where

- Σ is a finite alphabet,
- $A \subset \Sigma^+ \times \Sigma^+$ is the finite set of axioms of the form $\begin{pmatrix} uv \\ u \end{pmatrix}$ or $\begin{pmatrix} u \\ uv \end{pmatrix}$ with $u \in \Sigma^+, v \in \Sigma^*,$

– $T \subset \Sigma^+ \times \Sigma^+$ is the finite set of assembly units,

– $E \subset \Sigma^+ \times \Sigma^+$ is the finite set of ending assembly units of the form $\begin{pmatrix} uv \\ v \end{pmatrix}$ or $\begin{pmatrix} v \\ uv \end{pmatrix}$ with $u \in \Sigma^*$, $v \in \Sigma^+$.

A *derivation step* of a SAS S as above is denoted by $\Rightarrow$, and defined as follows. We can add a unit $\begin{pmatrix} xu_2 \\ yv_2 \end{pmatrix}$ for some $x, y \in \Sigma$ to the double stranded word $\begin{pmatrix} u_1 \\ v_1 \end{pmatrix}$, denoted as

$$\begin{pmatrix} u_1 \\ v_1 \end{pmatrix} \Rightarrow \begin{pmatrix} u_1 u_2 \\ v_1 v_2 \end{pmatrix},$$

if and only if $bgn\left(\begin{pmatrix} xu_2 \\ yv_2 \end{pmatrix} \right) = \begin{pmatrix} x \\ y \end{pmatrix} = end\left(\begin{pmatrix} u_1 \\ v_1 \end{pmatrix} \right)$, and if $|u_1 u_2| \geq |v_1 v_2|$, then $u_1 u_2$ can be written as $u_1 u_2 = v_1 v_2 u'$ for some $u' \in \Sigma^*$, or the other way around, if $|u_1 u_2| \leq |v_1 v_2|$, then $u_1 u_2 v' = v_1 v_2$ for some $v' \in \Sigma^*$.

A sequence of derivation steps is a *derivation*. A derivation of a string assembling system $S = (\Sigma, A, T, E)$ is *successful*, if the following holds. The derivation

1. begins with an axiom unit from A,
2. continues by adding assembling units from T, and
3. ends by adding a unit from E, in such a way that
4. the upper and lower strings of the string pair which is produced have equal length (which implies that they are identical).

If the reflexive and transitive closure of $\Rightarrow$ is denoted by $\Rightarrow^*$, then the language generated by S is

$$L(S) = \left\{ w \in \Sigma^+ \,\middle|\, \begin{pmatrix} u_1 \\ v_1 \end{pmatrix} \Rightarrow^* \begin{bmatrix} u_1 u_2 \ldots u_n \\ v_1 v_2 \ldots v_n \end{bmatrix} = \begin{bmatrix} w \\ w \end{bmatrix} \text{ is a successful derivation} \right\}.$$

In this paper we will consider several variants of SAS introduced in [6]. In a *one-set string assembling system* (one-set SAS in short), the distinction between the three different types of assembly units is lifted, that is, we have $A = T = E$ for the system $S = (\Sigma, A, T, E)$. In this case, we also write S as $S = (\Sigma, T)$.

A string assembling system is called free, if the requirement that the last and the first letters of the assembly units that are glued together must match is lifted. More formally, a *free string assembling system* (free SAS in short) is a construct $S = (\Sigma, A, T, E)$ where

– Σ is a finite alphabet, as usual, but
– $A, T, E \subseteq \Sigma^* \times \Sigma^*$, thus, the empty string is allowed to be part of the building units, and

the derivation step is defined as

$$\begin{pmatrix} u_1 \\ v_1 \end{pmatrix} \xRightarrow{f} \begin{pmatrix} u_1 u_2 \\ v_1 v_2 \end{pmatrix},$$

where $\begin{pmatrix} u_1 \\ v_1 \end{pmatrix}$ and $\begin{pmatrix} u_2 \\ v_2 \end{pmatrix}$ are assembly units, and if $|u_1u_2| \geq |v_1v_2|$, then $u_1u_2 = v_1v_2u'$ for some $u' \in \Sigma^*$, or the other way around, if $|u_1u_2| \leq |v_1v_2|$, then $u_1u_2v' = v_1v_2$ for some $v' \in \Sigma^*$.

Successful derivations are defined in the same way as in SAS. Starting with an axiom unit from A, the double stranded string can be appended with units from T, and the process must be finished with a unit from E, resulting in $\begin{bmatrix} w \\ w \end{bmatrix}$ for some $w \in \Sigma^*$, a double stranded string with identical upper and lower strands.

A string assembling system is called pure, if both of the above modifications are considered. A *pure string assembling system* (pure SAS in short) is a free SAS $S = (\Sigma, A, T, E)$ with $A = T = E$ which we also write as $S = (\Sigma, T)$.

The classes of languages generated by SAS, one-set SAS, free SAS, and pure SAS are denoted by $\mathcal{L}(\text{SAS})$, $\mathcal{L}(\text{one-set SAS})$, $\mathcal{L}(\text{freeSAS})$, and $\mathcal{L}(\text{pureSAS})$, respectively. If unary languages (languages over a singleton alphabet) are considered, we write $\mathcal{L}_{unary}(X)$ for $X \in \{\text{SAS, one-set SAS, freeSAS, pureSAS}\}$.

3   Small Watson-Crick Automata and Variants of String Assembling Systems

As already mentioned above, a first attempt was made in [7] to establish a relationship between WK automata and SAS. Since, according to [5], languages generated by SAS can be accepted by nondeterministic one-way two-head finite automata, and since one-way two-head finite automata can be simulated by WK automata, it is clear that languages of SAS can be accepted by WK automata. The strictness of the inclusion can be shown using a language not in $\mathcal{L}(\text{SAS})$ (according to [5]) but accepted by a WK automaton, so we have

$$\mathcal{L}(\text{SAS}) \subset \mathcal{L}(\text{WK}).$$

Thus, in order to discover more interesting relationships, restricted variants must be considered. Looking at stateless WK automata, we have

$$\mathcal{L}(\text{SAS}) \not\subseteq \mathcal{L}(\text{WK}_{|Q|=1}),$$

from [7], as there are languages generated by SAS that cannot be accepted by stateless WK automata.

The inclusion of $\mathcal{L}(\text{WK}_{|Q|=1})$ in $\mathcal{L}(\text{SAS})$ was not shown in [7], but a certain relationship between the language classes was established, as follows. According to [5], for all languages L accepted by stateless one-way two-head finite automata, a corresponding SAS generating L' can be constructed in such a way that all $w \in L$ corresponds to $w' \in L'$ with $h(w') = w$ for a homomorphism deleting four symbols from w'. A similar statement in [7] shows that an analogous result holds if L is a language accepted by a stateless WK automaton (even a homomorphism deleting just one symbol is sufficient to establish the correspondence between $w \in L$ and $w' \in L'$). As languages of stateless one-way two-head automata are strictly included in the class of languages accepted by stateless WK automata, this later result can be seen as somewhat "stronger" than the previous one from [5] relating SAS and one-way two-head finite automata.

To continue the exploration of the relationship of stateless WK automata and variants of SAS, let us start by establishing the following equality.

Proposition 1.

$$\mathcal{L}(\text{pure SAS}) = \mathcal{L}(\text{WK}_{|Q|=1}).$$

Proof. Let $S = (\Sigma, T)$ be a pure SAS and $M = (\Sigma, \rho_{id}, \{q\}, q, \{q\}, \delta)$ be a stateless WK automaton.

Since S uses the derivation step $\stackrel{f}{\Rightarrow}$ and any added unit can be considered as an ending unit, any derivation $\begin{pmatrix} u \\ v \end{pmatrix} \stackrel{f}{\Rightarrow}^* \begin{pmatrix} w \\ w \end{pmatrix}$ where the upper and lower strands have the same length (and hence they are the same) is successful, thus $w \in L(S)$.

Similarly, M is stateless, so whenever a configuration $\begin{bmatrix} w \\ w \end{bmatrix} q \begin{bmatrix} w' \\ w' \end{bmatrix}$ occurs, then $w \in L(M)$.

The state transition relation δ of M can be defined as $q \in \delta\left(\begin{pmatrix} u \\ v \end{pmatrix}, q\right)$ for every $(u, v) \in T$, and vice versa, the set of assembly units T can be defined as $\left\{(u, v) \Big| q \in \delta\left(\begin{pmatrix} u \\ v \end{pmatrix}, q\right)\right\}$. This way for any successful derivation

$$\begin{pmatrix} u_1 \\ v_1 \end{pmatrix} \stackrel{f}{\Rightarrow} \begin{pmatrix} u_1 u_2 \\ v_1 v_2 \end{pmatrix} \stackrel{f}{\Rightarrow} \ldots \stackrel{f}{\Rightarrow} \begin{pmatrix} u_1 u_2 \ldots u_k \\ v_1 v_2 \ldots v_k \end{pmatrix}, \ (u_i, v_i) \in T, \ 1 \le i \le k,$$

there is a sequence of transitions

$$q \begin{bmatrix} u_1 u_2 \ldots u_k \\ v_1 v_2 \ldots v_k \end{bmatrix} \Rightarrow \begin{pmatrix} u_1 \\ v_1 \end{pmatrix} q \begin{pmatrix} u_2 \ldots u_k \\ v_2 \ldots v_k \end{pmatrix} \Rightarrow \ldots \Rightarrow \begin{bmatrix} u_1 u_2 \ldots u_k \\ v_1 v_2 \ldots v_k \end{bmatrix} q,$$

and vice versa. $\square$

It is known from [6] that $\mathcal{L}(\text{pureSAS}) \subset \mathcal{L}(\text{freeSAS})$, so the above proposition also tells us that

$$\mathcal{L}(\text{WK}_{|Q|=1}) \subset \mathcal{L}(\text{freeSAS}). \tag{1}$$

As we have already mentioned, it is shown in [7] that for any $L \in \mathcal{L}(\text{WK}_{|Q|=1})$ we have an $L' \in \mathcal{L}(\text{SAS})$, such that $L' = \{\$\}L$ for some marker $\$$ not in the alphabet of L. Based on relation (1) above, we can strengthen this result in the next theorem. This statement might also be interesting in connection with the problem left open in [6] of whether $\mathcal{L}(\text{freeSAS})$ is strictly included in $\mathcal{L}(\text{SAS})$ or they are incomparable.

Theorem 1. *For any $L \in \mathcal{L}(\text{freeSAS})$ over some alphabet Σ, there is an $L' \in \mathcal{L}(\text{SAS})$, such that*

$$L' = \{\$\}L,$$

where $\$ \notin \Sigma$.

Proof. Given a free SAS $S = (\Sigma, A, T, E)$ we construct a SAS $S' = (\Sigma', A', T', E')$ such that $L(S') = \{\$\}L(S)$ as follows.

- $\Sigma' = \Sigma \cup \{\$\}$,
- $A' = \{(\$u, \$v) \mid (u, v) \in A\}$,
- $T' = \{(xu, yv) \mid (u, v) \in T, \ x, y \in \Sigma \cup \{\$\}\}$,
- $E' = \{(xu, yv) \mid (u, v) \in E, \ x, y \in \Sigma \cup \{\$\}\}$.

First we show that the word $\$w$ can by generated by S' for any $w \in L(S)$. There is a successful derivation by S that starts with the axiom $(u_0, v_0) \in A$, adds some units $(u_1, v_1), (u_2, v_2), \ldots, (u_{k-1}, v_{k-1}) \in T$ and ends with the ending unit $(u_k, v_k) \in E$, such that $u_0 u_1 u_2 \ldots u_k = v_0 v_1 v_2 \ldots v_k = w$. Then there is a sequence of units $(\$u_0, \$v_0) \in A'$, $(x_1 u_1, y_1 v_1), \ldots, (x_{k-1} u_{k-1}, y_{k-1} v_{k-1}) \in T'$, $(x_k u_k, y_k v_k) \in E'$, such that $\begin{pmatrix} x_i \\ y_i \end{pmatrix} = end\left(\begin{pmatrix} x_{i-1} u_{i-1} \\ y_{i-1} v_{i-1} \end{pmatrix} \right)$, $1 \leq i \leq k$, which can be assembled into the word $\$w$, that is, $\$w \in L(S')$.

Now we show that w can by generated by S for any $\$w \in L(S')$. There is a successful derivation

$$\begin{pmatrix} \$u_a \\ \$v_a \end{pmatrix} \Rightarrow \begin{pmatrix} \$u_a u_1 \\ \$v_a v_1 \end{pmatrix} \Rightarrow \ldots \Rightarrow \begin{pmatrix} \$u_a u_1 \ldots u_k \\ \$v_a v_1 \ldots v_k \end{pmatrix} \Rightarrow \begin{pmatrix} \$u_a u_1 \ldots u_k u_e \\ \$v_a v_1 \ldots v_k v_e \end{pmatrix}$$

by S' such that $\$u_a u_1 \ldots u_k u_e = \$v_a v_1 \ldots v_k v_e = \$w$. This implies that there is a sequence of units $(u_a, v_a) \in A$, $(u_1, v_1), \ldots, (u_k, v_k) \in T$, $(u_e, v_e) \in E$ such that $u_a u_1 \ldots u_k u_e = v_a v_1 \ldots v_k v_e = w$, that is, $w \in L(S)$. $\square$

Continuing to study the relationship of free SAS and WK automata, let us begin with restricting the number of states. We can show that automata with only three states already characterize a language class that is strictly larger than the one that is generated by free SAS.

Theorem 2.
$$\mathcal{L}(\text{free SAS}) \subset \mathcal{L}(\text{WK}_{|Q|=3}).$$

Proof. For any free SAS $S = (\Sigma, A, T, E)$ we can construct a WK automaton $M = (\Sigma, \rho_{id}, \{q_A, q_T, q_E\}, q_A, \{q_E\}, \delta)$ such that $L(M) = L(S)$, with the state transition relation δ defined as follows.

- $\delta\left(q_A, \begin{pmatrix} u \\ v \end{pmatrix} \right) = q_T$ for all axioms $(u, v) \in A$,

- $\delta\left(q_T, \begin{pmatrix} u \\ v \end{pmatrix} \right) = q_T$ for all assembly units $(u, v) \in T$,

- $\delta\left(q_T, \begin{pmatrix} u \\ v \end{pmatrix} \right) = q_E$ for all ending units $(u, v) \in E$.

For any $w \in L(S)$ there is a successful derivation by S

$$\begin{pmatrix} u_a \\ v_a \end{pmatrix} \xRightarrow{f} \begin{pmatrix} u_a u_1 \\ v_a v_1 \end{pmatrix} \xRightarrow{f} \ldots \xRightarrow{f} \begin{pmatrix} u_a u_1 \ldots u_k \\ v_a v_1 \ldots v_k \end{pmatrix} \xRightarrow{f} \begin{pmatrix} u_a u_1 \ldots u_k u_e \\ v_a v_1 \ldots v_k v_e \end{pmatrix},$$

where $(u_a, v_a) \in A$, $(u_i, v_i) \in T$ $(1 \le i \le k)$ and $(u_e, v_e) \in E$, such that $u_a u_1 \ldots u_k u_e = v_a v_1 \ldots v_k v_e = w$. Since there are transitions $\delta\left(q_A, \begin{pmatrix} u_a \\ v_a \end{pmatrix}\right) = q_T$, $\delta\left(q_T, \begin{pmatrix} u_e \\ v_e \end{pmatrix}\right) = q_E$ and $\delta\left(q_T, \begin{pmatrix} u_i \\ v_i \end{pmatrix}\right) = q_T$ corresponding to the axiom (u_a, v_a), the ending unit (u_e, v_e) and the assembly units (u_i, v_i), there is a transition sequence of M

$$q_A \begin{pmatrix} u_a u_1 \ldots u_k u_e \\ v_a v_1 \ldots v_k v_e \end{pmatrix} \Rightarrow \begin{pmatrix} u_a \\ v_a \end{pmatrix} q_T \begin{pmatrix} u_1 \ldots u_k u_e \\ v_1 \ldots v_k v_e \end{pmatrix} \Rightarrow \ldots$$

$$\ldots \Rightarrow \begin{pmatrix} u_a u_1 \ldots u_k \\ v_a v_1 \ldots v_k \end{pmatrix} q_T \begin{pmatrix} u_e \\ v_e \end{pmatrix} \Rightarrow \begin{pmatrix} u_a u_1 \ldots u_k u_e \\ v_a v_1 \ldots v_k v_e \end{pmatrix} q_E,$$

that is, $w \in L(M)$.

Similarly, for any $w \in L(M)$ there is a transition sequence

$$q_A \begin{pmatrix} u_a u_1 \ldots u_k u_e \\ v_a v_1 \ldots v_k v_e \end{pmatrix} \Rightarrow \begin{pmatrix} u_a \\ v_a \end{pmatrix} q_T \begin{pmatrix} u_1 \ldots u_k u_e \\ v_1 \ldots v_k v_e \end{pmatrix} \Rightarrow \ldots$$

$$\ldots \Rightarrow \begin{pmatrix} u_a u_1 \ldots u_k \\ v_a v_1 \ldots v_k \end{pmatrix} q_T \begin{pmatrix} u_e \\ v_e \end{pmatrix} \Rightarrow \begin{pmatrix} u_a u_1 \ldots u_k u_e \\ v_a v_1 \ldots v_k v_e \end{pmatrix} q_E,$$

such that $u_a u_1 \ldots u_k u_e = v_a v_1 \ldots v_k v_e = w$. Since there is a corresponding axiom $(u_a, v_a) \in A$ for the first transition, an ending unit $(u_e, v_e) \in E$ for the last transition, and assembly units $(u_i, v_i) \in T$ $(1 \le i \le k)$ for the rest of the transitions, we can generate w by choosing the axiom, adding the assembly units in the correct order, then closing the derivation by adding the ending unit, that is, $w \in L(S)$.

To show the strictness of the inclusion, consider the unary language $L = \{a\} \cup \{a^{2n} \mid n \ge 2\}$ which according to [5] (Theorem 3.6), cannot be generated by any SAS, and by [6] (Proposition 15) it cannot be generated by any free SAS either. It is not difficult to check that L can be accepted by the WK automaton with three states $M = (\{a\}, \rho_{id}, \{q_0, q_f, q_{f'}\}, q_0, \{q_f, q_{f'}\}, \delta)$, where

$$\delta\left(q_0, \begin{pmatrix} a \\ a \end{pmatrix}\right) = q_f, \quad \delta\left(q_0, \begin{pmatrix} aaaa \\ aaaa \end{pmatrix}\right) = q_{f'}, \quad \delta\left(q_{f'}, \begin{pmatrix} aa \\ aa \end{pmatrix}\right) = q_{f'}.$$

□

Although the relationship of languages generated by three state WK automata and "ordinary" SAS is not clear, we can obtain a similar result, if we restrict our attention to unary languages.

Theorem 3.

$$\mathcal{L}_{unary}(\text{SAS}) \subset \mathcal{L}_{unary}(\text{WK}_{|Q|=3}).$$

Proof. For any unary SAS $S = (\{a\}, A, T, E)$ we can construct a WK automaton $M = (\{a\}, \rho_{id}, \{q_A, q_T, q_E\}, q_A, \{q_E\}, \delta)$ such that $L(M) = L(S)$, with δ:

$$- \ \delta\left(q_A, \begin{pmatrix} u \\ v \end{pmatrix}\right) = q_T \text{ for all } (u,v) \in A, \ u,v \in \Sigma^+,$$

$$- \ \delta\left(q_T, \begin{pmatrix} u \\ v \end{pmatrix}\right) = q_T \text{ for all } (au, av) \in T, \ u,v \in \Sigma^*,$$

$$- \ \delta\left(q_T, \begin{pmatrix} u \\ v \end{pmatrix}\right) = q_E \text{ for all } (au, av) \in E, \ u,v \in \Sigma^*.$$

To see this, consider that for any $w \in L(S)$ there is a successful derivation of S

$$\begin{pmatrix} u_a \\ v_a \end{pmatrix} \Rightarrow \begin{pmatrix} u_a u_1 \\ v_a v_1 \end{pmatrix} \Rightarrow \dots \Rightarrow \begin{pmatrix} u_a u_1 \dots u_k \\ v_a v_1 \dots v_k \end{pmatrix} \Rightarrow \begin{pmatrix} u_a u_1 \dots u_k u_e \\ v_a v_1 \dots v_k v_e \end{pmatrix},$$

where $(u_a, v_a) \in A$, $(au_i, av_i) \in T$ $(1 \le i \le k)$ and $(au_e, av_e) \in E$, such that $u_a u_1 \dots u_k u_e = v_a v_1 \dots v_k v_e = w$. To accept w, M first reads (u_a, v_a) according to the corresponding axiom $(u_a, v_a) \in A$ and transitions from the initial state q_A to the state q_T. After that M reads (u_i, v_i) and remains in q_T whenever S adds $(au_i, av_i) \in T$. Finally it reads (u_e, v_e) according to the corresponding ending unit $(au_e, av_e) \in E$ and transitions from q_T to the final state q_E, thus $w \in L(M)$.

Conversely, for any $w \in L(M)$ there is a transition sequence in M

$$q_A \begin{bmatrix} u_a u_1 \dots u_k u_e \\ v_a v_1 \dots v_k v_e \end{bmatrix} \Rightarrow \begin{pmatrix} u_a \\ v_a \end{pmatrix} q_T \begin{pmatrix} u_1 \dots u_k u_e \\ v_1 \dots v_k v_e \end{pmatrix} \Rightarrow \dots \Rightarrow \begin{bmatrix} u_a u_1 \dots u_k u_e \\ v_a v_1 \dots v_k v_e \end{bmatrix} q_E,$$

such that $u_a u_1 \dots u_k u_e = v_a v_1 \dots v_k v_e = w$. For the first and the last transition step we choose the axiom $(u_a, v_a) \in A$ and the ending unit $(au_e, av_e) \in E$, respectively, and for the rest of the transition steps we choose $(au_i, av_i) \in T$, $1 \le i \le k$. This way the word $u_a u_1 \dots u_k u_e = v_a v_1 \dots v_k v_e = w$ can be generated by assembling these units, thus $w \in L(S)$.

The strictness of the inclusion is implied by the fact that the language $\{a\} \cup \{a^{2n} \mid n \ge 2\}$ cannot be generated by any SAS, but it can be accepted a WK automaton with three states, as it is shown in the proof of Theorem 2 above. $\square$

If we consider free SAS and unary languages, we can further decrease the number of states of the simulating WK automata (although the strictness of the inclusion is not clear in this case).

Theorem 4.
$$\mathcal{L}_{unary}(\text{free SAS}) \subseteq \mathcal{L}_{unary}(\text{WK}_{|Q|=2}).$$

Proof. According to [6] (Lemma 14), for each unary free SAS an equivalent free SAS can be constructed such that its only ending unit is (λ, λ). Based on this fact we can construct a WK automaton $M = (\{a\}, \rho_{id}, \{q_A, q_T\}, q_A, \{q_T\}, \delta)$, such that $L(M) = L(S)$, with the following transition rules.

$$- \ \delta\left(q_A, \begin{pmatrix} u \\ v \end{pmatrix}\right) = q_T \text{ for all axioms } (u,v) \in A,$$

$$- \ \delta\left(q_T, \begin{pmatrix} u \\ v \end{pmatrix}\right) = q_T \text{ for all units } (u,v) \in T. \qquad \square$$

Although the relationship of the corresponding languages classes is unclear in the general case of languages over arbitrary alphabets, we can show that WK automata with two states can accept languages which cannot be generated by SAS or free SAS.

Theorem 5.

$$\mathcal{L}(\text{WK}_{|Q|=2}) \not\subseteq \mathcal{L}(\text{X}) \text{ for } X \in \{\text{SAS, free SAS}\}.$$

Proof. Let $M = (\{a, b\}, \rho_{id}, \{q_0, q_1\}, q_0, \{q_0, q_1\}, \delta)$ be a WK automaton, where

$$(1)\; \delta\left(q_0, \begin{pmatrix} a \\ \lambda \end{pmatrix}\right) = q_0, \;(2)\; \delta\left(q_0, \begin{pmatrix} b \\ a \end{pmatrix}\right) = q_0, \;(3)\; \delta\left(q_0, \begin{pmatrix} \lambda \\ b \end{pmatrix}\right) = q_0,$$

$$(4)\; \delta\left(q_0, \begin{pmatrix} a \\ a \end{pmatrix}\right) = q_1, \;(5)\; \delta\left(q_1, \begin{pmatrix} a \\ a \end{pmatrix}\right) = q_1.$$

We show that $L(M)$ cannot be generated by any SAS. Consider the following words: $w_a = a^k$, $w = a^n b^n$, $w' = a^m b^n$, where $n, m, k \geq 1$, $m > n$. It is clear that $w_a, w \in L(M)$.

To see that $w' \notin L(M)$, consider the following. Every a before the first b must be read by applying the first and second transition rules, so in the case of w' we have no choice but to apply the first transition rule m times, then to continue we must read bs on the upper strand. The only possible way to do this is applying the second transition rule n times. After that, the upper head reaches the end of the strand. Since $m > n$, there are as on the lower strand that have not been read yet. The only transition rule where we do not read anything on the upper strand is the third one, but it cannot be applied because it tries to read bs on the lower string. Thus $w' \notin L(M)$.

Now suppose there is an SAS $S = (\Sigma, A, T, E)$ which generates $L(M)$. S must be able to generate a^k, so there must be an axiom $(u_a, v_a) \in A$ and an ending unit $(au_e, av_e) \in E$, as well as assembly unit(s) $T_a \subset T$. Since k can be arbitrarily large and A, T and E are finite sets, one or more units form T_a must be used several times to build a string pair $(u_{a}u_{t}, av_{t})$ such that $u_a u_t u_e = v_a v_t v_e = a^k$.

The SAS S must be able to generate $a^n b^n$ as well, and since n can be an arbitrarily large number there must be an axiom $(u'_a, v'_a) \in A$, where $u'_a, v'_a \in \{a\}^+$, with which S can start the generation.

We cannot allow units of the form (a^i, a^i), $i > 1$ in T_a, because it can be added to the axiom (u'_a, v'_a), allowing to generate the word $a^{n+i-1} b^n \notin L(M)$, since $n+i-1 > n$. Moreover, the strings in (u_t, v_t) cannot have the same length, that is, $u_t \neq u_v$ for the same reason. T_a cannot have exclusively units of the form (a^i, a^j), $i > j$ or (a^i, a^j), $i < j$, because then the value $|u_t - v_t|$ would increase without limit as k increases, which would require to have axioms or ending units (or both) with arbitrarily large upper or lower strings.

So T_a must have at least one unit of the form (aa^i, aa^{i+j}) and one of the form (aa^{k+l}, aa^k), where $i, k \geq 0$, $j, l \geq 1$. But if we assemble l (aa^i, aa^{i+j}) units then we get $\begin{pmatrix} aa^{li} \\ aa^{l(i+j)} \end{pmatrix}$, and we also can assemble j (aa^{k+l}, aa^k) units and we get $\begin{pmatrix} aa^{j(k+l)} \\ aa^{jk} \end{pmatrix}$. Assembling these two string pairs we get $\begin{pmatrix} aa^{li}a^{j(k+l)} \\ aa^{l(i+j)}a^{jk} \end{pmatrix} =$ $\begin{pmatrix} aa^{li+jk+jl} \\ aa^{li+lj+jk} \end{pmatrix} = \begin{pmatrix} aa^{li+jk+jl} \\ aa^{li+jk+jl} \end{pmatrix}$, that is a string pair where the upper and lower strings are the same, hence their lengths are the same, which is not allowed.

So we cannot generate the words $w_a, w \in L(M)$ with S without also generating the word $w' \notin L(M)$.

Similarly we show that $L(M)$ cannot be generated by any free SAS. Suppose there is a free SAS $S' = (\Sigma, A', T', E')$ that generates $L(M)$. S' must be able to generate a^k, so there must be an axiom $(u_a, v_a) \in A'$, as well as assembly unit(s) $T'_a \subset T'$. S' must be able to generate $a^n b^n$ as well, so there must be another axiom $(u'_a, v'_a) \in A'$, where $u'_a, v'_a \in \{a\}^*$, with which S' can start the generation. T'_a cannot have units of the form (a^i, a^i), $i > 0$, but in order to be able to generate the word a^k for arbitrarily large k, T'_a must have at least one unit of the form (a^i, a^{i+j}) and one of the form (a^{k+l}, a^k), where $i, k \geq 0$, $j, l \geq 1$. But then assembling l (a^i, a^{i+j}) and j (a^{k+l}, a^k) units we get $\begin{pmatrix} a^{li+jk+jl} \\ a^{li+jk+jl} \end{pmatrix}$, which is not allowed.

So we cannot generate the words $w_a, w \in L(M)$ with S' either without also generating the word $w' \notin L(M)$. □

4   Conclusions

We have studied variants of string assembling systems and their relationship to Watson-Crick automata with a small number of states. We have shown that the classes of languages of stateless WK automata and pure SAS coincide, so they are strictly included in the class of languages of free SAS. We have also shown that the class of languages of free SAS are "almost" (modulo a starting marker) included in the class of SAS languages, but strictly included in the class of languages of WK automata with three states. In case of unary languages, the above inclusion also holds for WK automata with two states, but considering languages over arbitrary alphabets we only know that two state WK automata can accept languages which cannot be generated by neither SAS, nor free SAS. As an open problem we would like to mention our conjecture that the above two classes are incomparable.

It would also be interesting to obtain a more general result concerning SAS and WK automata with a bounded number of states. We believe that for any k, there is a SAS language that cannot be accepted by WK automata having at most k states, but to prove such a statement further investigations will be necessary.

References

1. Freund, R., Păun, G., Rozenberg, G., Salomaa, A.: Watson-Crick finite automata. In: Rubin, H., Wood, D.H. (eds.) DNA Based Computers, Proceedings of a DIMACS Workshop. DIMACS Series in Discrete Mathematics and Theoretical Computer Science, vol. 48, pp. 297–327. DIMACS/AMS (1997)
2. Kari, L., Păun, G., Rozenberg, G., Salomaa, A., Yu, S.: DNA computing, sticker systems, and universality. Acta Inform. **35**(5), 401–420 (1998)
3. Kari, L., Seki, S., Sosík, P.: DNA computing - foundations and implications. In: Rozenberg, G., Bäck, T., Kok, J.N. (eds.) Handbook of Natural Computing, pp. 1073–1127. Springer, Heidelberg (2012). https://doi.org/10.1007/978-3-540-92910-9_33
4. Kuske, D., Weigel, P.: The role of the complementarity relation in Watson-Crick automata and sticker systems. In: Calude, C., Calude, E., Dinneen, M.J. (eds.) Developments in Language Theory, 8th International Conference, DLT 2004, Proceedings. Lecture Notes in Computer Science, vol. 3340, pp. 272–283. Springer (2004)
5. Kutrib, M., Wendlandt, M.: String assembling systems. RAIRO Theor. Inform. Appl. **46**(4), 593–613 (2012)
6. Kutrib, M., Wendlandt, M.: Variants of string assembling systems. Nat. Comput. **23**, 131–156 (2024)
7. Murvai, A., Vaszil, G.: String assembling systems and Watson-Crick finite automata. In: Brejová, B., Ciencialová, L., Holena, M., Mráz, F., Pardubská, D., Plátek, M., Vinar, T. (eds.) Proceedings of the 21st Conference Information Technologies - Applications and Theory (ITAT 2021). CEUR Workshop Proceedings, vol. 2962, pp. 210–216. CEUR-WS.org (2021). https://ceur-ws.org/Vol-2962/paper44.pdf
8. Păun, G., Rozenberg, G., Salomaa, A.: DNA Computing - New Computing Paradigms. Texts in Theoretical Computer Science. An EATCS Series. Springer (1998)
9. Rozenberg, G., Salomaa, A. (eds.): Handbook of Formal Languages, Volume 1: Word, Language, Grammar. Springer (1997). https://doi.org/10.1007/978-3-642-59136-5
10. Salomaa, A.: Formal Languages. Academic Press (1973)
11. Sempere, J.M.: On the languages accepted by Watson-Crick finite automata with delays. Mathematics **9**(8) (2021). https://doi.org/10.3390/math9080813

From Petri Nets to Virus Machines

David Orellana-Martín[1,2]([✉]) [iD], Álvaro Romero-Jiménez[1,2] [iD],
Agustín Riscos-Núñez[1,2] [iD], and Mario J. Pérez-Jiménez[1,2] [iD]

[1] Research Group on Natural Computing, Department of Computer Science
and Artificial Intelligence, Universidad de Sevilla, Avda. Reina Mercedes s/n,
41012 Seville, Spain
{dorellana,romero.alvaro,ariscosn,marper}@springer.com
[2] SCORE lab, I3US, Universidad de Sevilla, Avda. Reina Mercedes s/n,
41012 Seville, Spain

Abstract. Petri nets are a classical mathematical model used for several tasks, such as simulation of business processes, modelling of complex systems and so on. This model is based on a bipartite directed graph, where the set of places and the set of transitions mark the partition. There exists marks placed in each place in a specific way, whose representation depends on the problem being solved. A virus machine is a novel model of computation inspired by the spread and replication of viruses in real life, and has been used for applications such as cryptography and power systems fault diagnosis, among others. A virus machine can be represented by three well-differentiated graphs that mark the spaces where the viruses exist and move through, called hosts and channels, the control instructions, that direct the behaviour of the virus machine, and the instruction-channel graph that represents the control of the opening and closing of the channels. In this work, we use an extension of virus machines to simulate a specific variant of Petri nets, where there exist some restrictions. In fact, a direct protocol for the simulation is explicitly given.

Keywords: Petri nets · Virus machines · Simulation

1 Introduction

Petri nets are well-studied mathematical models used for numerous applications [4]. Introduced in [5], there are several variants such as coloured Petri nets [3], reset arcs [1] and inhibitor arcs [14], among others. These variants introduce new ingredients to the basic model to increase the expressiveness of the model.

In 2015 [12], virus machines were introduced as a Turing complete model, besides other interesting approaches of demonstrating their computational power [10,11]. In the last years, some interesting applications have been studied by means of virus machines such as cryptography [6] and power systems [13]. Some interesting variants have been presented, such as virus machines with host

© The Author(s), under exclusive license to Springer Nature Switzerland AG 2025
E. Formenti and J. Durand-Lose (Eds.): MCU 2024, LNCS 15270, pp. 103–114, 2025.
https://doi.org/10.1007/978-3-031-81202-6_7

excitation [7] and stochastic virus machines [9]. In particular, in [13], two different semantics are taken into account while using channel parallelism. On the one
hand, if an instruction opening different channels needs a virus to pass through
at least one channel to select the greatest-value path, then the virus machine is
said to be using the OR semantics. On the other hand, if a virus needs to pass
through all channels connected to the instruction, then the virus machine is said
to be using the AND semantics. In this work, we mix both the AND semantics
with the parallel virus machines presented in [8].

The rest of the paper is organized as follows: Next section will be devoted to
introduce some terms that will be needed for the paper to be self-contained. In
Sects. 3 and 4, we will introduce both Petri nets in their basic description and
parallel virus machines with AND parallelism, a novel extension mixing some
ingredients from previous models. Section 5 is devoted to the introduction of the
protocol for simulating Petri nets by virus machines, and the paper finishes with
some conclusions of the work and interesting future research lines.

2   Preliminaries

In this section, some notations are included to make the paper self-contained.

Let us recall the set-based definition of natural numbers. By definition, $0 = \emptyset$,
and each number $n = n - 1 \cup \{n - 1\}$. Thus, $n = \{0, \ldots, n - 1\}$ and it is a set
that contains exactly n elements. An alphabet is a non-empty set of elements
called *symbols*. A string s over an alphabet Σ is a mapping from $n \in \mathbb{N}$ to Σ,
where n is called the *length* of s; that is, for each $k \in n$, an element from Σ is
selected. The empty string, with length 0 is denoted by λ.

A multiset over an alphabet Σ is an ordered pair (Σ, f) such that f is a
mapping from Σ to $\mathbb{N}$. We represent a multiset (Σ, f) as $\{a_1^{f(a_1)}, \ldots, a_k^{f(a_k)}\}, a_i \in \Sigma, f(a_i) > 0 \ (1 \leq i \leq k)$.

3   Petri Nets

In this section, we recall the description of Petri nets as defined in [2], but
including interesting remarks that will be useful for this work.

A Petri net of degree (σ, τ) is a tuple

$$N = (S, T, F, m_0)$$

where:

1. S is the set of *places* and T is the set of *transitions*, where $S \cap T = \emptyset, |S| = \sigma, |T| = \tau$;
2. F is a relation over $(S \times T) \cup (T \times S)$ to $\mathbb{N}$;
3. m_0 is an initial marking of N, indicating the number of *marks* in each place
   in the initial configuration.

A Petri net $N = (S, T, F, m_0)$ of degree (s, t) can be seen as a directed bipartite weighted graph G where the partition corresponds to $\{S, T\}$, where S is the set of states (depicted as circles) and T is the set of transitions (depicted as black rectangles), where the weight of an arc between two nodes x_1 and x_2 is $F(x_1, x_2)$. If $F(x_1, x_2) = 0$, then no arc is drawn from x_1 to x_2. A marking m is a function from S to $\mathbb{N}$ that indicates the number of *marks* in each place. We denote as $^\bullet x$ (respectively, $x^\bullet$) the set Y such that $F(y, x) > 0, y \in Y$ (resp., $F(x, y) > 0$), called the *preset* (resp., *postset*) of x.

Let m be a marking of a Petri net N. A finite set $U \in \mathcal{P}(T)$ of transitions is *enabled* under m (denoted as $m[U\rangle$) if $\forall s \in S \sum_{t \in T} U(t) \cdot F(s, t) \leq m(s)$; that is, if all the transitions $t_i \in U$ can take $F(s_j, t_i)$ marks from places s_j. Enabled transitions can move marks from places of their preset to places of their postset. This process is called the *firing* of a transition. If a finite set U is enabled under m, then it may be fired, reaching a marking m' such that

$$m'(s) = m(s) + \sum_{t \in T} U(t) \cdot (F(t, s) - F(s, t)),$$

for all $s \in S$. Let $\mathcal{U}$ be the set of sets of transitions *enabled* by a marking m. We say that U is maximal if it does not exist $U' \in \mathcal{U}$ such that $U \subset U'$. A *step firing sequence* of N is a (finite or infinite) sequence such that:

1. m_0 is a step firing sequence, and
2. if $m_0[U_1\rangle m_1 \ldots m_{n-1}[U_n\rangle m_n$ is a step firing sequence and $m_n[U_{n+1}\rangle m'$ is a step, then also $m_0[U_1\rangle m_1 \ldots m_n[U_n\rangle m'$ is a step firing sequence.

The length of the step firing $m_0[U_1\rangle m_1 \ldots m_{n-1}[U_n\rangle m_n$ is n. The empty sequence is associated to the step firing sequence m_0.

4 Virus Machines

In this section, we introduce the definition of virus machines when parallelism both in instructions [8] and in channels [13] is allowed.

A parallel virus machine with AND channel parallelism of degree (p, q) is a tuple

$$\Pi = (\Gamma, H, I, D_H, D_I, G_C, n_1, \ldots, n_p, I_0, h_{out})$$

where:

1. $\Gamma = \{v\}$ is a singleton alphabet, where the only element is called a *virus*;
2. $H = \{h_1, \ldots, h_p\}$, the set of *hosts*, and $I = \{i_1, \ldots, i_q)$, the set of *control instructions* are ordered sets such that $H \cap I = \emptyset, v \notin H \cup I, h_{out} \notin \Gamma \cup I$ and $I_0 \subseteq I$;

3. $D_H = (H \cup \{h_{out}\}, E_H, w_H)$ is a weighted directed graph where $E_H \subseteq H \times (H \cup \{h_{out}\})$ such that $(h, h) \notin E_H, h \in H, out - degree(h_{out}) = 0$ and w_H is a mapping from E_H to $\mathbb{N} \setminus \{0\}$, called the *hosts graph*;

4. $D_I = (I, E_I, w_I)$ is a weighted directed graph where $E_I \subseteq I \times I, out - degree(i) \leq 2$ and w_I is a mapping from E_I to $\mathbb{N} \setminus \{0\}$, called the *control instructions graph*;

5. $G_C = (V_C, E_C)$ is a directed bipartite graph where $V_C = I \cup E_H$, being $\{I, E_H\}$ the partition associated, called the *instructions-channels graph*;

6. $n_j \in \mathbb{N}, 1 \leq j \leq p$ is the number of viruses initially placed in host h_j.

A parallel virus machine with channel parallelism $\Pi = (\Gamma, H, I, D_H, D_I, G_C, n_1, \ldots, n_a, I_0, h_{out})$ of degree (p, q) can be seen as a set of p hosts, each host h_j containing initially n_j viruses, and a set of q instructions. The hosts are connected through *channels* that are initially closed. The instruction graph marks the flow of the computation, each instruction having the ability to *open* the channels it is attached to. A configuration of a parallel virus machine is given by the number of viruses in each host in a specific moment t, the set of *active* instructions and the number of viruses in the environment, denoted $C_t = (n_{1,t}, \ldots, n_{p,t}, I_t, n_{0,t})$. The initial configuration of Π is given by $C_0 = (n_1, \ldots, n_p, I_0, 0)$. A configuration is halting if $I_t = \emptyset$. A computational step of a virus machine Π in a configuration $C_t = (n_{1,t}, \ldots, n_{p,t}, I_t, n_{0,t})$ will occur as follows: each instruction $i \in I_t$ will open all the channels it is attached to. From the point of view of the hosts, if a channel (h_i, h_j) is opened, if $n_{i,t} = 0$, then no viruses will pass through it, and if $n_{i,t} > 0$, then one virus will be removed from the initial host and $w_H(h_i, h_j)$ viruses will be added to the receiving host. We must take into account that if k channels going out of h_i are opened, then two different scenarios may arise: On the one hand, if $n_{i,t} \geq k$, then a virus will pass through each channel and k viruses will be removed from such a host; On the other hand, if $n_{i,t} < k$, then all the viruses will be removed from that host and the channels where the viruses pass through are selected in a non-deterministic way. From the point of view of the instructions, if for each channel that is opened by an instruction i_j a virus passes, then the next instruction will be i_k such that $(i_j, i_k) \in E_I$ and $\nexists i_m \in I$ such that $(i_j, i_k) \in E_I$ and $w_I(i_j, i_k) < w_I(i_j, i_m)$; that is, it will select the greatest-value path. Otherwise, it will select the lower-value path; that is, the next instruction will be i_k such that $(i_j, i_k) \in E_I$ and $\nexists i_m \in I$ such that $(i_j, i_k) \in E_I$ and $w_I(i_j, i_k) > w_I(i_j, i_m)$. If the out-degree of i_j is 2 and both paths have the same weight, then the path will be selected in a non-deterministic way. If the out-degree of i_j is 0, then i_j will not have a following instruction. Each instruction of I_t is executed at the same time. A *transition* or *computational step* of a parallel virus machine with AND channel parallelism Π from C_t to C_{t+1} is made by the execution of all the instructions from I_t as stated above, and it is denoted as $C_t \Rightarrow_\Pi C_{t+1}$. A computation of a virus machine Π is a sequence of configurations $\mathcal{C} = (C_0, C_1, \ldots, C_n)$, where C_0 is the initial configuration of Π and for each t, $C_t \Rightarrow_\Pi C_{t+1}$. A halting computation is a computation such that $n \in \mathbb{N}$, and its last configuration C_n is a halting configuration (that is, $I_n = \emptyset$).

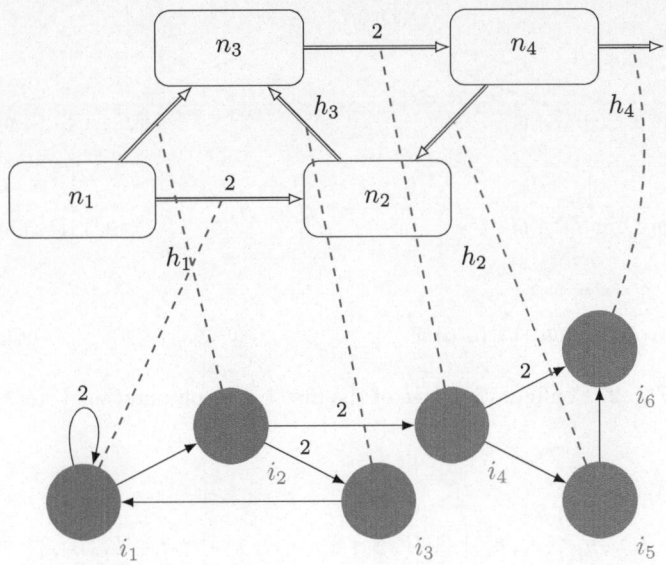

Fig. 1. Example of a basic virus machine of degree $(4, 6)$

An example of a virus machine of degree $(4, 6)$ is depicted in Fig. 1. Let us think that the initial configuration is $C_0 = (2, 0, 0, 1, \{i_1, i_2\}, 0)$. In the first computational step, both i_1 and i_2 open the channels going out from h_1. Since two viruses are present in h_1, a virus passes through each of these channels. Concerning i_1, the next instruction is selected going through the highest-weight path, being i_1; Concerning i_2, since both paths going out from it have the same weight, the selection of the next instruction is made in a non-deterministic way. Thus, two different configurations can arise from the initial one: $C_1 = (0, 2, 1, 1, \{i_1, i_3\}, 0)$ or $C_1' = (0, 2, 1, 1, \{i_1, i_4\}, 0)$. A tree of computations of this virus machine with that initial configuration is depicted in Fig. 2.

In the right branch, it can be appreciated that since instruction i_6 has no next instructions, then a single instruction will be running until the computation halts (or it goes forever in the loop $i_1 \rightarrow i_2 \rightarrow i_3$). It is easy to see that the number of active instructions is staying the same or decreasing; that is, $|I_t| \geq |I_{t+1}|$.

5   Simulation of Petri Nets with Virus Machines

In this section we introduce a way to simulate Petri nets by virus machines. More specifically, we will simulate Petri nets when the set of transitions enabled is *maximal*; that is, if $\mathcal{U}$ is the set of sets of enable transitions, then we select a set $U \in \mathcal{U}$ such that there does not exist $U' \in \mathcal{U}$ where $U \subset U'$, $F(x, y) \leq 1$. Let $N = (S, T, F, m_0)$ such that $S = \{s_1, \ldots, s_p\}$ and $T = \{t_1, \ldots, t_r\}$. The virus machine simulating N is

$$\Pi = (\Gamma, H, I, D_H, D_I, G_C, n_1, \ldots, n_a, I_0, h_{out})$$

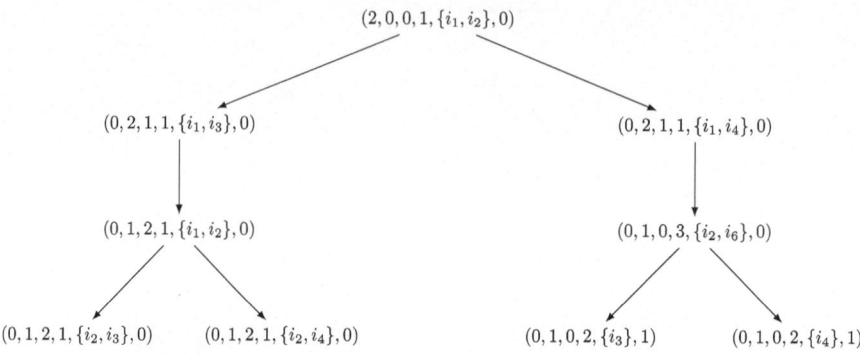

Fig. 2. Configuration tree of the first three computational steps

such that:

1. $\{h_{s_1}, \ldots, h_{s_p}, h_{t_1}, \ldots, h_{t_r}\} \subseteq H$ and for each $s \in^\bullet t, t \in T, \{h_{s-t}\} \in H$;
2. $I = \{i_{t_1}, i_{t_{1_n}}, i_{t'_{1_n}}, i_{t_{1_y}}, i_{t'_{1_y}}, \ldots, i_{t_r}, i_{t_{r_n}}, i_{t'_{r_n}}, i_{t_{r_y}}, i_{t'_{r_y}}\}$;
3. $D_H = (H, E_H, w_H)$, where:
   - for each $s \in^\bullet t, t \in T, \{(h_s, h_{s-t}), (h_{s-t}, h_s), (h_{s-t}, h_t)\} \subseteq E_H$. Let $k_1 = |^\bullet t|$ and $k_2 = |t^\bullet|$. Then, $w_H(h_{s-t}, h_t) = 1$ for $k_1 - 1$ channels except for one whose value is $max(1, k_2 - k_1 + 1)^1$;
   - for each $s \in t^\bullet, t \in T, (h_t, h_s) \in E_H$, and $w_H(h_t, h_s) = 1$;
4. $I_H = (I, E_I, w_I)$, where:
   - for each $t \in T, \{(i_t, i_{t_n}), (i_{t_n}, i_{t'_n}), (i_{t'_n}, i_t), (i_t, i_{t_y}), (i_{t_y}, i_{t'_y}), (i_{t'_y}, i_t)\}$;
   - $w_I(i_t, i_{t_n}) = w_I(i_{t_n}, i_{t'_n}) = w_I(i_{t'_n}, i_t) = w_I(i_{t_y}, i_{t'_y}) = w_I(i_{t'_y}, i_t) = 1, w_I(i_t, i_{t_y}) = 2$;
5. $G_C = (H \cup I, E_C)$, where:
   - for each $s \in^\bullet t, t \in T, \{(i_t, (h_s, h_{s-t}), (i_{t_n}, (h_{s-t}, h_s)), (i_{t_y}, (h_{s-t}, h_t))\} \in E_C$
   - for each $s \in t^\bullet, t \in T, (i_{t'_y}, (h_t, h_s)) \in E_C$;
6. $n_s = m_0(s), n_{s-t} = n_t = 0$, for $s \in S$ and $t \in T$;
7. for each $t \in T, i_t \in I_0$;
8. h_{out} is the environment.

The simulation for a single transition as depicted in Fig. 3 can be seen in Fig. 4. Let m_k be a marking of a Petri net N. This marking is simulated in the configuration C_{3k} of the virus machine Π. If the transition t is *not enabled*, then at least one of the places in $^\bullet t$ has no marks. In this case, the transition will not move any mark from any place to any other place. The virus machine will work as follows: i_t is executed, but since not all hosts $h_s (s \in^\bullet t)$ have viruses, then the lowest-value path is selected, thus the next instruction selected is i_{t_n} in the $3k + 2$ step, which will send back the viruses from h_{s-t} to h_s, in order to

---

[1] This is made in order to have enough viruses to sent to the hosts simulating the postset of t.

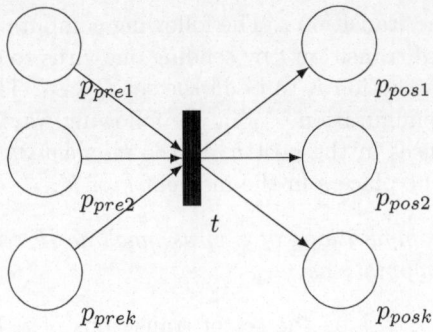

Fig. 3. A basic transition of Petri nets

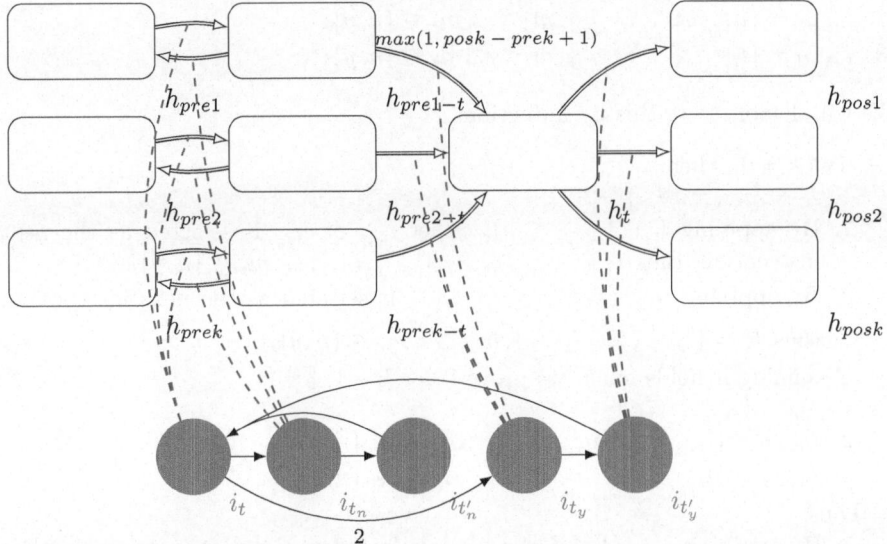

Fig. 4. A parallel virus machine with AND channel parallelism simulating a transition of Petri nets

keep the original viruses in their respective hosts. The computational step that finishes the simulation of a *not enabled* transition is a waiting step simulated by the instruction $i_{t'_n}$, that is not attached to any channel, and will select back the instruction i_t, to start simulating the next *firing* of the Petri net. If the transition t is *enabled*, then all the places in $^\bullet t$ have at least one mark. Then, all the hosts $h_s(s \in^\bullet t)$ transmit a virus to h_{s-t}, and since all the channels connected to i_t have a virus passing by them, then the next selected instruction is i_{t_y}, as it is connected by the greatest-value path. In the configuration C_{3k+1}, all h_{s-t} such that $s \in^\bullet t$ contain exactly one virus, which will be transmitted in the step $3k + 2$, but one of them will transmit $|t^\bullet| - |^\bullet t| + 1$ viruses. This special behaviour is made in order to have enough viruses for the hosts representing the postset of places of the transition t. The following computational step will finish the firing of an *enabled* transition t by sending one virus to each host $h_s(s \in t^\bullet)$, and leading to the instruction i_t to be in the set $I_{3(k+1)}$. The marking m_k of N is simulated by the configuration C_{3k} in the following way: $m_k(s) = n_{s,3k}$; that is, the number of viruses in the host h_s in the moment $3k$ of Π represents the number of marks in the place s in the moment k of N.

Lemma 1. *All the computations of a virus machine Π simulating a Petri net N are non-halting computations.*

Proof. Let $T = \{t_1, \ldots, t_r\}$ be the set of transitions of t. For each $k \in \mathbb{N}$, the following holds:

1. $I_{3k} = \{i_{t_1}, \ldots, i_{t_r}\}$;
2. $I_{3k+1} = \{i_{t_{1_{m_1}}}, \ldots, i_{t_{1_{m_r}}}\}, m_1, \ldots, m_r \in \{n, y\}$;
3. $I_{3k+2} = \{i_{t'_{1_{m_1}}}, \ldots, i_{t'_{1_{m_r}}}\}, m_1, \ldots, m_r \in \{n, y\}$;

We will demonstrate this by induction:

- Let $k = 0$. Then:
  1. $I_0 = \{i_{t_1}, \ldots, i_{t_r}\}$
  2. By applying $i_{t_j} (1 \leq j \leq r)$, either $i_{t_{j_n}}$ or $i_{t_{j_y}}$ is selected as the next instruction, thus $I_1 = \{i_{t_{1_{m_1}}}, \ldots, i_{t_{1_{m_r}}}\}, m_1, \ldots, m_r \in \{n, y\}$
  3. By applying $i_{t_{j_{m_j}}} (1 \leq j \leq r)$, $i_{t'_{j_{m_j}}}$ is selected as the next instruction, thus $I_2 = \{i_{t'_{1_{m_1}}}, \ldots, i_{t'_{1_{m_r}}}\}, m_1, \ldots, m_r \in \{n, y\}$.
- Assuming it holds for k, we prove it for $k + 1$.
  1. $I_{3k} = \{i_{t_1}, \ldots, i_{t_r}\}$;
  2. $I_{3k+1} = \{i_{t_{1_{m_1}}}, \ldots, i_{t_{1_{m_r}}}\}, m_1, \ldots, m_r \in \{n, y\}$;
  3. $I_{3k+2} = \{i_{t'_{1_{m_1}}}, \ldots, i_{t'_{1_{m_r}}}\}, m_1, \ldots, m_r \in \{n, y\}$;
  Thus:
  1. By applying $i_{t'_{j_{m_j}}} (1 \leq j \leq r)$, i_t is selected as the next instruction, thus $I_{3(k+1)} = \{i_{t_1}, \ldots, i_{t_r}\}$;
  2. By applying $i_{t_j} (1 \leq j \leq r)$, either $i_{t_{j_n}}$ or $i_{t_{j_y}}$ is selected as the next instruction, thus $I_{3(k+1)+1} = \{i_{t_{1_{m_1}}}, \ldots, i_{t_{1_{m_r}}}\}, m_1, \ldots, m_r \in \{n, y\}$;
  3. By applying $i_{t_{j_{m_j}}} (1 \leq j \leq r)$, $i_{t'_{j_{m_j}}}$ is selected as the next instruction, thus $I_{3(k+1)+2} = \{i_{t'_{1_{m_1}}}, \ldots, i_{t'_{1_{m_r}}}\}, m_1, \ldots, m_r \in \{n, y\}$;

$\square$

Because of this, we impose the following condition as a halting condition for such a virus machine Π. If $C_{3k} = C_{3(k+1)}$, then the virus machine halts. Since $I_{3k} = I_{3(k+1)}$, the rest of the configuration is equal if $n_{j,3k} = n_{j,3(k+1)}$, that is, if no *enabled* transitions have been simulated. We must take into account that when simulating an enabled transition t, some viruses could be left over in h_t, but if such a transition is not enabled, these viruses will not move to $h_s(s \in t^\bullet)$, thus the configuration still remains the same in C_{3k} and $C_{3(k+1)}$. Apart from that, let us think at a place such that $\exists t_1, t_2 \in T, t_1 \neq t_2, s \in^{\bullet} t_1 \cap^{\bullet} t_2$, and let the marking $m_k(s) = 1$. Then, in the first step of the simulation, both channels (h_s, h_{s-t_1}) and (h_s, h_{s-t_2}) will be opened, but the virus present in h_s will be moved through only one of these channels. Let us think that the channel non-deterministically selected is the channel (h_s, h_{s-t_1}), and that a virus pass through all the channels $(h_{s'}, h_{s'-t_1}), s' \in^{\bullet} t_1$ and $(h_{s''}, h_{s''-t_2}) \in^{\bullet} t \setminus \{s\}$. Then, the transition t_1 will be simulated as *enabled* and t_2 will not be enabled, as it should be since only one mark was present in the marking m_k.

5.1   Removing Some Restrictions from the Original Model

There exists an easy way to avoid the restriction on having to select a *maximal* set of transitions to be enabled, and to avoid the restriction of having $F(t, s) \leq 1, t \in T, s \in t^{\bullet}$. For the first restriction, we include two new instructions for each instruction t, that are $i_{t''_n}$ and i_{t_m}. Apart from that, channels $(h_{s-t}, h_s), \forall s \in^{\bullet} t$ are connected to $i_{t'_n}$ and not to i_{t_n}. Besides, new edges have been created in the control instruction graph. For the second restriction, we include $F(t, s)$ as the weights of the channels going out of h_t. All these changes are depicted in Fig. 5.

Formally, the elements of Π described previously in this section that are changed in this case are I, D_I and G_C. The new description of these elements is as follows:

1. $D_H = (H, E_H, w_H)$, where:
   - for each $s \in^{\bullet} t, t \in T, \{(h_s, h_{s-t}), (h_{s-t}, h_s), (h_{s-t}, h_t)\} \subseteq E_H$. Let $k_1 = |^{\bullet}t|$ and $k_2 = |t^{\bullet}|$. Then, $w_H(h_{s-t}, h_t) = 1$ for $k_1 - 1$ channels except for one whose value is $max(1, k_2 - k_1 + 1)^2$;
   - for each $s \in t^{\bullet}, t \in T, (h_t, h_s) \in E_H$, and $w_H(h_t, h_s) = F(t, s)$ (this is, in fact, is the only change made to D_H with respect to the previous one);
2. $I = \{i_{t_1}, i_{t_{1_n}}, i_{t'_{1_n}}, i_{t''_{1_n}}, i_{t_{1_m}}, i_{t_{1_y}}, i_{t'_{1_y}}, \ldots, i_{t_r}, i_{t_{r_n}}, i_{t'_{r_n}}, i_{t''_{r_n}}, i_{t_{r_m}}, i_{t_{r_y}}, i_{t'_{r_y}}\}$;
3. $I_H = (I, E_I, w_I)$, where:
   - for each $t \in T, \{(i_t, i_{t_n}), (i_{t_n}, i_{t'_n}), (i_{t'_n}, i_{t''_n}), (i_{t''_n}, i_t), (i_t, i_{t_m}), (i_{t_m}, i_{t'_n}), (i_{t_m}, i_{t_y}), (i_{t_y}, i_{t'_y}), (i_{t'_y}, i_t)\}$;
   - $w_I(i_t, i_{t_n}) = w_I(i_{t_n}, i_{t'_n}) = w_I(i_{t'_n}, i_{t''_n}) = w_I(i_{t''_n}, i_t) = w_I(i_{t_m}, i_{t'_n}) = w_I(i_{t_m}, i_{t_y}) = w_I(i_{t_y}, i_{t'_y}) = w_I(i_{t'_y}, i_t) = 1, w_I(i_t, i_{t_m}) = 2$;
4. $G_C = (H \cup I, E_C)$, where:
   - for each $s \in^{\bullet} t, t \in T, \{(i_t, (h_s, h_{s-t})), (i_{t''_n}, (h_{s-t}, h_s)), (i_{t_y}, (h_{s-t}, h_t))\} \in E_C$
   - for each $s \in t^{\bullet}, t \in T, (i_{t'_y}, (h_t, h_s)) \in E_C$;

In this case, the simulation of a single *firing* would be described in four computational steps. That is, the marking m_k of a Petri net N will be represented in the configuration $C_{4k} = (n_{1,4k}, \ldots, n_{p,4k}, I_{4k}, n_{0,4k})$ of Π as $m_k(s) = n_{h_s,4k}$. In the case that the transition is *not enabled*, the behaviour is similar to that

---

[2] This is made in order to have enough viruses to sent to the hosts simulating the postset of t.

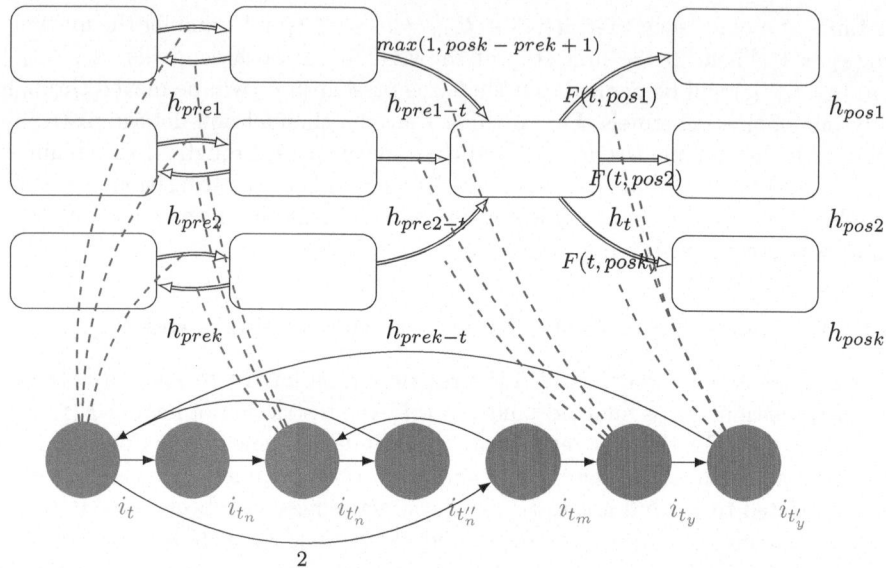

Fig. 5. A module of a virus machine simulating t, i_{t_m} decides whether the transition is *fired* if it was enabled

one explained in the previous case. If the transition t is *not enabled*, then at least one of the places in $^\bullet t$ has no marks. The virus machine will work as follows: i_t is executed, but since not all hosts $h_s (s \in^\bullet t)$ have viruses, then the lowest-value path is selected, thus the next instruction selected is i_{t_n} in the $3k + 2$ step. In the next step, the instruction $i_{t'_n}$ will send back the viruses from h_{s-t} to h_s, in order to keep the original viruses in their respective hosts. The computational step that finishes the simulation of a *not enabled* transition is a waiting step simulated by the instruction $i_{t''_n}$, that is not attached to any channel, and will select back the instruction i_t, to start simulating the next *firing* of the Petri net. If the transition t is *enabled*, then all the places in $^\bullet t$ have at least one mark. Then, all the hosts $h_s (s \in^\bullet t)$ transmit a virus to h_{s-t}, and since all the channels connected to i_t have a virus passing through them, then the next selected instruction is i_{t_m}, as it is connected by the greatest-value path. In this moment, a non-deterministic selection will decide if the transition is *fired* or not. If the next instruction is $i_{t'_n}$, then the transition will not be fired, and it will return the viruses to the original hosts to wait for the next firing to be simulated, and the simulation of the current firing will be finished with the execution of the instruction $i_{t''_n}$. If the next instruction is i_{t_y}, then the firing will be simulated, and the behaviour is similar to the previous case. All the viruses from $h_{s-t}(s \in^\bullet t)$ will be submitted to h_t, being one of them replicated to $|t^\bullet| - |^\bullet t| + 1$ viruses. The following computational step will finish the firing of an *enabled* transition t by sending one virus to each host $h_s (s \in t^\bullet)$, and leading to the instruction i_t to be in the set $I_{4(k+1)}$. In this case, since all the transitions can "decide" to not be fired, then an infinite computation exists such that no transitions are executed, thus having to remove the special halting condition defined above.

With this change, the type of Petri nets that can be simulated is less restrictive than the previous one, and with this approach we can simulate Petri nets where $F(s,t) \leq 1, t \in T, s \in {}^{\bullet} t$.

6   Conclusions and Future Work

A first approach to Petri nets through virus machines seems an interesting idea from the point of view of simulation. In this work, a rather simplified model of Petri nets has been studied for being simulated with virus machines. For that purpose, a protocol to obtain virus machines that simulates a restricted version of Petri nets has been obtained. In the future, three interesting research lines are open. First, simulating more generic types of Petri nets is interesting, including some ingredients such as weights and non-determinism. Second, simplifying the virus machines used to simulate Petri nets is a good idea in order to use a lower computational power and have efficient software simulations. Last, simulating virus machines by Petri nets, that would lead to interesting uses of proof schemas used in Petri nets into the framework of virus machines.

Disclosure of Interests. The authors have no competing interests to declare that are relevant to the content of this article.

References

1. Araki, T., Kasami, T.: Some decision problems related to the reachability problem for Petri nets. Theoret. Comput. Sci. **3**(1), 85–104 (1976)
2. Ciobanu, G., Michele Pinna, G.: Catalytic and communicating Petri nets are Turing complete. Inf. Comput. **239**, 55–70 (2014)
3. Jensen, K.: A brief introduction to coloured Petri Nets. In: Brinksma, E. (ed.) TACAS 1997. LNCS, vol. 1217, pp. 203–208. Springer, Heidelberg (1997). https://doi.org/10.1007/BFb0035389
4. Pawlewski, P.: Petri nets applications. InTech, Poland (2010)
5. Petri, C.A.: Kommunikation mit Automaten (Ph.D. thesis). University of Bonn (1962)
6. Ramírez-de-Arellano, A., Orellana-Martín, D., Pérez-Jiménez, M.J.: Attacking cryptosystems by means of virus machines. Nat. Sci. Rep. **13**, 21831 (2023)
7. Ramírez-de-Arellano, A., Orellana-Martín, D., Pérez-Jiménez, M.J.: Bridges between spiking neural membrane systems and virus machines. Int. J. Neural Syst. (2024)
8. Ramírez-de-Arellano, A., Orellana-Martín, D., Pérez-Jiménez, M.J.: Parallel Virus Machines. J. Membrane Comput. (accepted)
9. Ramírez-de-Arellano, A., Rodríguez-Gallego, J.A., Orellana-Martín, D., Ivanov, S.: Stochastic virus machines. In: Proceedings of the 19th Brainstorming Week on Membrane Computing, pp. 79–90. RGNC REPORT 1/2023, Sevilla (2023)

10. Romero-Jiménez, Á., Valencia-Cabrera, L., Pérez-Jiménez, M.J.: Generating Diophantine sets by virus machines. In: BIC-TA 2015. CCIS, vol. 562, pp. 331–341. Springer, Heidelberg (2015). https://doi.org/10.1007/978-3-662-49014-3_30
11. Romero-Jiménez, Á., Valencia-Cabrera, L., Riscos-Núñez, A., Pérez-Jiménez, M.J.: Computing partial recursive functions by virus machines. In: Rozenberg, G., Salomaa, A., Sempere, J.M., Zandron, C. (eds.) CMC 2015. LNCS, vol. 9504, pp. 353–368. Springer, Cham (2015). https://doi.org/10.1007/978-3-319-28475-0_24
12. Valencia-Cabrera, L., Pérez-Jiménez, M.J., Chen, X., Wang, B., Zeng, X.: Basic virus machines. In: 16th International Conference on Membrane Computing (CMC16), pp. 323–342 (2015)
13. Wu, H., Ramirez-de-Arellano, A., Orellana-Martín, D., Wang, T., Wang, T., Pérez-Jiménez, M.J.: Channel parallel virus machine with production rules for power system fault diagnosis. J. Membrane Comput. (submitted)
14. Zaitsev, D.A.: Toward the minimal universal Petri net. IEEE Trans. Syst. Man Cybern.: Syst. **44**(1), 47–58 (2013)

On the Powers of the Collatz Function

Didier Caucal[1,2] and Chloé Rispal[2(✉)]

[1] National Center for Scientific Research, University Gustave Eiffel, Paris, France
didier.caucal@gmail.com, Chloe.rispal@univ-eiffel.fr
[2] Computer Laboratory Gaspard Monge, University Gustave Eiffel, Paris, France

Abstract. For all natural numbers a, b and $d > 0$, we consider the function $f_{a,b,d}$ which associates n/d with any integer n when it is a multiple of d, and $an + b$ otherwise; in particular $f_{3,1,2}$ is the Collatz function. To realize these functions by transducers (automata labelled by pairs of words), the coding in reverse base 2 is generally used. For the Collatz function, it gives a simple 5-states transducer but it is not suitable for the composition and so far, no one has been able to specify, for all integers p, a generic transducer computing its composition p times. Coding in direct base ad with $b < a$, we realize the functions $f_{a,b,d}$ by synchronous sequential transducers. This particular form makes explicit the composition of such a transducer p times to compute $f_{a,b,d}^p$ in terms of p and a, b, d. We even give an explicit construction of an infinite transducer realizing the closure under composition of $f_{a,b,d}$.

1 Introduction

Many functions on integers have been described by automata (transducers) as word functions using an integer base. In general, the properties of sequences produced by transducers are studied [2,6] but in this work, we address mainly properties of the realized functions themselves.

In this paper, we are interested in the family of functions $f_{a,b} : \mathbb{N} \longrightarrow \mathbb{N}$ defined for all natural numbers a, b and any integer $n \geq 0$ by

$$f_{a,b}(n) = \begin{cases} \frac{n}{2} & \text{if } n \text{ is even,} \\ an + b & \text{otherwise.} \end{cases}$$

In particular, $f_{3,1}$ is the Collatz function [5]. The Collatz conjecture states that, for any integer n, there exists $p \geq 0$ such that the composition of the Collatz function p times applied to n equals 1: $f_{3,1}^p(n) = 1$. This conjecture remains open despite recent progress [12]. A new conjecture on this function has been proposed [3]. In this paper, our aim is to give an explicit deterministic transducer realizing the p-th power $f_{a,b}^p$ in terms of p.

To realize the function $f_{a,b}$, the transducer must compute the operations of division by 2, multiplication by a and addition of b. A first natural approach is to take the base 2 with the least significant digit to the left to see right away if the input is even and, if not, to realize multiplication by a and addition of b starting from the left. Basic arithmetic operations have already been described by transducers [7]. The Collatz function can be realized easily by a 5-states

E. Formenti and J. Durand-Lose (Eds.): MCU 2024, LNCS 15270, pp. 115–129, 2025.
https://doi.org/10.1007/978-3-031-81202-6_8

sequential transducer. Introduced by Ginsburg, sequential transducers compute functions deterministically. Their transitions are labelled by a letter in input and a word in output. They have been extended with a terminal function associating an output word to each terminal state [8]. The sequential transducer in reverse base 2 for the Collatz function can be composed a few times to realize $f_{3,1}^2$, $f_{3,1}^3$ and so on, but so far, no one has been able to specify, for all integers p, a generic transducer computing its composition p times.

To solve this problem, we chose the direct base $2a$. When $b < a$, which is the case of the Collatz function, we obtain a 2-states deterministic sequential transducer realizing $f_{a,b}$. This new transducer, which in addition is letter-to-letter, can be composed to get an explicit transducer realizing $f_{a,b}^p$ in terms of p. The difficulty in defining its terminal function has been overcome using a key lemma given in [1].

For all natural integers $b < a$ and $d > 0$, we generalize the previous transducers for the functions $f_{a,b,d} : \mathbb{N} \longrightarrow \mathbb{N}$ defined for any integer $n \geq 0$ by

$$f_{a,b,d}(n) = \begin{cases} \frac{n}{d} & \text{if } n \text{ is a mutiple of } d, \\ an + b & \text{otherwise.} \end{cases}$$

Using the base ad, and for all integer p, we obtain a generic transducer computing $f_{a,b,d}^p$ in terms of p. Finally, for any natural numbers a, b, d with $b < a \neq 1$ and $d \neq 0$, we give an explicit construction of a transducer realizing the closure under composition of $f_{a,b,d}$.

2   Transducers in Reverse Base 2

In this section, we first recall basic definitions. Then, we look at the transducers realizing the functions $f_{a,b,d}$ using the reverse base 2. Although this approach seems natural, we notice that those transducers are not appropriate for composition.

Let N be a finite alphabet. We denote by N^* the set of words over letters of N, and we write ε for the empty word.

A *transducer* $\mathcal{T}$ is defined by a finite subset of $Q \times N^* \times N^* \times Q$ of labelled edges where Q is a finite set of states, by a set $I \subseteq Q$ of initial states, and by a set $F \subseteq Q$ of final states. So a transducer is a finite automaton labelled by pairs of words. Any transition (p, u, v, q) of a transducer $\mathcal{T}$ will be denoted by $p \xrightarrow[\mathcal{T}]{u/v} q$ or by $p \xrightarrow{u/v} q$ when $\mathcal{T}$ is understood.

A path $p_0 \xrightarrow{u_1/v_1} p_1 \dots p_{n-1} \xrightarrow{u_n/v_n} p_n$ with $u = u_1 \dots u_n$ and $v = v_1 \dots v_n$ is labelled u/v and is denoted by $p_0 \xRightarrow[\mathcal{T}]{u/v} p_n$. A path is *successful* if it leads from an initial state to a final one. A pair $(u, v) \in N^* \times N^*$ is recognized by a transducer if there exists a successful path labelled u/v. For instance, the following transducer:

with a unique initial state on the left and a unique final state on the right recognizes the relation $\{ (0^n1^m, 1^n0^{2m}) \mid n \geq 0, m > 0 \}$.

Let $\beta > 1$ and let $\widehat{\beta} = \{0, \ldots, \beta - 1\}$ be the alphabet of its *digits*. Any word $u \in \widehat{\beta}^*$ is a (respectively reverse) *representation in base* β of the integer $[u]_\beta$ (respectively ${}_\beta[u]$) defined by

$$[c_n \ldots c_0]_\beta = \sum_{i=0}^{n} c_i \beta^i = {}_\beta[c_0 \ldots c_n]$$

for any $n \geq 0$ and $c_0, \ldots, c_n \in \widehat{\beta}$.

Representations of integers are extended to relations. A relation $R \subseteq \widehat{\beta}^* \times \widehat{\beta}^*$ is a representation (respectively reverse representation) in base β of the binary relation $[R]_\beta$ (respectively ${}_\beta[R]$) on $\mathbb{N}$:

$$[R]_\beta = \{ ([u]_\beta, [v]_\beta) \mid (u, v) \in R \} \text{ and } {}_\beta[R] = \{ ({}_\beta[u], {}_\beta[v]) \mid (u, v) \in R \}.$$

The functions $f_{a,b}$ on integers can be seen as relations on words and defined by transducers. First, let us see what transducers can be obtained for the functions $f_{a,b}$ using a coding in reverse base 2. For some simple functions such as $f_{1,1}$, we get a transducer for the composition p times using an acceleration. This is not possible in the general case. Consider the function $f_{1,1} : \mathbb{N} \longrightarrow \mathbb{N}$ defined for any integer $n \geq 0$ by

$$f_{1,1}(n) = \begin{cases} \frac{n}{2} & \text{if } n \text{ is even,} \\ n+1 & \text{otherwise.} \end{cases}$$

The first natural approach is to take the base 2 with the least significant digit to the left. In reverse base 2, $f_{1,1}$ is realized by the following word function:

$$0u \longrightarrow u \qquad \text{for any binary word } u$$
$$1u \longrightarrow 0(u+1)$$

This word function is realized by the following 3 states transducer:

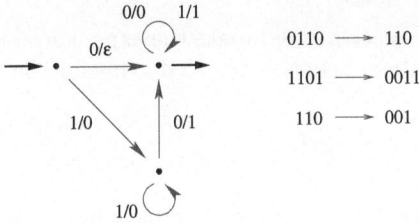

Fig. 1. Transducer realizing $f_{1,1}$ in reverse base 2

Taking the product, we can construct an automaton for $f_{1,1}^p$ having 3^p states but we do not know how to define it in terms of p. To solve this problem, for any natural integers a, b of same parity, we consider the *acceleration* $f'_{a,b}$ defined for any natural number n by

$$f'_{a,b}(n) = \begin{cases} \frac{n}{2} & if \ n \text{ is even,} \\ \frac{an+b}{2} & \text{otherwise.} \end{cases}$$

In the particular case of $f'_{1,1}$, we get the property below.

Lemma 1. *For all* $n, p \geq 0$, $f_{1,1}^{\prime p}(n) = \lceil \frac{n}{2^p} \rceil$.

Proof. By induction on $p \geq 0$.

$p = 0$: For all $n \geq 0$, $f_{1,1}^{\prime 0}(n) = n = \lceil \frac{n}{2^0} \rceil$.

$p \geq 0$: If n is even then $f_{1,1}^{\prime p+1}(n) = f_{1,1}^{\prime p}(\frac{n}{2}) = \lceil \frac{n}{2^{p+1}} \rceil$ by induction hypothesis. Otherwise n is odd and can be written $n = 2^{p+1}k + r$ for some $k \geq 0$ and $0 < r < 2^{p+1}$. We have

$$f_{1,1}^{\prime p+1}(n) = f_{1,1}^{\prime p}(\tfrac{n+1}{2}) = \lceil \tfrac{n+1}{2^{p+1}} \rceil = k + \lceil \tfrac{r+1}{2^{p+1}} \rceil = k + 1 = k + \lceil \tfrac{r}{2^{p+1}} \rceil = \lceil \tfrac{n}{2^{p+1}} \rceil.$$

◀

So for any $n, p \geq 0$, $f_{1,1}^{\prime p}(n) = \begin{cases} \frac{n}{2^p} & if \ n \text{ is a multiple of } 2^p, \\ \lfloor \frac{n}{2^p} \rfloor + 1 & \text{otherwise.} \end{cases}$

In reverse base 2, we get the function

$$0^p u \longrightarrow u \qquad \text{for any } u \in \{0, 1\}^*$$
$$v u \longrightarrow u + 1 \quad \text{for } |v| = p \text{ and } v \neq 0^p$$

which is recognized by the following transducer:

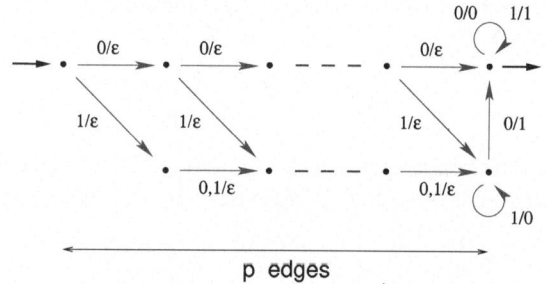

Fig. 2. Transducer realizing $f_{1,1}^{\prime p}$ in reverse base 2

In this case, the acceleration breaks the exponential number 3^p of states into the linear number $2p + 1$. Let us try to do this for the Collatz function:

$$f_{3,1}(n) = \begin{cases} \frac{n}{2} & if \ n \text{ is even,} \\ 3n + 1 & \text{otherwise.} \end{cases}$$

Using the reverse base 2, we get the following transducer among others [10].

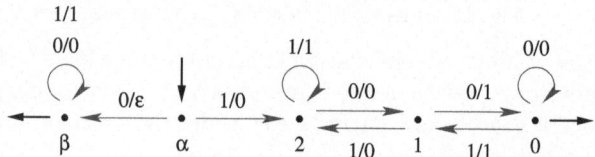

Fig. 3. The Collatz function in reverse base 2

The states 0, 1, 2 manage the carry of the multiplication by 3.

From this transducer, it follows some results to describe the behaviour of the Collatz function by automata [9] and regular expressions [11].

Contrary to the previous case, we cannot get a transducer in reverse base 2 for $f_{3,1}^p$ in terms of p, not even for its acceleration $f_{3,1}'^p$.

3   Transducer for $f_{a,b}$ in base $2a$

In the following, we will use the base a and a particular case of transducer, namely deterministic synchronized transducers, very convenient to make the composition. For any $0 \leq b < a$ of same parity, we give a transducer in standard base a realizing the acceleration $f_{a,b}'$. Since $f_{a,b} = f_{2a,2b}'$, we obtain a transducer in base $2a$ for $f_{a,b}$.

A (input-)*deterministic synchronized transducer* $\mathcal{T} = (Q, T, i, \omega)$ is defined by a finite set Q of *states*, a subset T of $Q \times \hat{a} \times \hat{a} \times Q$ of transitions, an initial state $i \in Q$ and a final partial function $\omega : Q \to \hat{a}^*$. We denote by $q \xrightarrow{w}$ when q is a final state such that $\omega(q) = w$. The set of transitions is *input-deterministic* meaning that if $p \xrightarrow{c/d} q$ and $p \xrightarrow{c/e} r$ then $d = e$ and $q = r$. The transducer $\mathcal{T}$ *realizes* the binary relation

$$\langle \mathcal{T} \rangle = \{ (u, vw) \in \hat{a}^* \times \hat{a}^* \mid \exists q \in Q \ (i \xRightarrow{u/v}_{\mathrm{T}} q \xrightarrow{w}) \}.$$

For instance, the following deterministic synchronized transducer $\mathcal{T}_{2,1}$:

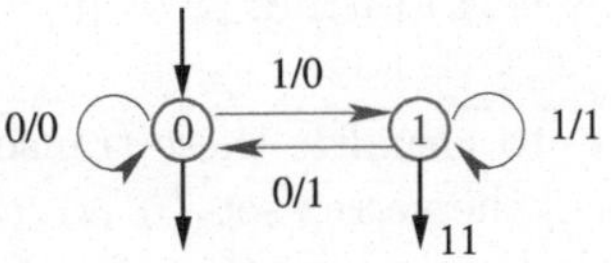

Fig. 4. Transducer realizing $f_{2,1}$ in base 2

realizes the following word function $\langle \mathcal{T}_{2,1} \rangle$:

$$\varepsilon \longrightarrow \varepsilon$$
$$u0 \longrightarrow 0u \quad \text{for any } u \in \{0,1\}^*$$
$$u1 \longrightarrow 0u11$$

which is, in direct base 2, a representation of $f_{2,1} = [\langle \mathcal{T}_{2,1} \rangle]_2$.

To generalize this transducer to any base a and $b < a$, we need the standard deterministic synchronized transducer

$$/_{a,d,r} = (\hat{d}, :_{a,d}, \{0\}, \omega_{a,d,r})$$

of division by d in base a with remainder r where

$$\omega_{a,d,r}(r) = \epsilon \text{ and } i \xrightarrow{b/c}_{:a,d} j \text{ if } ia + b = cd + j \text{ for all } i,j \in \hat{d} \text{ and } b,c \in \hat{a}.$$

The transition relation can be extended to paths.

Lemma 2. *For all* $i, j \in \hat{d}$ *and* $u, v \in \hat{a}^*$, *we have*

$$i \xRightarrow{u/v}_{:a,d} j \quad \Longleftrightarrow \quad i\,a^{|u|} + [u]_a = [v]_a d + j \text{ and } |u| = |v|.$$

Proof. Each implication can be checked easily by induction on $|u| \geq 0$.

$\Longrightarrow$: As $:_{a,d}$ is a subset of $\hat{d} \times \hat{a} \times \hat{a} \times \hat{d}$, $|u| = |v|$.

Let us check the equality by induction on $|u| \geq 0$.

$|u| = 0$: We have $u = \varepsilon = v$ and $i = j$ hence the equality.

Let $i \overset{ub/vc}{\Longrightarrow} j$ with $b, c \in \hat{a}$ and the implication true for u. There exists k such that $i \overset{u/v}{\Longrightarrow} k \overset{b/c}{\longrightarrow} j$. Thus $i\,a^{|u|} + [u]_a = [v]_a d + k$ and $ka + b = cd + j$. Hence

$$i\,a^{|ub|} + [ub]_a = b + (i\,a^{|u|} + [u]_a)a = b + ([v]_a d + k)a = [v]_a da + (ka + b)$$
$$= [v]_a da + cd + j = [vc]_a d + j .$$

$\Longleftarrow$: by induction on $|u| \geq 0$.

$|u| = 0$: We have $u = \varepsilon = v$ and $i = j$ hence $i \overset{u/v}{\Longrightarrow} j$.

Suppose the implication true for $|u|$ and $i\,a^{|ub|} + [ub]_a = [vc]_a d + j$ with $|u| = |v|$ and $0 \leq b, c < a$. So, we have $(i\,a^{|u|} + [u]_a)a + b = [v]_a ad + cd + j$.

By Euclidean division of $cd + j$ by a, we have $cd + j = ka + b'$ with $b' < a$. As $b < a$, we have $b = b'$ hence $i\,a^{|u|} + [u]_a = [v]_a d + k$.

As $|u| = |v|$ and by induction hypothesis, $i \overset{u/v}{\Longrightarrow} k$. As $cd + j = ka + b$, we get $k \overset{b/c}{\longrightarrow} j$ hence $i \overset{ub/vc}{\Longrightarrow} j$. ◀

Thus $/_{a,d,r}$ realizes $\{\ (u,v) \mid u, v \in \downarrow_a^* \wedge |u| = |v| \wedge [u]_a = [v]_a d + r\ \}$.

Let us propose a way to visualize these transducers to highlight basic symmetries. The d integers of the vertex set $\{0, \ldots, d-1\}$ of $:_{a,d}$ are equidistant on a counterclockwise circle in a way that the diameter between 0 and $d-1$ is horizontal with 0 at the top right. Here is a representation for respectively $d = 1, 2, 3, 4$:

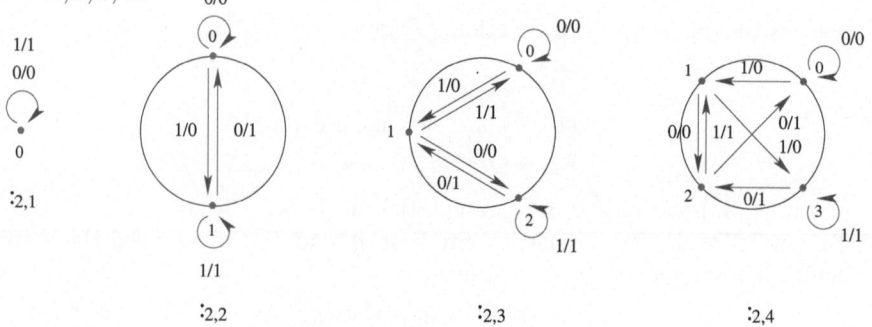

Fig. 5. Visualization of the division

Using division by 2 in base a, we give a deterministic synchronized transducer for the acceleration $f'_{a,b}$ for any $0 \leq b < a$ of same parity.

Proposition 1. *For all $0 \le b < a$ with $a > 1$ and a, b of same parity,*
$$\mathcal{T}'_{a,b} = (\{0,1\}, :_{a,2}, \{0\}, \omega'_{a,b}) \text{ with } \omega'_{a,b}(0) = \varepsilon \text{ and } \omega'_{a,b}(1) = \tfrac{a+b}{2}$$
is a deterministic synchronized transducer realizing a representation in base a of $f'_{a,b}$.

Proof. As $:_{a,2}$ is input-deterministic and input-complete (for all $p \in \{0,1\}$ and $b \in \widehat{a}$, there exists a unique transition starting from p of input b), for all $u \in \widehat{a}^*$, there exists a unique $v \in \widehat{a}^*$ and $j \in \{0,1\}$ such that $0 \xRightarrow{u/v} :_{a,2} j$.
By Lemma 2, we have $[u]_a = 2[v]_a + j$.
For $j = 0$, $[u]_a$ is even and $[v]_a = \frac{[u]_a}{2} = f'_{a,b}([u]_a)$.
For $j = 1$, $[u]_a$ is odd and since $\frac{a+b}{2} < a$, we have

$$[v\omega'_{a,b}(1)]_a = a[v]_a + \tfrac{a+b}{2} = a\,\tfrac{[u]_a - 1}{2} + \tfrac{a+b}{2} = \tfrac{a[u]_a + b}{2} = f'_{a,b}([u]_a). \blacktriangleleft$$

Thus $\mathcal{T}'_{3,1} = (\{0,1\}, :_{3,2}, \{0\}, \omega'_{3,1})$ with $\omega'_{3,1}(0) = \epsilon$ and $\omega'_{3,1}(1) = 2$ realizes in base 3 the acceleration $f'_{3,1}$ of the Collatz function:

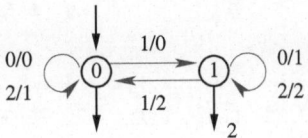

Fig. 6. Acceleration of the Collatz function in base 3

The transitions $:_{3,2} = \{\, i \xrightarrow{b/c} j \mid i*3 + b = c*2 + j \,\}$ realize division by 2 in base 3: for all $u, v \in \widehat{3}^*$, if $0 \xRightarrow{u/v} j$ then $[u]_3 = [v]_3 2 + j$.
If $j = 0$ then $[u]_3$ is even and $[v]_3 = \frac{[u]_3}{2} = f'_{a,b}([u]_3)$.
If $j = 1$, then $[u]_3$ is odd and $[v2]_3 = \frac{[u]_3 - 1}{2} * 3 + 2 = \frac{3[u]_3 + 1}{2} = f'_{a,b}([u]_3)$.
Translating this transducer in a word rewriting system, we get a variant of the system defined by [13].

Finally, the transducer $\mathcal{T}'_{6,2}$ realizes in base 6 the Collatz function $f_{3,1} = f'_{6,2}$:

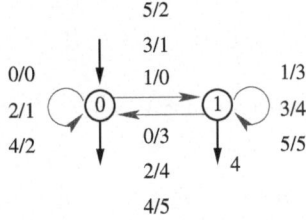

Fig. 7. The Collatz function in base 6

More generally for any $0 \le b < a$, the function $f_{a,b} = f'_{2a,2b}$ is represented in base $2a$ by the deterministic synchronized transducer $\mathcal{T}'_{2a,2b}$.

4   Transducers for $f_{a,b}^p$ in Base $2a$

By composition of the previous transducer in base a realizing the acceleration $f'_{a,b}$, we obtain a deterministic synchronized transducer realizing $f_{a,b}^{\prime p}$.

Deterministic synchronized transducers are closed under composition : the composition of $\mathcal{T} = (Q, T, i, \omega)$ by $\mathcal{T}' = (Q', T', i', \omega')$ is the transducer $\mathcal{T} \circ \mathcal{T}' = (Q \times Q', T \circ T', (i, i'), \omega \circ \omega')$ defined by

$$T \circ T' = \{ (p, p') \xrightarrow{b/c} (q, q') \mid \exists\, d\ (p \xrightarrow[T]{b/d} q \wedge p' \xrightarrow[T']{d/c} q') \}\ \text{and}$$

$\omega \circ \omega'((p, p')) = v.\omega'(q')$ for any $p \in \mathrm{dom}(\omega)$, any $q' \in \mathrm{dom}(\omega')$ and any $p' \xRightarrow{\omega(p)/v}_{T'} q'$.

For instance, the transducer $\mathcal{T}_{3,1}^{\prime 2}$ is represented as follows:

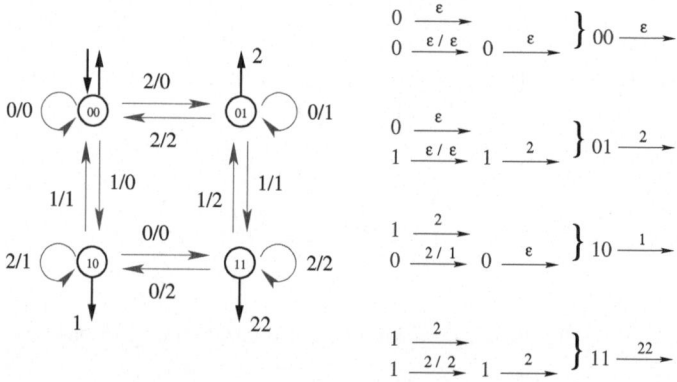

Fig. 8. The composition of transducers

Note that its set of transitions realizes division by 4 in base 3 by coding each vertex in reverse base 2. Precisely, the relation $:_{a,d} \circ :_{a,d'}$ is in bijection with the relation $:_{a,dd'}$ by coding any vertex (i, i') where $0 \le i < d$ and $0 \le i' < d'$ by the integer $_d[(i, i')] = i + i'd$.

Lemma 3. For all $a > 1$ and $d, d' > 0$, $_d[:_{a,d} \circ :_{a,d'}]$ is equal to $:_{a,dd'}$.

Proof. For all $0 \le i, j < d$ and $0 \le i', j' < d'$, we have

$$(i, i') \xrightarrow{b/c}_{:_{a,d} \circ :_{a,d'}} (j, j')$$

$$\Longleftrightarrow \exists\, 0 \le e < a\ \text{such that}\ i \xrightarrow{b/e}_{:_{a,d}} j\ \text{and}\ i' \xRightarrow{e/c}_{:_{a,d'}} j'$$

$$\Longleftrightarrow \exists\, 0 \le e < a\ \text{such that}\ ia + b = ed + j\ \text{and}\ i'a + e = cd' + j'$$

$$\Longleftrightarrow ia + b = (cd' + j' - i'a)d + j$$

$$\Longleftrightarrow (i + i'd)a + b = cdd' + j + j'd$$

$$\Longleftrightarrow {}_d[(i, i')] \xrightarrow{b/c}_{:_{a,dd'}} {}_d[(j, j')] . \blacktriangleleft$$

More generally, to realize the function $f'^p_{a,b}$, we first do division by 2^p and then the numerator is performed by the terminal function. This is possible by the property below [1] using the number

$$\eta_{a,b,p}(n) = |\{\, 0 \leq i < p \mid f'^i_{a,b}(n) \text{ odd } \}|$$

of odd integers among the first p powers of $f'_{a,b}$ applied to n.

Lemma 4. *For all natural numbers a, b, p, q, r with a, b of same parity,*

$$f'^p_{a,b}(q2^p + r) = q\, a^{\eta_{a,b,p}(r)} + f'^p_{a,b}(r) \quad \text{and} \quad \eta_{a,b,p}(q2^p + r) = \eta_{a,b,p}(r).$$

Proof. By induction on $p \geq 0$.

$p = 0$: $\eta_{a,b,0}$ is the constant mapping 0 and $f'^0_{a,b}$ is the identity.

$p \implies p+1$: For r even, we have

$$\begin{aligned}
f'^{p+1}_{a,b}(q2^{p+1} + r) &= f'^p_{a,b}(f'_{a,b}(q2^{p+1} + r)) = f'^p_{a,b}(q2^p + \tfrac{r}{2}) \\
&= q\, a^{\eta_{a,b,p}(\frac{r}{2})} + f'^p_{a,b}(\tfrac{r}{2}) = q\, a^{\eta_{a,b,p+1}(r)} + f'^{p+1}_{a,b}(r)
\end{aligned}$$

and $\eta_{a,b,p+1}(q2^{p+1} + r) = \eta_{a,b,p}(q2^p + \tfrac{r}{2}) = \eta_{a,b,p}(\tfrac{r}{2}) = \eta_{a,b,p+1}(r)$.

For r odd, we have

$$\begin{aligned}
f'^{p+1}_{a,b}(q2^{p+1} + r) &= f'^p_{a,b}(f'_{a,b}(q2^{p+1} + r)) = f'^p_{a,b}(aq2^p + \tfrac{ar+b}{2}) \\
&= f'^p_{a,b}(aq2^p + f'_{a,b}(r)) = q\, a^{1+\eta_{a,b,p}(f'_{a,b}(r))} + f'^p_{a,b}(f'_{a,b}(r)) \\
&= q\, a^{\eta_{a,b,p+1}(r)} + f'^{p+1}_{a,b}(r)
\end{aligned}$$

and

$$\begin{aligned}
\eta_{a,b,p+1}(q2^{p+1} + r) &= 1 + \eta_{a,b,p}(f'_{a,b}(q2^{p+1} + r)) = 1 + \eta_{a,b,p}(aq2^p + f'_{a,b}(r)) \\
&= 1 + \eta_{a,b,p}(f'_{a,b}(r)) = \eta_{a,b,p+1}(r). \blacktriangleleft
\end{aligned}$$

This property helps to calculate the terminal function of transducers realizing $f'^p_{a,b}$. Take for example the path $00 \overset{200/011}{\Longrightarrow} 01$ of the previous transducer $T'^2_{3,1}$. It calculates the quotient $[011]_3$ of $[200]_3$ by 2^2 and its rest $_2[01]$. By Lemma 4, we get $f'^2_{3,1}([200]_3) = f'^2_{3,1}([011]_3 * 2^2 +_2[01]) = [011]_3 * 3 + f'^2_{3,1}(_2[01])$. So the terminal function in $_2[01]$ must be $\omega'_{3,1}(_2[01]) = f'^2_{3,1}(_2[01]) = 2$.

We denote by $_2[T'^p_{a,b}]$ the transducer where each vertex $x \in \{0,1\}^p$ is replaced by the integer $_2[x]$. Then $_2[T'^p_{a,b}]$ is the transducer of division by 2^p in base a with a terminal function defined by the 2^p first values of $f'^p_{a,b}$. For any vertex, the length of its final word is the number of odd numbers among the first p values of its orbit.

Theorem 1. *For all $p \geq 0$ and $0 \leq b < a \neq 1$ with a, b of same parity, the function $f'^p_{a,b}$ is recognized by the transducer*

$$_2[T'^p_{a,b}] = (\{0, \ldots, 2^p - 1\}, :_{a,2^p}, \{0\}, \omega'_p)$$

of division by 2^p in base a with the terminal function defined for any $0 \leq i < 2^p$ by $\omega'_p(i) \in \hat{a}^*$, $[\omega'_p(i)]_a = f'^p_{a,b}(i)$ and $|\omega'_p(i)| = \eta_{a,b,p}(i)$.

Proof. By induction on $p \geq 0$.

$p = 0$: $\mathcal{T}_{a,b}^{\prime 0} = (\{\varepsilon\}, \{\varepsilon\}, \omega, \{\varepsilon \xrightarrow{c/c} \varepsilon \mid c \in \widehat{a}\})$ with $\omega(\varepsilon) = \varepsilon$.

$p \implies p+1$: we have $\mathcal{T}_{a,b}^{\prime p+1} = \mathcal{T}_{a,b}^{\prime} \circ \mathcal{T}_{a,b}^{\prime p}$.

By Lemma 3, the relation $_2[:_{a,2} \; o \; :_{a,2^p}]$ is equal to $:_{a,2^{p+1}}$. We have to show that $\omega_{p+1}^{\prime}$ is the terminal function of $_2[\mathcal{T}_{a,b}^{\prime p+1}]$.

As $\omega_{a,b}^{\prime}(0) = \varepsilon$, we get $\omega_{p+1}^{\prime}(_2[0u]) = \omega_p^{\prime}(_2[u])$ for any $u \in \{0,1\}^p$ hence $\omega_{p+1}^{\prime}(2i) = \omega_p^{\prime}(i)$ for all $0 \leq i < 2^p$.

By induction hypothesis, we get
$$[\omega_{p+1}^{\prime}(2i)]_a = [\omega_p^{\prime}(i)]_a = f_{a,b}^{\prime p}(i) = f_{a,b}^{\prime p+1}(2i) \quad \text{and}$$
$$|\omega_{p+1}^{\prime}(2i)| = |\omega_p^{\prime}(i)| = \eta_{a,b,p}(i) = \eta_{a,b,p+1}(2i).$$

Similarly $\omega_{a,b}^{\prime}(1) = \frac{a+b}{2}$ and for any $0 \leq i < 2^p$, there exists unique j and c such that $i \xrightarrow{\frac{a+b}{2}/c}_{:_{a,2^p}} j$ thus $\omega_{p+1}^{\prime}(2i+1) = c.\omega_p^{\prime}(j)$.

Moreover $f_{a,b}^{\prime}(2i+1) = ia + \frac{a+b}{2} = c2^p + j$.

By Lemma 4 and induction hypothesis,
$$\begin{aligned}
[\omega_{p+1}^{\prime}(2i+1)]_a &= [c.\omega_p^{\prime}(j)]_a &&= c \, a^{|\omega_p^{\prime}(j)|} + [\omega_p^{\prime}(j)]_a \\
&= c \, a^{\eta_{a,b,p}(j)} + f_{a,b}^{\prime p}(j) = f_{a,b}^{\prime p}(c2^p + j) \\
&= f_{a,b}^{\prime p+1}(2i+1)
\end{aligned}$$

and

$$\begin{aligned}
|\omega_{p+1}^{\prime}(2i+1)| &= 1 + |\omega_p^{\prime}(j)| &&= 1 + \eta_{a,b,p}(j) \\
&= 1 + \eta_{a,b,p}(c2^p + j) = 1 + \eta_{a,b,p}(f_{a,b}^{\prime}(2i+1)) \\
&= \eta_{a,b,p+1}(2i+1). \blacktriangleleft
\end{aligned}$$

Here is a representation in base 5 of $f_{5,1}^{\prime 3}$ by the transducer $\mathcal{T}_{5,1}^{\prime 3}$:

Note that the final word of the state 100 is 04 and not 4, and the accepting path $000 \xrightarrow{4/0} 001 \xrightarrow{2/2} 011 \xrightarrow{3/4} 100 \xrightarrow{04}$ of input word 423 and output word 02404 represents $f_{5,1}^{\prime 3}(113) = 354$ in base 5.

The function $f_{a,b}^p$ realized in base $2a$ by the deterministic synchronized transducer $\mathcal{T}_{a,b}^p = \mathcal{T}_{2a,2b}^{\prime p}$.

5   Transducers for $f_{a,b,d}^p$ in Base ad

For all natural numbers a, b, d with $d \neq 0$, we consider the functions $f_{a,b,d}$: $\mathbb{N} \longrightarrow \mathbb{N}$ defined for any integer $n \geq 0$ by

$$f_{a,b,d}(n) = \begin{cases} \frac{n}{d} & \text{if } n \text{ is a mutiple of } d, \\ an + b & \text{otherwise.} \end{cases}$$

So $f_{a,b} = f_{a,b,2}$. For $b < a$, we generalize the previous transducers realizing $f_{a,b}$. We define a deterministic synchronized transducer realizing $f_{a,b,d}$ from the transducer computing division by d in base ad.

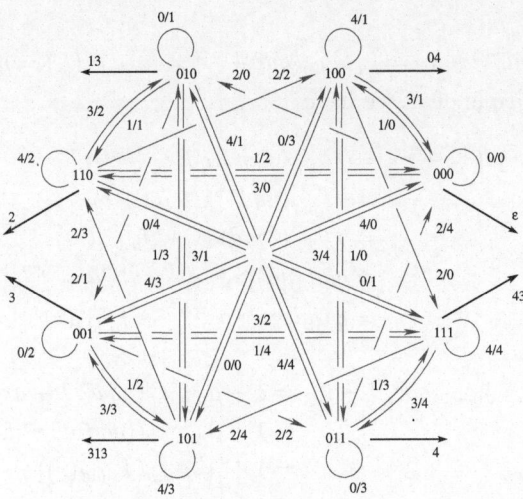

Fig. 9. Transducer realising $f_{5,1}^{\prime 3}$ in base 5

Proposition 2. *For all $0 \le b < a \ne 1$ and $d > 0$, the deterministic synchronized transducer*
$$\mathcal{T}_{a,b,d} = (\{0, \ldots, d-1\}, :_{ad,d}, \{0\}, \omega_{a,b})$$
with $\omega_{a,b}(0) = \varepsilon$ and $\forall \, 0 < j < d$, $\omega_{a,b}(j) = aj + b$ realizes a representation in base ad of $f_{a,b,d}$.

Sketch of Proof. If an initial path ends to the state j, the input represents an integer n multiple of d plus j and the output represents $\frac{n-j}{d}$. The final digit in $j \ne 0$ is $aj + b$ since $ad\frac{n-j}{d} + aj + b = an + b = f_{a,b,d}(n)$. ◄

For all natural numbers $a, b, p, n \ge 0$, $\eta_{a,b,p}(n)$ is generalized to the number
$$\mu_{a,b,d,p}(n) = |\{\, 0 \le i < p \mid f_{a,b,d}^{\,i}(n) \text{ not multiple of } d \,\}|$$
of integers that are not multiples of d among the first p numbers of the orbit from n of $f_{a,b,d}$. Let us adapt Lemma 4 to the powers of $f_{a,b,d}$.

Lemma 5. *For all natural numbers a, b, d, p, q, r with $d > 0$, we have*
$$f_{a,b,d}^{p}(qd^p + r) = q\,(ad)^{\mu_{a,b,d,p}(r)} + f_{a,b,d}^{p}(r) \text{ and } \mu_{a,b,d,p}(qd^p + r) = \mu_{a,b,d,p}(r).$$
Proof. By induction on $p \ge 0$.
$p = 0$: immediate because $\mu_{a,b,d,0}$ is the constant mapping 0 and $f_{a,b,d}^{0}$ is the identity.
$p \implies p+1$: For r multiple of d, we have
$$\begin{aligned}
f_{a,b,d}^{p+1}(qd^{p+1} + r) &= f_{a,b,d}^{p}(f_{a,b,d}(qd^{p+1} + r)) & = f_{a,b,d}^{p}(qd^p + \tfrac{r}{d}) \\
&= q\,(ad)^{\mu_{a,b,d,p}(\frac{r}{d})} + f_{a,b,d}^{p}(\tfrac{r}{d}) = q\,(ad)^{\mu_{a,b,d,p+1}(r)} + f_{a,b,d}^{p+1}(r)
\end{aligned}$$

and

$$\mu_{a,b,d,p+1}(qd^{p+1} + r) = \mu_{a,b,d,p}(qd^p + \tfrac{r}{d}) = \mu_{a,b,d,p}(\tfrac{r}{d}) = \mu_{a,b,d,p+1}(r).$$

For r not multiple of d, we have

$$
\begin{aligned}
f_{a,b,d}^{p+1}(qd^{p+1} + r) &= f_{a,b,d}^p(f_{a,b,d}(qd^{p+1} + r)) \\
&= f_{a,b,d}^p(aqd^{p+1} + ar + b) \\
&= f_{a,b,d}^p((qad)d^p + f_{a,b,d}(r)) \\
&= qad\,(ad)^{\mu_{a,b,d,p}(f_{a,b,d}(r))} + f_{a,b,d}^p(f_{a,b,d}(r)) \\
&= q\,(ad)^{\mu_{a,b,d,p+1}(r)} + f_{a,b,d}^{p+1}(r)
\end{aligned}
$$

and

$$
\begin{aligned}
\mu_{a,b,d,p+1}(qd^{p+1} + r) &= 1 + \mu_{a,b,d,p}(aqd^{p+1} + ar + b) \\
&= 1 + \mu_{a,b,d,p}((qad)d^p + f_{a,b,d}(r)) \\
&= 1 + \mu_{a,b,d,p}(f_{a,b,d}(r)) \\
&= \mu_{a,b,d,p+1}(r). \blacktriangleleft
\end{aligned}
$$

Similarly to Theorem 1, we get an explicit description of the transducer $\mathcal{T}_{a,b,d}^p$ realizing $f_{a,b,d}^p$ for all p.

Theorem 2. *For all integers $p \geq 0$ and $0 \leq b < a \neq 1$ and $d > 0$, the function $f_{a,b,d}^p$ is realized by the transducer*

$$_d[\mathcal{T}_{a,b,d}^p] = (\{0, \ldots, d^p - 1\}, :_{ad,d^p}, \{0\}, \omega_p)$$

with the terminal function defined for any $0 \leq i < d^p$, by $\omega_p(i) \in \widehat{ad}^*$, $[\omega_p(i)]_{ad} = f_{a,b,d}^p(i)$ and $|\omega_p(i)| = \mu_{a,b,d,p}(i)$.

Proof. By induction on $p \geq 0$.

$p = 0$: $\mathcal{T}_{a,b,d}^0 = (\{\varepsilon\}, \{\varepsilon\}, \omega, \{\varepsilon \xrightarrow{c/c} \varepsilon \mid c \in \widehat{ad}\})$ with $\omega(\varepsilon) = \varepsilon$.

$p \implies p+1$: we have $\mathcal{T}_{a,b,d}^{p+1} = \mathcal{T}_{a,b,d} \circ \mathcal{T}_{a,b,d}^p$.

By Lemma 3, the transition relation $_d[:_{ad,d} \ o \ :_{ad,d^p}]$ is equal to $:_{ad,d^{p+1}}$. We have to show that ω_{p+1} is the terminal function of $_d[\mathcal{T}_{a,b,d}^{p+1}]$. As $\omega_{a,b}(0) = \varepsilon$, we get $\omega_{p+1}(_d[0u]) = \omega_p(_d[u])$ for any $u \in \downharpoonleft_d^p$ i.e. $\omega_{p+1}(di) = \omega_p(i)$ for all $0 \leq i < d^p$. By induction hypothesis, we get

$$[\omega_{p+1}(di)]_{ad} = [\omega_p(i)]_{ad} = f_{a,b,d}^p(i) = f_{a,b,d}^{p+1}(di)$$

and

$$|\omega_{p+1}(di)| = |\omega_p(i)| = mu_{a,b,d,p}(i) = \mu_{a,b,d,p+1}(di).$$

Let $0 \leq i < d^p$ and $0 < j < d$. So $\omega_{a,b}(j) = aj + b \leq a(d-1) + b < ad$. There exists unique k and c such that $i \xrightarrow[:_{ad,d^p}]{aj+b/c} k$ thus $\omega_{p+1}(di + j) = c.\omega_p(k)$.

Moreover $f_{a,b,d}(di + j) = iad + aj + b = cd^p + k$.

By Lemma 5 and induction hypothesis,

$$\begin{aligned}
[\omega_{p+1}(di+j)]_{ad} &= [c.\omega_p(k)]_{ad} \\
&= c\,(ad)^{|\omega_p(k)|} + [\omega_p(k)]_{ad} \\
&= c\,(ad)^{\mu_{a,b,d,p}(k)} + f_{a,b,d}^p(k) \\
&= f_{a,b,d}^p(cd^p + k) \\
&= f_{a,b,d}^{p+1}(di+j)
\end{aligned}$$

and

$$\begin{aligned}
|\omega_{p+1}(di+j)| &= 1 + |\omega_p(k)| \\
&= 1 + \mu_{a,b,d,p}(k) \\
&= 1 + \mu_{a,b,d,p}(cd^p + k) \\
&= 1 + \mu_{a,b,d,p}(f_{a,b,d}(di+j)) \\
&= \mu_{a,b,d,p+1}(di+j). \blacktriangleleft
\end{aligned}$$

6 Transducers for $f_{a,b,d}^*$

We present a simple infinite deterministic synchronized transducer realizing the composition closure of $f_{a,b,d}$ for $b < a \neq 1$ and $d > 0$.

To construct this transducer we just take the union of the transition sets $(:_{a,2})^p$ of the division by 2^p in base a, plus the set of initial states 0^p, plus a terminal function defined according to b by length induction that is from the vertices of the division by 2^p to the vertices of the division by 2^{p-1}.

Proposition 3. *For all $0 \leq b < a$ with $a > 1$ and a,b of the same parity,*
$$\mathcal{T}_{a,b}'^* = (\{0,1\}^*, 0^*, \omega_{a,b}', :_{a,2}^*) \text{ where for all } u \in \{0,1\}^*,$$
$$\omega_{a,b}'(0u) = \omega_{a,b}'(u) \text{ and } \omega_{a,b}'(1u) = c.\omega_{a,b}'(v) \text{ for } 1u \xrightarrow{b/c} :_{a,2}^* 0v.$$

Proof. We have seen in the proof of Theorem 1 that for all $p \geq 0$, the terminal function ω_{p+1}' of $\mathcal{T}_{a,b}'^{p+1}$ is defined recursively for all $0 \leq i < 2^p$ by

$$\omega_{p+1}'(2i) = \omega_p'(i)$$
$$5\omega_{p+1}'(2i+1) = c.\omega_p'(j) \text{ for } i \xrightarrow{\frac{a+b}{2}/c} :_{a,2^p} j$$

and we have

$$\begin{aligned}
i \xrightarrow{\frac{a+b}{2}/c} :_{a,2^p} j &\iff ia + \tfrac{a+b}{2} = c2^p + j \\
&\iff (2i+1)a + b = c2^{p+1} + 2j \\
&\iff 2i+1 \xrightarrow{b/c} :_{a,2^{p+1}} 2j. \blacktriangleleft
\end{aligned}$$

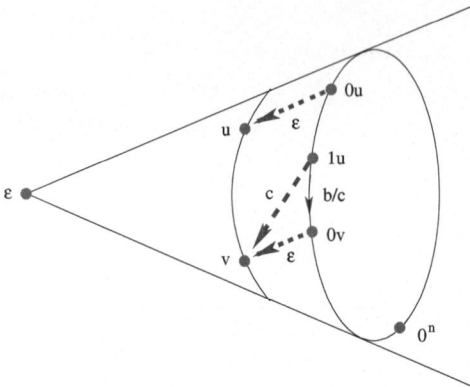

Fig. 10. The iteration of the composition $f_{a,b}^{\prime*}$ in base a

We visualize $\mathcal{T}_{a,b}^{\prime*}$ by a cone with ε at the tip and circular sections. The p-th section is the previously given representation of the Euclidean division $(:_{a,2})^p$ in base a by 2^p of initial state 0^p. The terminal function $\omega_{a,b}^{\prime}$ is represented as follows: with a transition $0u \xrightarrow{\varepsilon} u$ from any node starting by 0, and a transition $1u \xrightarrow{c} v$ from any node starting by 1 for the transition $1u \xrightarrow{b/c} 0v$ of the division by $2^{|u|+1}$ in base a. Note that these transitions of the terminal function can only be used at the end of an accepting path.

Similarly to Proposition 3, we get an explicit description of the transducer $\mathcal{T}_{a,b,d}^{*}$.

Theorem 3. *For all integers $0 \le b < a \ne 1$ and $d > 0$, the function $f_{a,b}^{\prime*}$ is realized by the transducer*

$$\mathcal{T}_{a,b,d}^{*} = (\downarrow_{d}^{*}, 0^{*}, \omega_{a,b,d}, :_{ad,d}^{*}) \text{ with for all } u \in \widehat{d}^{*} \text{ and } 0 < i < d,$$
$$\omega_{a,b,d}(0u) = \omega_{a,b,d}(u) \text{ and } \omega_{a,b,d}(iu) = c.\omega_{a,b,d}(v) \text{ for } iu \xrightarrow{bd/c} :_{ad,d}^{*} 0v.$$

Theorem 3 states that under the condition $b < a \ne 1$, we realize the composition closure of $f_{a,b,d}$ by taking the union of the divisions $(:_{ad,d})^p$ by d^p in base ad of initial state 0^p, plus a recurrent terminal function on p dependent on ab.

7   Conclusion

This work focuses on the description of functions on integers and their powers by deterministic transducers. This has been possible for the functions $f_{a,b,d}$ by the choice of the base ad but only under the restriction that $b < a$. The generalization to any integers a and b requires a new approach.

For any natural numbers a, b, d with $b < a \ne 1$ and $d \ne 0$, we have given an explicit construction of a transducer realizing the closure under composition of $f_{a,b,d}$. In its geometric representation, the disposition of the vertices is well appropriate for both the transitions of the Euclidean divisions and those of the terminal function. It might be a new approach to consider the circularity of the functions $f_{a,b,d}$ namely the existence of paths $0^p \xrightarrow{uv/0^{|v|}u} x$ where v is the terminal word of the vertex x in the transducer of the division by d^p in base ad. However, the circularity of the Collatz function is already considered as a difficult subproblem of the Collatz conjecture. With this approach and for the acceleration $f'_{3,1,2}$ of the Collatz function, it comes down to a deeper understanding of the Euclidean divisions by 2^p in base 3 and its transitions of input 1 [4].

Acknowledgments. We would like to thank Pierre Simonnet who was at the origin of this article: he recalled us the transducer of the Collatz function in base 2 and highlighted the fact that its compositions can not be explicited [10].

References

1. Allouche, J.-P.: T. Tao et la conjecture de Syracuse. Gazette de la SMF 168, pp. 34–39 (2021)
2. Allouche, J.-P., Shallit, J.: Automatic Sequences: Theory, Applications, Generalizations, 588 p. Cambridge University Press (2003)
3. Eliahou, S., Fromentin, J., Simonetto, R.: Is the syracuse falling time bounded by 12?. In: Nathanson, M.B. (ed.) Combinatorial and Additive Number Theory V. CANT. Springer Proceedings in Mathematics & Statistics, vol. 395, pp. 139–152 (2022). https://doi.org/10.48550/arXiv.2107.11160
4. Erdös, P.: Some unconventional problems in number theory. Math. Mag. **52**(2), 67–70 (1979). https://doi.org/10.2307/2689842
5. Lagarias, J.: The ultimate challenge: the 3x+1 problem. Am. Math. Soc. (2010). https://doi.org/10.1090/mbk/078
6. Muscholl, A., Puppis, G.: The many facets of string transducers. In: Nichermeir, R., Paul, C. (eds.) 36th STACS. Lecture Notes in Computer Science, vol. 1563, pp. 32–46 (2019). https://doi.org/10.4230/LIPIcs.STACS.2019.2
7. Reitwiesner, G.W.: Binary Arithmetic. Advances in Computers, vol. 1, pp. 231–308. Academic Press, New York (1960). https://doi.org/10.1016/S0065-2458(08)60610-5
8. Schützenberger, M.-P.: Sur une variante des fonctions séquentielles. Theoret. Comput. Sci. **4**(1), 47–57 (1977). https://doi.org/10.1016/0304-3975(77)90055-X
9. Shallit, J., Wilson, D.: The "3x + 1" problem and finite automata. Bull. EATCS **46**, 182–185 (1992)
10. Simonnet, P.: Personal communication (2019)
11. Stérin, T.: Binary expression of ancestors in the Collatz graph. In: Schmitz, S., Potapov, I. (eds.) RP 2020. LNCS, vol. 12448, pp. 115–130. Springer, Cham (2020). https://doi.org/10.1007/978-3-030-61739-4_8
12. Tao, T.:Almost all orbits of the Collatz map attain almost bounded values. arXiv:1909.03562 (2019).https://doi.org/10.48550/arXiv.1909.03562
13. Yolcu, E., Aaronson, S., Heule, M.J.H.: An automated approach to the Collatz conjecture. In: Platzer, A., Sutcliffe, G. (eds.) CADE 2021. LNCS (LNAI), vol. 12699, pp. 468–484. Springer, Cham (2021). https://doi.org/10.1007/978-3-030-79876-5_27

On the Entanglement and Mixedness of Quantum Boolean Function Circuits

Zornitza Prodanoff[✉], Iliya Kulbaka, and Natasha Interlichia

School of Computing, University of North Florida, Jacksonville, FL 32224, USA
{zprodano,n01427009,n01488786}@unf.edu

Abstract. Understanding the entanglement and mixedness introduced into a quantum system by quantum Boolean functions (BFs) circuits holds a significant potential in quantum information theory. This study provides an overview and empirical findings on *purity, negativity,* and *von Neumann entropy* with the aim to reveal an insight into the internal structure of the corresponding unitary operators. Approximately 5,000 quantum circuits were examined for BFs of different types, e.g., *balanced, symmetric, bent, etc.* and of various properties such as *algebraic degree, algebraic immunity, resiliency order,* and others. While previous research typically focuses on input superposition alone through addition of Hadamard gates (Superposition scenario), we introduce additional entanglement through random statevector generation (Random Statevector scenarios). Results show a slight increase in von Neumann entropy and negativity for the Random Statevector scenario as compared to the Superposition scenario. Surprisingly, further measurement increases were observed when adding classical randomness via random qubit rotations (Random Qubit Rotations scenario) instead of random statevector generation. The observed trends include lower mean values and wider ranges of negativity and von Neumann entropy for BFs of higher algebraic degree in the Superposition scenario. Additionally, plateaued functions of lower algebraic degree exhibit purity measurements with wider spread in the Random Statevector scenario as compared to the Superposition scenario. We hope that this work may inspire new theoretical studies on quantum BF circuits. For example, a deeper understanding of quantum BF circuits with high mixedness and entanglement may lead to the development of novel quantum error correction techniques.

Keywords: Boolean function · quantum computing · Disjunctive Normal Form (DNF) · Algebraic Normal Form (ANF) · reversible computing · Zhegalkin polynomial · von Neumann entropy · quantum negativity

1 Introduction

After Benioff proposed the notion of quantum computing in 1980 [3] and Feynman has famously addressed the challenges of simulating quantum systems using

This study was supported by the IBM Quantum Researchers program.

E. Formenti and J. Durand-Lose (Eds.): MCU 2024, LNCS 15270, pp. 130–152, 2025.
https://doi.org/10.1007/978-3-031-81202-6_9

classical computers, emphasizing the need for a new computational paradigm in his seminal paper [13], Feynman proposed an extension of the Classical Church-Turing Thesis in the context of quantum computing, known as the Quantum Strong Church-Turing Thesis [13]. Namely, that any computational process that can be efficiently computed can be efficiently simulated by a quantum Turing machine (or equivalently, by a quantum circuit). The term "efficiently" generally refers to computational tasks that can be performed in polynomial time. In classical computing, this corresponds to tasks that a classical Turing machine can solve in polynomial time. For quantum computing, this means tasks that a quantum Turing machine or a quantum circuit can solve in polynomial time. David Deutsch proposed the theoretical connection between quantum computing and Boolean Functions (BFs) by reexamining the Church-Turing principle in the context of computational universality [8]. Deutsch's study is recognized today as the first published paper to describe a quantum algorithm with a provable speedup over any possible classical algorithm. It introduced the concept of a quantum oracle, a crucial component in many quantum algorithms and laid the foundation for the development of more sophisticated quantum algorithms, such as the Deutsch-Jozsa algorithm used to distinguish between quantum implementations of *balanced* vs. *constant* BFs. Multiple studies have since expanded on the topic to include specific circuit examples and implementation details rooted in physics and linear algebra, for example [2, 10, 16, 18]. In addition, since BFs can be used to specify any classical computational problem, it is not surprising that there is a growing number of studies on classifying previously unknown sub-classes of BFs. Some well studied subclasses of BFs using primarily their Disjunctive Normal Form (DNF) representation include: *balanced, symmetric, bent, monotone, plateaued*, BFs having *linear structure*, and other. Some of those, which are more relevant to this study, are more formally defined in Sect. 4.1. As already demonstrated by the Deutsch-Jozsa algorithm, one general speculation on whether quantum speed-up and other goals could be achieved for quantum algorithms implementing BFs, would depend on the specific properties of the underlying BF as already demonstrated by the Deutsch-Jozsa algorithm. Noted, however, that the input provided to the quantum circuit is another important determinant of the outcomes.

Through this study, we venture to provide an empirical demonstration of the specific levels of quantum entanglement and mixedness within quantum circuits that implement several BFs of some specific properties. We expect that the internal quantum circuit dynamics are dependent on those properties and that some information about them can be revealed by measuring the level of quantum entanglement of their respective subsystems. Our hope is to provide valuable insights that could be useful for the purposes of further theoretical study on this topic. Such specific insights could be potentially beneficial in the context of several relevant areas, including quantum information theory and algorithmic time complexity analysis in the quantum domain.

2   BFs in Quantum Computing

A Boolean function (BF) $f : \{0,1\}^n \rightarrow \{0,1\}$ is specified with Boolean *formulas*, that is, an expression, using n variables $v_1, v_2, \ldots, v_n$ and logical connectives. A *literal* is a variable or its negation (usually denoted as $\bar{v}$ or v'). A Boolean formula is in *disjunctive normal form* (DNF) if it is a sum of products, i.e., a disjunction ($\vee$ or $+$) of clauses, where each clause is a conjunction ($\wedge$ or $\cdot$) of literals (denoted by juxtaposition). BFs and classical circuits can be directly related through their representations: truth tables, logical expressions and algebraic expressions. Using those alternative representations, BFs can be translated into equivalent circuit diagrams, and vice versa. Moreover, according to the Quantum Strong Church-Turing Thesis any classical circuit can be simulated by a quantum circuit and consequentially, quantum circuits can simulate and implement BFs.

The most convenient BF representation for the purposes of designing corresponding quantum circuits is Algebraic Normal Form (ANF), also known as Zhegalkin polynomials [32]. It uses a representation of functions over a finite (Galois) field of two elements GF(2), and can be written in the following sum of product expansion form:

$$f(v_1 \ldots v_n) = a_1 \mathbf{1} \oplus a_2 v_1 \oplus a_3 v_2 \oplus a_{n+1} v_n \oplus a_{n+2} v_1 v_2 \oplus \cdots \oplus a_k v_{n-1} v_n \oplus a_{k+1} v_1 v_2 v_3 \oplus \cdots \oplus a_{2^n} v_1 v_2 v_3 \ldots v_n$$

where $\oplus$ denotes addition modulo 2, logical conjunction is presented as juxtaposition, Boolean coefficients $a_1, \ldots, a_{2^n} \in \{0, 1\}$, and $v_1, v_2, \ldots, v_n$ represent the Boolean input variables, while $\mathbf{1}$ represents the true term. Note that the ANF representation of f includes the true term $\mathbf{1}$ only if $a_1 = 1$. Each logical conjunctions term $v_1 \ldots v_m$ preceded by a coefficient a_i is referred to as a *monomial*. Note that the n-bit string $x = v_1 \ldots v_n$ represents one of the 2^n possible combinations of values of the binary input variable $v_1, \ldots, v_n$. For example, $f = \mathbf{1} \oplus v_2 \oplus v_3 v_4$ has two monomials v_2 and $v_3 v_4$ as well as a true term $\mathbf{1}$. Methods to convert a BF from DNF into ANF and vice versa have been proposed already. Further discussion and a polynomial-time algorithm for such conversion is offered in Sect. 2.1.

2.1   BFs as Quantum Circuits

A single *qubit* models a quantum mechanical system whose state can be described in the form of a wave function in a complex Hilbert space. The wave function $\psi(r, t)$ describes the probabilities of all possible states at position r and at time t and can describe a physical phenomenon such as the spin state of an electron. Hence, $\psi(r, t)$ can be thought of as a vector in a Hilbert space denoted in Dirac notation as $|\psi\rangle$. Qubits can be represented as states of vectors on a Bloch sphere by representing their vector amplitudes as real numbers, such as α_0 and α_1, that is, in the form $|\psi\rangle = \alpha_0 |0\rangle + \alpha_1 |1\rangle$ or more simply as $|\psi\rangle = \begin{bmatrix} \alpha_0 \\ \alpha_1 \end{bmatrix}$, where the $|0\rangle$ and $|1\rangle$ vectors extend to the North and South pole respectively. The specific geometric representation of the state of a qubit can be expressed by using Euler's identity: $e^{i\phi} = cos\phi + isin\phi$ for an arbitrary angle ϕ in a plane. However, a

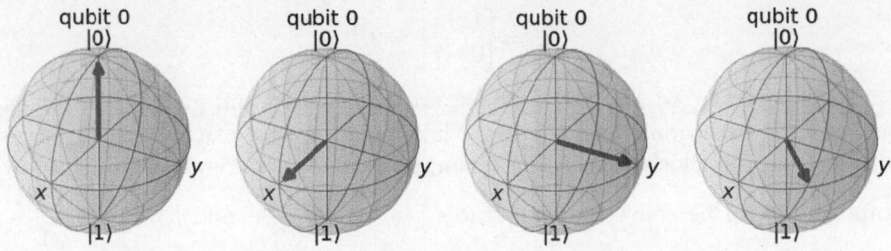

Fig. 1. Quantum states for a single qubit [left to right]: initialized to $|0\rangle$, $|+\rangle$ after application of H-gate, $|i\rangle$ after application of H-gate and S-gate, and $\begin{bmatrix} \dfrac{1}{\sqrt{2}} \\ \dfrac{1}{2}(1+i) \end{bmatrix}$ after application of H-gate and T-gate.

representation of perpendicular vectors that are 180° apart (and not 90) allows for a convenient analogy between single-qubit quantum operations and rotations among the axes on the Bloch sphere as depicted in Fig. 1 and hence we express that by using a factor of 2 as $|\psi\rangle = \alpha_0|0\rangle + \alpha_1|1\rangle = e^{i\gamma}(\cos\frac{\theta}{2}|0\rangle + e^{i\lambda}\sin\frac{\theta}{2}|1\rangle)$, where $\alpha_0, \alpha_1, \theta, \gamma$ and $\lambda, \in \mathbb{R}$. We observe that the normalization condition can be expressed as:

$$\|\alpha_0\|^2 + \|\alpha_1\|^2 = e^{i\gamma}e^{-i\gamma}\cos^2\frac{\theta}{2} + e^{i\gamma}e^{-i\gamma}e^{i\lambda}e^{-i\lambda}\sin^2\frac{\theta}{2} = 1. \tag{1}$$

Note that the square of the global phase $e^{i\gamma}$ can be ignored as it does not affect the result. If the vector $|\psi\rangle$ has a unit length, i.e. its inner product $\langle\psi|\psi\rangle = 1$, its state is referred to as *pure*. Vectors extending to the points on the surface of the Bloch sphere represent pure qubit states, while vectors extending to interior to the sphere points are referred to as *mixed* states as explained later in this section.

Vector rotations operations could be achieved through the application of single-qubit quantum gates:

$$H = \frac{1}{\sqrt{2}}\begin{bmatrix} 1 & 1 \\ 1 & -1 \end{bmatrix} \tag{2}$$

$$T = \begin{bmatrix} 1 & 0 \\ 0 & e^{\frac{i\pi}{4}} \end{bmatrix} \tag{3}$$

$$S = \begin{bmatrix} 1 & 0 \\ 0 & i \end{bmatrix} = T^2 \tag{4}$$

$$X = \begin{bmatrix} 0 & 1 \\ 1 & 0 \end{bmatrix} = HT^4H \tag{5}$$

$$Y = \begin{bmatrix} 0 & -i \\ i & 0 \end{bmatrix} = T^2HT^4HT^6 \tag{6}$$

$$Z = \begin{bmatrix} 1 & 0 \\ 0 & -1 \end{bmatrix} = T^4 \qquad (7)$$

The operators X, Y, and Z above are known as Pauli gates. Conversion between the orthogonal bases is a trivial operation and can be visualized as rotations on the Bloch sphere. For example, as shown in Fig. 1, a qubit vector state of $|0\rangle$ can be converted into states $|+\rangle =: \dfrac{|0\rangle + |1\rangle}{\sqrt{2}}$ and $|i\rangle =: \dfrac{|0\rangle + i|1\rangle}{\sqrt{2}}$ respectively by applying single qubit gates. States $|+\rangle$ and $|i\rangle$ are examples of *superposition* states as the vectors are considered to be both in state 1 and 0 at the same time, but when being measured they assume state one of those states with a probability given by Eq. 1. Their corresponding orthogonal superposition states are $|-\rangle =: \dfrac{|0\rangle - |1\rangle}{\sqrt{2}}$ and $|-i\rangle =: \dfrac{|0\rangle - i|1\rangle}{\sqrt{2}}$ respectively.

Lets consider the combined state of the two Bloch spheres on the left in Fig. 1. They represent vectors in pure states $|0\rangle$ and $|+\rangle$. That combined state of a system of two entities is described as their tensor product $|0\rangle \otimes |+\rangle$ often written in a qubit string format as $|0+\rangle = \dfrac{1}{\sqrt{2}}(1|00\rangle + 1|01\rangle + 0|10\rangle + 0|11\rangle) = \dfrac{1}{\sqrt{2}}(|00\rangle + |01\rangle)$. Note that states $|10\rangle$ and $|11\rangle$ have zero probability of being measured. Such state is referred to as being a *product* state as it could be expressed as the tensor product of $|0\rangle \otimes |+\rangle$, where the individual qubit states $|0\rangle$ and $|+\rangle$ are pure states. Application of the little-endian variant of the *Controlled NOT* gate with matrix $\begin{bmatrix} 1 & 0 & 0 & 0 \\ 0 & 0 & 0 & 1 \\ 0 & 0 & 1 & 0 \\ 0 & 1 & 0 & 0 \end{bmatrix}$ to the same qubit string $|0+\rangle$ yields $\dfrac{1}{\sqrt{2}}(|00\rangle + |11\rangle)$, where states $|01\rangle$ and $|10\rangle$ have a zero probability of being measured (see Sect. 2.1 for elaboration on little-endian qubit ordering.) Such state models the quantum physical phenomenon of particle *entanglement*. It is an example of an *entangled* state since measuring the first qubit as $|0\rangle$ always leads to measuring the second qubit as $|0\rangle$ and measuring the first qubit as $|1\rangle$ always leads to measuring the second qubit as $|1\rangle$. This phenomenon is known as a *collapse* of the entangled state upon measurement. States that are not entangled are referred to as *separable*. A separable state is a composite quantum state of multiple single-qubit subsystems that can be expressed as a product state, i.e., the overall state of the system can be written as a tensor product of the states of individual single-qubit subsystems. For example, a separable states ρ_{AB} of a bipartite system A and B can be written as:

$$\rho_{AB} = \sum_i p_i \rho_i^A \otimes \rho_i^B$$

where p_i are probabilities and ρ_i^A and ρ_i^B are density matrices describing the states of subsystems A and B representing a single qubit each. Note that in general subsystems are often denoted with a capital Latin alphabet letter, e.g. A.

Due to non-ideal operation of the Hadamard gate and potential for errors in the quantum hardware, when it is applied to the $|0\rangle$ pure state, for example, it may not produce a rotation resulting in the $|+\rangle$ state in 100% of the cases and only in 80%, for example. In the other 20% cases the system could be with 10% probability in state $|\psi_1\rangle = \frac{\sqrt{3}}{2}|0\rangle + \frac{1}{2}|1\rangle$ and a different 10% probability in a third state of $|\psi_2\rangle = \frac{1}{2}|0\rangle + \frac{\sqrt{3}}{2}|1\rangle$. This is an example of quantum interference, or a probabilistic scenario, where the qubit is said to be in a *mixed* state, or a mix of those three states with their respective probabilities.

Consider another example of mixed states, where a single qubit could be in states $|+\rangle$ and $|-\rangle$ with probability of $\frac{1}{2}$ each. It demonstrates a model of the physical phenomenon of *destructive interference*, or the case when two identical waves are superimposed exactly out of phase. Taking a closer look at the positive and negative amplitudes, we observe that they cancel out for the state of $|0\rangle$:

$$\rho = \frac{1}{2}|+\rangle\langle+| + \frac{1}{2}|-\rangle\langle-| = \frac{1}{2}\begin{bmatrix} \frac{1}{2} & \frac{1}{2} \\ \frac{1}{2} & \frac{1}{2} \end{bmatrix} + \frac{1}{2}\begin{bmatrix} \frac{1}{2} & -\frac{1}{2} \\ -\frac{1}{2} & \frac{1}{2} \end{bmatrix} = \begin{bmatrix} \frac{1}{2} & 0 \\ 0 & \frac{1}{2} \end{bmatrix} \tag{8}$$

Here, the *density matrix* ρ is used to describe the state of the quantum system. It encapsulates not only pure states but also mixed states, offering a more general framework for quantum states than wavefunctions alone. A pure state can be described by $\rho = |\psi\rangle\langle\psi|$, where $|\psi\rangle$ is the state vector in the Hilbert space. For mixed states, ρ is a probabilistic mixture of pure states, $\rho = \sum_i p_i |\psi_i\rangle\langle\psi_i|$, where p_i are the probabilities that the system is in one of the pure states $|\psi_i\rangle$. The density matrix ρ is Hermitian ($\rho = \rho^\dagger$), has trace one ($\text{Tr}(\rho) = 1$), and is positive semi-definite (i.e. all its eigenvalues are non-negative). These properties ensure that probabilities derived from ρ are real and sum up to 1.

Constructing Quantum Circuits from BFs. Consider that each variable v_i of a Boolean formula in DNF is represented with the same symbol in ANF. The following symbolic representations are used. Exclusive or operation (XOR) is denoted as $\oplus$. Logical not $\neg v_i$ (sometimes written as $\bar{v}_i$) is not used. Instead, negation is represented by a XOR operation with a purely true term (denoted as 1), e.g. $1 \oplus v_i$. No special symbol is used to represent logical conjunction, e.g. $v_1 \wedge v_2$ is written as the juxtaposition $v_1 v_2$. Logical disjunction $v_1 \vee v_2$ also written as $v_1 + v_2$ is represented as $v_1 \oplus v_2$. The distributive property of logical conjunction is written as usual, e.g. $(v_1 \oplus v_2)(v_3 \oplus v_4) = v_1 v_3 \oplus v_1 v_4 \oplus v_2 v_3 \oplus v_2 v_4$.

The respective ANF representation of any Boolean formula φ can be arrived to by following the procedures in Algorithms 1 and 9 with respective time complexity of $o(2^{2n})$ and $O(n2^n)$. Note that for practical purposes this worst case computational complexity is usually considered in terms of the number of bits needed to represent an input to an algorithm. Hence, we could view the complexity of Algorithm 9 published in [20] as linear (in terms of the number of DNF formula clauses or truth table rows [25]) regardless of its exponential complexity (in terms of the number of input variables). For ease of visualization, we only present the brute-force conversion of φ_1 from [15, Example 2] in Table 1. Note

---

Algorithm 1: Pseudocode for brute-force DNF to ANF conversion with complexity $o(n^2)$

---

    input : BF φ of n literals in DNF: φ_{DNF}
    output: BF φ of n literals in ANF: φ_{ANF}

1 **begin**
2     $TT_{DNF}[1...2^n] \leftarrow \varphi_{DNF}$ // populate output column of φ_{DNF} truth table
3   **for** $i \leftarrow 1$ *to* 2^n **do**
4         $CT_{ANF}[i][1] = TT_{DNF}[i]$ // initialize first row and column of conversion table
5         $CT_{ANF}[1][i] \leftarrow 0$
6   **for** $j \leftarrow 1$ *to* 2^n **do**
7         $Counter \leftarrow 0$
8   **for** $i \leftarrow 1$ *to* $2^n - j$ **do**
9   **if** $CT_{ANF}[i][j] \neq CT_{ANF}[i+1][j]$ **then**
10              $CT_{ANF}[i][j+1] \leftarrow 1$
11   **else**
12               $CT_{ANF}[i][j+1] \leftarrow 0$
13               $Counter + +$
14   **if** $Counter = j$ **then**
15   **return** $\min(\varphi_{ANF})$ // conversion is completed if column j contains all 0s
16   **return** $\min(\varphi_{ANF})$
    // algorithm returns the list of index positions in $CT_{ANF}[1][]$ containing 1

---

that function F_1 represented with the formula φ_1 below is depicted in a truth-table form. Algorithm 1 is based on the method of operation of the elementary cellular automaton known as Rule 102 [31].

The ANF representation of the above BF F_i with formula φ_1 is computed as:

$$\varphi_1 = v_2 \oplus v_3 \oplus v_4 \oplus v_1 v_2 \oplus v_1 v_3 \oplus v_2 v_3 \oplus v_2 v_4 \oplus v_3 v_4 \oplus v_1 v_2 v_3 \oplus v_1 v_2 v_4 \oplus v_1 v_3 v_4 \oplus v_1 v_2 v_3 v_4$$

The IBM Qiskit [1] implementation of the quantum circuit for φ_1 is shown in Fig. 2. Note that Qiskit uses a little-endian qubit ordering where higher qubit indices are more significant in terms of (polynomial) bitstring ordering. Most published academic studies use an alternative approach, where controlled gates are presented with the assumption of more significant qubits as control bits, hence assuming a big-endian ordering. This study follows the latter, big-endian approach unless explicitly stated otherwise or unless depicting specific Qiskit implementations. As mentioned previously in Sect. 1, by the Quantum Strong Church-Turing Thesis [13], any Quantum Turing machine can efficiently simulate

---

Algorithm 2: Pseudocode for DNF to ANF conversion with complexity $o(n)$ [20]

---

input : BF φ of n literals in DNF: φ_{DNF}
output: BF φ of n literals in ANF: φ_{ANF}

1 **begin**

2     $CA_{ANF}[1...2^n] \leftarrow \varphi_{DNF}$ // populate conversion array with φ_{DNF} evaluation values

3     $k \leftarrow 1$

4   **for** $i \leftarrow 1$ *to* n **do**

5   **for** $s \leftarrow k$ *to* $2^n - k$ **do**

6   **for** $j \leftarrow s$ *to* $k - 1$ **do**

7              $CA_{ANF}[j] = CA_{ANF}[j] \oplus CA_{ANF}[j - k]$ // store partial $\sum$ in $CA_{ANF}[]$

8        $k = 2k$

9   **return** $\min(\varphi_{ANF})$

    // algorithm returns the list of index positions in $CA_{ANF}[]$ containing 1

---

any other model of computation. Consequently, for each BF in ANF representation there is at least one quantum circuit that can be designed to implement it. The bitwise classical representation of BF $F : \{0,1\}^n \rightarrow \{0,1\}$ is represented using qubits: $F : \{|0\rangle, |1\rangle\}^n \rightarrow \{|0\rangle, |1\rangle\}$ and is specified with Boolean formulas, using n variables $v_1, v_2, \ldots, v_n$. The transformation of formulas in ANF to quantum circuits has been formulated in [11]. The true term $\mathbf{1} = \begin{bmatrix} 1 \\ 1 \end{bmatrix}$ corresponds to the X-gate, acting on the output qubit q_4 as a bit flip operation. Term v_{j_k} corresponds to the $CNOT$ gate with j_k control qubit. The multiplication of m Boolean arguments $v_{j_1}, v_{j_2}, \ldots v_{j_k}$ corresponds to the $C^m NOT$ (*Toffoli*) gate with m number of control qubits, where $m = 1, 2, \ldots, n$ for n-number of input qubits. The number of possible gates is: one X-gate (with zero control bits) acting on the output qubit, n $CNOT$ gates, C_n^2 gates of type $C^2 NOT$, etc. Hence, the total number of all possible, X, $CNOT$, *Toffoli*, and multi-qubit controlled *Toffoli* gates to be used for the design of any BF through direct conversion from functions in ANF is $\Sigma_{k=0}^n C_n^k = 2^n$. The number of all possible Boolean quantum circuits is 2^{2^n} and it corresponds to the number of all possible BFs.

Table 1. DNF to ANF conversion of the BF from Example [15, Example 2].

v_1	v_2	v_3	v_4	F_1	0000	0001	0010	0011	0100	0101	0110	0111	1000	1001	1010	1011	1100	1101	1110	1111
					1	v_4	v_3	v_3v_4	v_2	v_2v_4	v_2v_3	$v_2v_3v_4$	v_1	v_1v_4	v_1v_3	$v_1v_3v_4$	v_1v_2	$v_1v_2v_4$	$v_1v_2v_3$	$v_1v_2v_3v_4$
0	0	0	0	0	0	1	1	1	1	1	1	1	0	0	1	0	1	1	1	1
0	0	0	1	1	1	0	0	0	0	0	0	1	0	1	1	1	0	0	0	
0	0	1	0	1	1	0	0	0	0	0	1	1	1	0	0	1	0	0		
0	0	1	1	1	1	0	0	0	0	1	0	0	1	0	1	1	0			
0	1	0	0	1	1	0	0	0	1	1	0	1	1	1	0	1				
0	1	0	1	1	1	0	0	1	0	1	1	0	0	1	1					
0	1	1	0	1	1	0	1	1	1	0	1	0	1	0						
0	1	1	1	1	1	1	0	0	1	1	1	1	1							
1	0	0	0	0	0	1	0	1	0	0	0	0								
1	0	0	1	1	1	1	1	0	0	0										
1	0	1	0	0	0	0	0	1	0	0										
1	0	1	1	0	0	0	1	1	0											
1	1	0	0	0	0	1	0	1												
1	1	0	1	1	1	1	1													
1	1	1	0	0	0	0														
1	1	1	1	0	0															

$$\varphi_1 = v_2 \oplus v_3 \oplus v_4 \oplus v_1v_2 \oplus v_1v_3 \oplus v_2v_3 \oplus v_2v_4 \oplus v_3v_4 \oplus v_1v_2v_3 \oplus v_1v_2v_4 \oplus v_1v_3v_4 \oplus v_1v_2v_3v_4$$

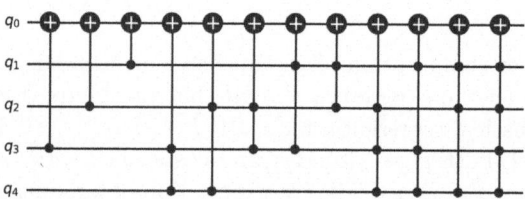

Fig. 2. Qiskit implementation of the quantum circuit from Table 1 ($v_1 \rightarrow q_4$, $v_2 \rightarrow q_3$, etc.)

3   Methods of Measuring Entanglement and Mixedness in Quantum Circuits

The state of a quantum circuit, including multi-qubit circuits, can be described using the density matrix ρ. A mixed state ρ can be decomposed into a sum of pure or mixed states with associated probabilities. A mixed state can also be entangled if and only if it's not separable [21]. The general form of a pure state decomposition for a mixed state is given by: $\rho = \sum_i p_i |\psi_i\rangle\langle\psi_i|$, where ρ is the density matrix representing the mixed state, $|\psi_i\rangle$ are the pure states in the decomposition, p_i are the probabilities associated with each pure state, $\langle\psi_i|$ denotes the *Hermitian adjoint* (conjugate transpose) of the state $|\psi_i\rangle$. A subsystem of the circuit can be a subset of the qubits in a pure state or alternatively in a mixed state itself. Such subsystem's state is represented as the reduced density matrix ρ_A, obtained by taking a partial trace of the density matrix ρ.

For a 2-qubit quantum circuit, the partial trace, denoted as Tr_B, of its density matrix ρ_{AB} with respect to subsystem B (one of the qubits) results in a reduced density matrix for subsystem A (the other qubit). This is represented as $\rho_A = Tr_B(\rho_{AB})$. This notion is used to quantify the levels of entanglement in the circuit as described next.

3.1   Measures of Entanglement and Mixedness

The measurements focused on in this study include *purity*, *negativity*, and *von Neumann entropy*. Purity is the first quantity used to describe the overall state of the circuit and individual qubits in order to further determine how aspects of the circuit affect entanglement. The purity of a quantum state $|\psi\rangle$ is given by the trace of the density operator squared:

$$P(\rho) = \text{Tr}(\rho^2)$$

where $\rho = |\psi\rangle\langle\psi|$ is the density operator associated with the state $|\psi\rangle$. Similarly, the purity of a subsystem (e.g. individual qubit) can be found by using the reduced density matrix representing that qubit. For example, if looking at one of the circuit qubits as a subsystem, denoted as A, the following expression represents the trace taken to find its purity:

$$P(\rho_A) = \text{Tr}(\rho_A^2).$$

For a 2-qubit system, the resulting value will be in the range .5 to 1, where .5 indicates a perfectly mixed state and 1 indicates a perfectly pure state. In general, for a pure state $|\psi\rangle$, the purity is equal to 1, while for a *maximally mixed state*, the purity is equal to $1/d$, where d is the dimensionality of the Hilbert space. Maximally mixed states are defined as states with no entanglement between subsystems.

When a mixed state represents a statistical ensemble of separable states, it would not exhibit entanglement. However, in other cases of mixed states entanglement is possible and some conclusions can be drawn about the degree of entanglement in the system. More specifically, a pure separable state is a state of a composite quantum system where each subsystem is in a pure state, and the overall state of the composite system is described by a pure state. A pure separable state is expressed as:

$$|\psi_{pure,\ separable}\rangle = |\psi_A\rangle \otimes |\psi_A\rangle.$$

Entanglement comes into play when the state of a composite system cannot be written as a convex combination of tensor products of states of the individual subsystems. In that case, the system is in an entangled state. Hence, entanglement is a characteristic of mixed states as well as pure states. A mixed separable state is a state of a composite quantum system where each subsystem may be in a mixed state. In this case, the overall state of the composite system is still separable, but it is represented by a density matrix that is a convex combination of tensor products of states for the individual subsystems. A mixed separable state is expressed as:

$$\rho = \sum_{ij,kl} p_{ij,kl} |\psi_{A_i}\rangle \otimes |\psi_{B_j}\rangle \langle \psi_{A_k}| \otimes \langle \psi_{B_l}|.$$

Its full transpose can be represented using subsystem states:

$$(|\psi_{A_i}\rangle \otimes |\psi_{B_j}\rangle \langle \psi_{A_k}| \otimes \langle \psi_{B_l}|)^T = |\psi_{A_k}\rangle \otimes |\psi_{B_l}\rangle \langle \psi_{A_i}| \otimes \langle \psi_{B_j}|,$$

and its partial transpose can be expressed as follows:

$$(|\psi_{A_i}\rangle \otimes |\psi_{B_j}\rangle \langle \psi_{A_k}| \otimes \langle \psi_{B_l}|)^{T_A} = |\psi_{A_k}\rangle \otimes |\psi_{B_j}\rangle \langle \psi_{A_i}| \otimes \langle \psi_{B_l}|.$$

The first measure of entanglement used in this study is negativity:

$$\mathcal{N}(\rho) = \frac{\|\rho^{T_A}\|_1 - 1}{2} = \left| \sum_{\mu_i < 0} \mu_i \right|$$

where ρ^{T_A} is the partial transpose of the density matrix ρ with respect to subsystem A, $\{\mu_1, \mu_2, \ldots, \mu_n\}$ is the set of eigenvalues of a matrix ρ^{T_A}, and $\|X\|_1 = Tr|X| = Tr\sqrt{X^\dagger X}$ denotes the trace norm or the sum of the singular values of the operator X. The term negativity is chosen to reflect the idea that the sum of negative eigenvalues are used to define it. The range for negativity is $0 \leq \mathcal{N} \leq \frac{1}{2}$ with $\mathcal{N}(\rho) = 0$ for separable states and $\mathcal{N} = \frac{1}{2}$ for *maximally entangled states*. In the context of quantum computing, maximally entangled are states having a reduced density matrix that is maximally mixed.

It is important to note that there are multiple definitions of negativity in the literature. The one we presented above was proposed in [28] based on prior work from [21] and [33]. Later works, e.g. [30], used an alternative definition:

$$\mathcal{N}_{alternative}(\rho) = 2 \left| \sum_{\mu_i < 0} \mu_i \right|$$

that results in a range for $0 \leq \mathcal{N} \leq 1$. `Qiskit` uses a third definition of negativity, implemented as part of the `Qiskit's qiskit.quantum.info` class:

$$\mathcal{N}_{\texttt{Qiskit}}(\rho) = \left| \sum_i s_i \right| \approx \mathcal{N}(\rho),$$

where s_i are the singular values of the matrix ρ^{T_A}. This is a reasonable approximation of the original definition of negativity proposed in [28] that is computationally efficient and we use it for all negativity computations as presented in Sect. 5.

Negativity can be used to measure the entanglement of the (whole) system state with respect of a subsystem or the entanglement of the subsystem with respect to its own subsystems. For example, the expression below could be used to determine the negativity of a 4-qubit system where A represents qubits $q0$ and $q3$, and a represents $q3$ as a subsystem of A:

$$\mathcal{N}(\rho_a) = \frac{\|\rho_a^{T_A}\|_1 - 1}{2}.$$

We use this idea to compute the negativity of the reduced density matrices in our experimentation.

The second measure of entanglement used in this study is *von Neumann entropy*. The concept could be introduced by taking the logarithm of a matrix as follows. The logarithm of a matrix A (denoted as $\log(A)$) is a matrix B such that $e^B = A$, where e^B represents the matrix exponential of B [14]. More formally, if A is an $n \times n$ invertible matrix, the matrix logarithm $\log(A)$ is defined as:

$$\log(A) = B \quad \text{if and only if} \quad e^B = A.$$

Here, the matrix exponential e^B is given by the power series:

$$e^B = \sum_{k=0}^{\infty} \frac{B^k}{k!}.$$

Recall that the Shannon entropy is used to find the compression ability of classical systems, giving an average number of bits needed to encode a message [27] and is expressed as:

$$H(X) = -\sum_x p(x) \log p(x),$$

where $p(x)$ is the probability of outcome x of a classical random variable X. The von Neumann entropy can be viewed as the quantum extension of Shannon entropy and is represented as:

$$S(\rho) = -\text{Tr}(\rho \log_2 \rho).$$

In general, for any type of state, ρ is a Hermitian, and hence could be diagonalized using a unitary transformation U into a diagonal matrix D, where the diagonal elements are the eigenvalues of ρ. That is, $\rho = UDU^\dagger$. Using the fact that $U^\dagger U = I$, the trace operation in the definition for $S(\rho)$, can be expanded as follows:

$$\begin{aligned}
\text{Tr}(\rho \log \rho) &= \text{Tr}(UDU^\dagger \log(UDU^\dagger)) \\
&= \text{Tr}(U^\dagger U D \log D) \\
&= \text{Tr}(D \log D) = -\sum_i \lambda_i \log \lambda_i.
\end{aligned}$$

where the density matrix ρ describes a quantum system with eigenvalues λ_i and the diagonal matrix D contains those eigenvalues.

For quantum systems that are a mixture of separable states, the von Neumann entropy reduces to the Shannon entropy. If the quantum state ρ is a classical probability distribution over a set of orthogonal computational basis states (i.e., a diagonal density matrix), then its von Neumann entropy is equivalent to the Shannon entropy of the classical probability distribution. In such case, the density matrix ρ represents a classical probability distribution as it is a diagonal matrix itself. That is, when the off-diagonal elements of ρ are zero, the state described by ρ is a classical probability distribution. In a diagonal density matrix, each diagonal element ρ_{ii} represents the probability of finding the system in the corresponding eigenstate (i.e. eigenvector) $|i\rangle$. This scenario is analogous to classical probability distributions, where the probabilities of different outcomes are represented by the entries of a probability vector.

For maximally mixed states, the von Neumann entropy measures only its mixedness since by definition such states do not have entanglement between subsystems. A maximally mixed state is described by a density matrix ρ that is proportional to the identity matrix I such that:

$$\rho = \frac{1}{d}I$$

where d is the dimension of the Hilbert space. In this state, all possible pure separable states are equally probable.

Fedus [12] lists the three main pieces of information that the von Neumann entropy provides. First, it can be used to find the maximum amount of bits that can be recovered from a message. Second, the entropy can determine the number of qubits needed to encode a message in a given quantum state (compression). The term compression is used in this context in order to indicate that the dimension of the Hilbert space is reduced when using a lesser number of qubits. Lastly, it quantifies the degree of entanglement for pure and mixed bipartite states.

The values of $S(\rho)$ range from 0 to $\log d$, where $d = 2^n$ is the dimension of the quantum circuit with n qubit inputs. For a pure state, $S(\rho) = 0$ indicates there is no entanglement and a value of $S(\rho) = \log d$ correlates with maximum entanglement [12]. For a mixed state, $S(\rho) > 0$ and is a combined indicator of the level of mixedness and/or entanglement. That is, the von Neumann entropy is zero for pure states that are also separable, and it increases as the state becomes more mixed or entangled.

It is important to note that negativity specifically focuses on entanglement, providing a measure of bipartite entanglement, that is, entanglement between a subsystem and the rest of the quantum system, while von Neumann entropy is related to entanglement, but presents a more general measure of uncertainty or mixedness in a quantum state and positive values are not exclusive to entangled states but can be calculated for mixed states, as well. If a composite system is in a pure and separable state, the von Neumann entropy of each subsystem is always zero, that is, if $|\psi\rangle = |\psi_A\rangle \otimes |\psi_B\rangle$, then $S(\rho_A) = S(\rho_B) = 0$. If a pure state of a composite system is entangled, the von Neumann entropy of each subsystem is nonzero. Entanglement introduces correlations between subsystems, and as a result, the reduced density matrix of each subsystem is a mixed state with a positive von Neumann entropy. If $|\psi\rangle$ is entangled, then $S(\rho_A) > 0$ and $S(\rho_B) > 0$. In general, negativity is a measure of entanglement, capturing the degree to which the state violates the condition of separability. It provides information about the presence and "strength" of entanglement but it does not directly quantify the mixedness or purity of the state. In contrast, the von Neumann entropy measures both the entanglement and the mixedness of a quantum state.

3.2   Examples of Pure, Separable, Entangled and Mixed States

Several examples are presented next. To determine if a state is maximally entangled, we consider bipartite entanglement between two subsystems. Let's consider the Bell state $|\Phi^+\rangle = \frac{1}{\sqrt{2}}(|00\rangle + |11\rangle)$ as an example. To compute the entropy of each subsystem, we first need to take the partial trace of one of the subsystems. The density matrix representing the state $|\Phi^+\rangle$ is given by:

$$\rho = |\Phi^+\rangle\langle\Phi^+| = \frac{1}{2}\begin{bmatrix} 1 & 0 & 0 & 1 \\ 0 & 0 & 0 & 0 \\ 0 & 0 & 0 & 0 \\ 1 & 0 & 0 & 1 \end{bmatrix}$$

and the partial trace over the second qubit is

$$\mathrm{Tr}_B(\rho) = \frac{1}{2}(1 + 0 + 0 + 1) = 1.$$

This represents the density matrix of the first qubit, which is maximally mixed. For a maximally mixed state in a two-dimensional Hilbert space, the density matrix ρ_A is given by:

$$\rho_A = \frac{1}{2}\begin{bmatrix} 1 & 0 \\ 0 & 1 \end{bmatrix}$$

The entropy S_A of the first qubit is then:

$$S_A = -\mathrm{Tr}(\rho_A \log \rho_A) = -\mathrm{Tr}\left(\frac{1}{2}\begin{bmatrix} 1 & 0 \\ 0 & 1 \end{bmatrix} \log \frac{1}{2}\begin{bmatrix} 1 & 0 \\ 0 & 1 \end{bmatrix}\right) = \log 2 = 1$$

The negativity of the state $|\Phi^+\rangle$ is given by:

$$\mathcal{N} = \frac{||\rho^{T_A}||_1 - 1}{2}$$

Taking the partial transpose with respect to the first qubit, we obtain:

$$\rho^{T_A} = \frac{1}{2}\begin{bmatrix} 1 & 0 & 0 & 0 \\ 0 & 0 & 1 & 0 \\ 0 & 1 & 0 & 0 \\ 0 & 0 & 0 & 1 \end{bmatrix}$$

The trace norm of ρ^{T_A} is the sum of the absolute values of its eigenvalues $||\rho^{T_A}||_1 = |1 + 1| = 2$ and the negativity is computed as $\mathcal{N} = \frac{2-1}{2} = \frac{1}{2}$. So, the negativity of each subsystem for the Bell state $|\Phi^+\rangle$ is $\frac{1}{2}$ and the subsystems' individual states are maximally mixed, while the overall system state is pure. This observation is the basis of our empirical evaluation design and highlights the necessity for using both those metrics, $\mathcal{N}$ and S for the purposes of understanding the state transformations that BF circuits produce.

As another example, consider the following positive von Neumann   entropy state that is not entangled:

$$|\psi_{separable}\rangle = \frac{1}{2}|0\rangle\langle 0|_A \otimes |0\rangle\langle 0|_B + \frac{1}{2}|1\rangle\langle 1|_A \otimes |1\rangle\langle 1|_B$$

In this state, each qubit is in a pure state (either $|0\rangle$ or $|1\rangle$), but the overall state is a statistical mixture of these pure states. The purity $P(\rho) = \frac{1}{2}$, negativity $\mathcal{N}(\rho) = 0$, and $S(\rho) = 1$.

4   Empirical Evaluation

The design of this empirical evaluation study is organized to include the quantum computing implementation of BFs of various properties such as algebraic degree, algebraic immunity, and resiliency order. Their definitions are presented next.

4.1   Preliminaries

Definition 1. *Given strings* $s, x \in \{0,1\}^n$, *their* partial order *is defined as* $s \leq x \iff s_i \leq x_i$ *for* $i \in \{1, ..., n\}$.

Definition 2. *(Hamming Weight) Given a binary string* $x \in \{0,1\}^n$ *where each bit in position* $i \in \{1, ..., n\}$ *is denoted as* v_i, *the Hamming weight of* x *is* $w_H(x) = \sum_{i=1}^{n} v_i$.

Definition 3. *The* algebraic degree *of a BF* F *is the number of variables in the highest order monomial in its ANF. That is, for strings* $\{u_i \in M | i \in \{1, ..., m\}\}$, *where* M *is the set of* m *monomials in the ANF representation of* f, *the algebraic degree of* f *is* $deg(f) = max_{i=1}^{m}\{w_H(u_i)\}$.

Partial order [5], algebraic degree [24], and Hamming weight [22], were formally introduced in 1940, 1948, and 1954 respectively.

Definition 4. *A BF* $f : \{0,1\}^n \to \{0,1\}$ *is said to have a* linear structure *if it can be expressed as a linear combination of its input variables and their complements, that is,* f *has a linear structure if it can be written in the form:*

$$f(v_1, v_2, \ldots, v_n) = \alpha_1 v_1 \oplus \alpha_2 v_2 \oplus \ldots \oplus \alpha_n v_n.$$

Remark 1. Note that the above definition is different than the definition of affine functions as a BF that has linear structure does not include a constant term, i.e. $a_0 = 1$. A comprehensive review on affine functions is presented in [23].

Definition 5. *The* Hamming *distance [17] between two BFs f and g is defined as $d_H(f,g) = w_H(f \oplus g)$.*

Definition 6. *The* Walsh-Hadamard Transform *of a BF f denoted as W_f, given s, can be represented as a $|s| \times |s|$ matrix and is defined as $W_f(s) = \frac{1}{2^{\frac{|s|}{2}}}(-1)^{ij}$, where ij denotes the bitwise dot product of the row and column indices i and j.*

The foundation work for the study of Walsh functions has been published in 1923 [29].

Definition 7. *The* nonlinearity *[6] of a BF f is the Hamming distance from this function to the set of all affine functions A_n. That is, $min\{d_H(f,g)|g \in A_n\} = 2^n - \frac{1}{2}max\{|W_f(u)| : u \in \{0,1\}^n\}$.*

Definition 8. *A* maximally nonlinear *BF in n variables, where n is even, is classified as* bent. *A bent function has a maximal possible Hamming distance from the set of all affine BFs with even number of variables. That is, a bent function has the maximal Walsh–Hadamard transform and nonlinearity of $2^n - \frac{2^n}{2}$.*

Definition 9. *A symmetric BF is a function $f : \{0,1\}^n \rightarrow \{0,1\}$ that remains unchanged under any permutation of its input variables. In other words, for any permutation π of the input variables $v_1, v_2, \ldots, v_n$, the function f satisfies:*

$$f(v_1, v_2, \ldots, v_n) = f(v_{\pi(1)}, v_{\pi(2)}, \ldots, v_{\pi(n)})$$

for all $v_1, v_2, \ldots, v_n \in \{0,1\}$.

Remark 2. The output of a symmetric function remains the same regardless of the order in which the input variables are arranged.

Definition 10. *A BF f is* monotone (increasing) *if $f(u) \le f(v)$ holds for its partial order $u \le v$.*

Definition 11. *The* correlation immunity *of a BF $f : \{0,1\}^n \rightarrow \{0,1\}$, denoted as $\mathcal{CI}(f)$, is defined as the maximum number of input bits that can be fixed such that the function is still immune to classical linear attacks.*

Definition 12. *The* resiliency order *of a BF $f : \{0,1\}^n \rightarrow \{0,1\}$, denoted as $\mathcal{R}(f)$, is defined as the minimum number of input bit flips required to change the output of the function.*

Definition 13. *A BF $f : \{0,1\}^n \rightarrow \{0,1\}$ is said to be* plateaued *if, for each input difference vector Δv, the output difference $\Delta f = f(v \oplus \Delta v) \oplus f(v)$ is constant for all nonzero vectors Δv, where v is an n-bit input variable vector and Δf is the output difference of f.*

Definition 14. Algebraic immunity has been defined as $AI(f) = min_{g \neq 0}\{\deg(g) \mid fg = 0 \text{ or } (f \oplus 1)g = 0\}$ *[7], where a function g such that $fg = 0$ is called an* annihilator *of f.*

Note that in the definition expression, g ranges over all non-zero BFs that annihilate f, i.e. that satisfy $fg = 0$. Considering every possible non-zero Boolean function g, the goal is to find the one with the smallest degree among these functions. The existence of low degree annihilators of BFs has been implicated in classical algebraic attacks [9]. BFs with large AI can resist classical algebraic attacks since large values of $AI(f)$ guarantee that there are no low degree annihilators of f. However, the quantum implementation of BF circuits changes the notion of algebraic attacks if such circuits are not limited to accepting classical input (i.e. computational basis states). As demonstrated in the next section, that fact leads to much variability in the negativity and von Neumann entropy of the quantum state and quantum interactions between its subsystems and may warrant further study.

In the simplest execution scenario, a quantum BF circuit accepts classical inputs in the form of computational basis states on all input qubits as well as its target qubit. As a result, its execution maps one computational basis state to another, ensuring the output is also a computational basis state with zero von Neumann entropy. This simple observation could be presented more formally as follows.

Theorem 1. *Let $\mathcal{C}$ be a quantum circuit that computes a BF $f : \{0,1\}^n \to \{0,1\}$. Assume that $\mathcal{C}$ acts on an initial state $|\psi_{in}\rangle$ that is pure state, and let $\rho_{out} = |\psi_{out}\rangle\langle\psi_{out}|$ be the density matrix representing the state of the system after the application of $\mathcal{C}$. Then, the von Neumann entropy of the output state ρ_{out} is $S(\rho_{out}) = 0$.*

Proof. A unitary operator, U, acting on a quantum state has the property that it preserves the inner product, meaning $U^\dagger U = UU^\dagger = I$, where $U^\dagger$ is the adjoint (or conjugate transpose) of U, and I is the identity operator. When a unitary operator U acts on a pure state $|\psi_{in}\rangle$, the resulting state $|\psi_{out}\rangle = U|\psi_{in}\rangle$ remains pure and its density matrix has only one non-zero eigenvalue $\lambda_i = 1$ and the rest are zero (λ_i for $i \neq 1$). We can express $S(\rho_{out})$ in terms of the eigenvalues λ_i as follows:

$$S(\rho_{out}) = -\sum_i (\lambda_i \cdot \log_2(\lambda_i)) = -(1 \cdot \log_2(1) + \sum_{i \neq 1}(0 \cdot \log_2(0))) = 0.$$

4.2   Evaluation Design

We used the default `Qiskit` quantum simulator `Qasm` in noiseless mode. Quantum gates are implemented using classical computations that approximate ideal quantum gates. The precision of these approximations determines the accuracy of quantum operations. To produce a large set of BF circuits, we first used integer counting in order to obtain binary values by the means of type casting using Python as the implementation programming language. The integer value was then converted into binary, which is then cast into a string for storage and later use. Measurements were produced for all possible BFs of up to $n = 8$ variables. Due to computing resource limitations, for BFs with $3 < i \leq 8$ variables, we produced no more than 1,000 quantum circuits for each value of i by employing random selection from a discrete uniform distribution and implementing it through the Python `randint()` method. We utilized the System of Algebra and Geometry Experimentation (SAGE) framework [26] to accomplish conversion of any binary function to ANF. More specifically, those binary strings represent the output column form a truth table definition of the function.

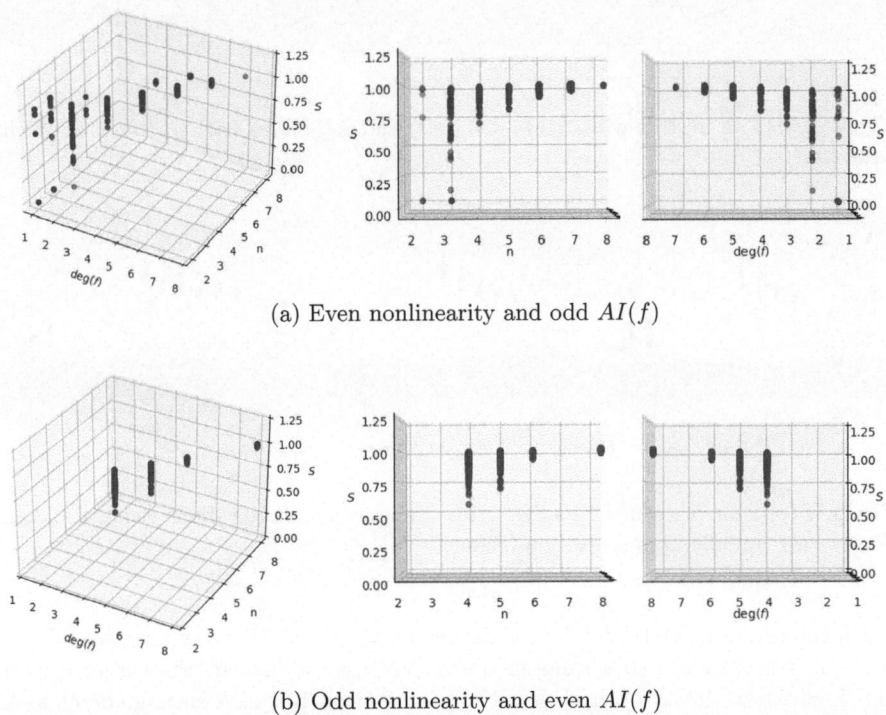

(a) Even nonlinearity and odd $AI(f)$

(b) Odd nonlinearity and even $AI(f)$

Fig. 3. $S(\rho_A)$ for all BFs with $n \leq 8$ for the Random Qubit Rotations scenario.

In an attempt to maximize the range of measurements, we introduce both classical randomization as well as superposition to the inputs of each BF circuit. This is a very important design choice since it results on an average in higher values for all measurements as compared to superposition alone. Note that this idea extends the general design of the Deutsch-Jozsa [8] and the Bernstein-Vazirani [4] algorithms that rely on introducing only quantum superposition to the input of the BF circuits. We tested three scenarios: Superposition, Random Qubit Rotations, and Random Statevector. In the Superposition scenario we introduced superposition through Hadamard gates applied to all input qubits except the target qubit. For the Random Qubit Rotations scenario, all BF circuit inputs were initialized to random individual bit rotations on the Bloch sphere except the target qubit and then fed individually into Hadamard gates (except

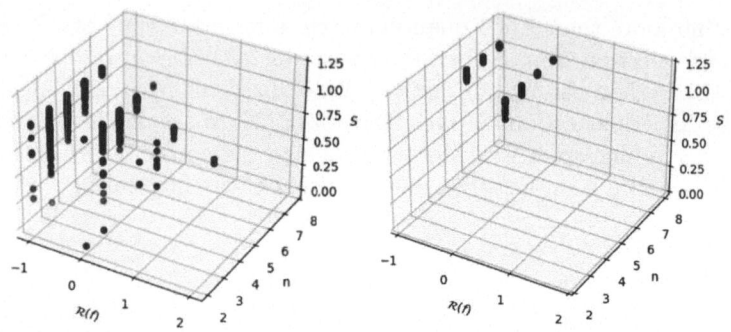

Fig. 4. $S(\rho_A)$ for all BFs with $AI(f) < 3$ (left) and $AI(f) \geq 3$ (right) (Random Qubit Rotations).

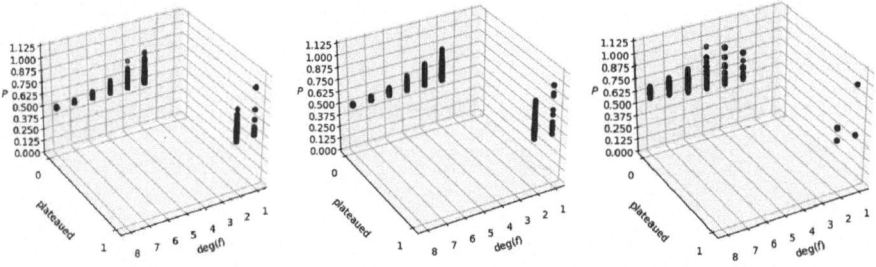

Fig. 5. $P(\rho_A)$ for plateaued BFs Scenarios: Random Qubit Rotations (left), Random Statevector (middle), Superposition (right).

again the target qubit). Finally, for the Random Statevector scenario, we initialized the system state to a random qiskit Statevector (except the target qubit) and hence introduced both classical randomization but also entanglement as a random state vector represents a pure state but not necessarily a separable one.

5   Results and Discussion

In the Random Qubit Rotations scenario, we observed an average increase of 0.0591869 for $\mathcal{N}(\rho_A)$, 0.1636744 for $S(\rho_A)$, and 0.0590092 for $\mathcal{N}_a(\rho_A)$ as compared to the Superposition scenario. In the Random Statevector scenario, we observed slightly lower average increase of 0.0584126 for $\mathcal{N}(\rho_A)$, 0.1611631 for $S(\rho_A)$, and 0.0580963 for $\mathcal{N}_a(\rho_A)$ as compared to the Superposition scenario. As expected, $P(\rho) = 1$ for all scenarios was measured as 1. The measured $S(\rho)$ for the final state of all whole system density matrices is 0, confirming the result from Theorem 1. Note that the individual qubit rotations are always limited to the precision of the integer type used to produce complex numbers. We used the default 7 digits after the decimal point to approximate real numbers, with single values (and not the double format of 15 decimal digits).

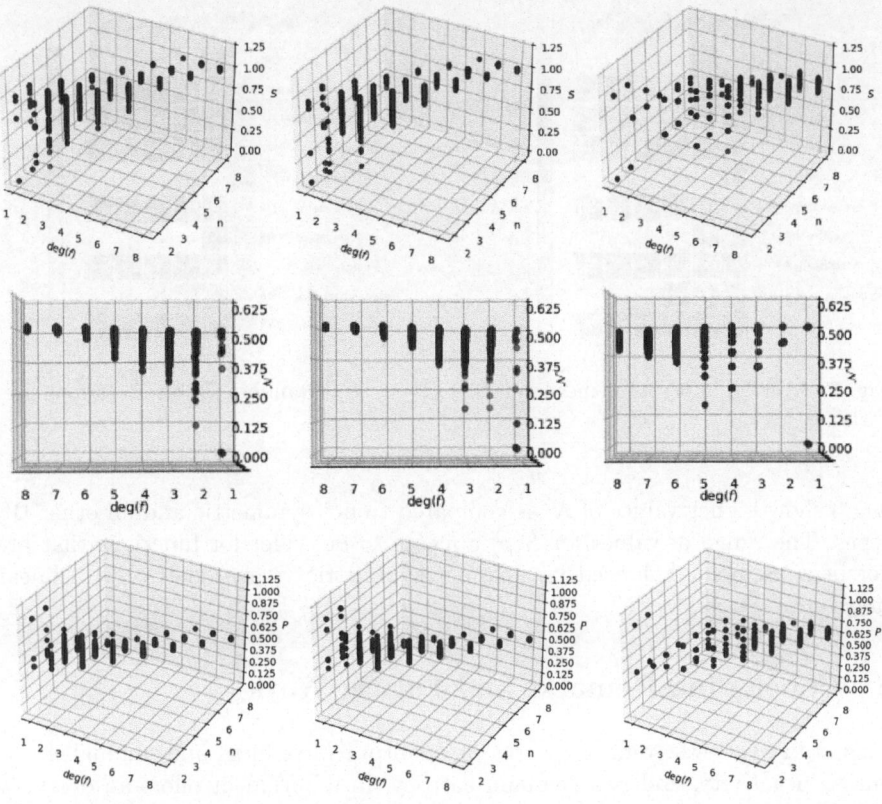

Fig. 6. Scatterplots for all BF circuits ($A = q0$ for results on $\mathcal{N}$). Scenarios: Random Qubit Rotations (left), Random Statevector (middle), Superposition (right).

Graphs were generated using Matplotlib [19]. Figures 3 and 4 show results for subsystem measurements of $S(\rho_A)$ and $\mathcal{N}_a(\rho_A)$, where negativity is measured for the subsystem of the reduced density matrix with A representing the subsystem and a a subsystem of subsystem A. Figure 3 depicts an interesting trend suggesting a potential lower bound of $S(\rho_A) = 0.5$ in subfigure (b). Figures 4 depicts the relationship between $S(\rho_A)$ and $\mathcal{R}(f)$ for $AI(f) < 3$ vs. $AI(f) \geq 3$. Results for and $\mathcal{N}_a(\rho_A)$ exhibit similar trends but in the range $\{0, ..., 0.5\}$ and were hence omitted. Reduced density matrix purity for plateaued BFs is presented in Fig. 5. As depicted, plateaued functions of lower algebraic degree exhibit purity measurements with wider spread in the Random Statevector scenario as compared to the Superposition scenario.

Overall scatter plot results are presented in Fig. 6. Average measurements for BFs with various properties are presented in Fig. 7. A general trend of a monotone increase for both $\mathcal{N}$ and S can be observed with the exception of functions that have linear structure. The range of values for $\mathcal{N}(\rho)$ appear to be slightly wider for balanced vs not balanced BFs. Symmetric BFs for $n = 2$ and

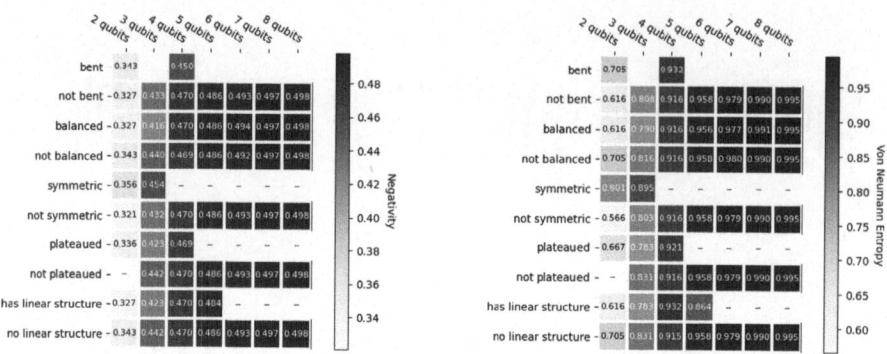

Fig. 7. Average subsystem measurements ($A = q0$) (Random Qubit Rotations scenario).

$n = 3$ show higher values of $\mathcal{N}$ as compared to not symmetric and all other BF types. The range of values for $S(\rho)$ appears to be wider for functions that are not bent vs. bent, balanced vs. not, not symmetric vs. symmetric, with linear structure vs. not.

6   Concluding Remarks and Future Work

This study reviews some measures of quantum mixedness and entanglement: purity, negativity, and von Nemann entropy. In addition, it offers an overview of BF properties and classification types. Empirical results are presented for purity, negativity, and von Nemann entropy for a set of about 5,000 quantum BF circuits of various properties and types under three different scenarios: Superposition, Random Statevector, and Random Qubit Rotations. Overall, slightly higher mean values of Von Neumann entropy and negativity were observed for the Random Qubit Rotations scenario. Other noticeable trends include lower mean values and wider ranges of those measurements for BFs of higher algebraic degree in the Superposition scenario and purity of wider spread in the Random Statevector scenario as compared to the Superposition scenario for plateaued functions of lower algebraic degree. Future work can include but is not limited to the theoretical study on the observed trends and applications in the context of quantum information theory.

Acknowledgements. The authors appreciate the valuable resources provided through the IBM Quantum Researcher's program.

References

1. Aleksandrowicz, G., et al.: Qiskit: an open-source framework for quantum computing (2019). https://doi.org/10.5281/zenodo.2573505. Accessed 15 Nov 2021

2. Barenco, A., et al.: Elementary gates for quantum computation. Phys. Rev. A **52**, 3457–3467 (1995)
3. Benioff, P.: The computer as a physical system: a microscopic quantum mechanical Hamiltonian model of computers as represented by turing machines. J. Stat. Phys. **22**, 563–591 (1980)
4. Bernstein, E., Vazirani, U.: Quantum complexity theory. SIAM J. Comput. **26**(5), 1411–1473 (1997)
5. Birkhoff, G.: Lattice Theory, American Mathematical Society Colloquium Publications, vol. 25. American Mathematical Society (1940)
6. Carlet, C.: Nonlinearity of Boolean functions and its applications. Boolean Methods Models **5**, 35–52 (2010)
7. Carlet, C.: Algebraic Immunity of Boolean Functions. In: van Tilborg, H.C.A., Jajodia, S. (eds) Encyclopedia of Cryptography and Security, pp. 31–32. Springer, Boston (2011). https://doi.org/10.1007/978-1-4419-5906-5_333
8. Deutsch, D.: Quantum theory, the church-turing principle and the universal quantum computer. Proc. Roy. Soc. London A **400**(1818), 97–117 (1985)
9. Du, Y., Zhang, F., Liu, M.: On the resistance of Boolean functions against fast algebraic attacks. In: Kim, H. (ed.) ICISC 2011. LNCS, vol. 7259, pp. 261–274. Springer, Heidelberg (2012). https://doi.org/10.1007/978-3-642-31912-9_18
10. Fastovets, D., Bogdanov, Y., Bogdanova, N., Lukichev, V.: Representation of Boolean functions in terms of quantum computation. In: Lukichev, V.F., Rudenko, K.V. (eds.) International Conference on Micro- and Nano-Electronics 2018. SPIE (2019). https://doi.org/10.1117/12.2522053
11. Fastovets, D., Bogdanov, Y., Bogdanova, N., Lukichev, V.: Representation of Boolean functions in terms of quantum computation. In: Proceedings of the International Conference on Micro- and Nano-Electronics (2019). https://doi.org/10.1117/12.2522053
12. Fedus, W.: Entropy in classical and quantum information theory (2015). https://api.semanticscholar.org/CorpusID:18933184
13. Feynman, R.P.: Simulating physics with computers. Int. J. Theor. Phys. **21**(6/7), 467–488 (1982)
14. Gantmacher, F.R.: The Theory of Matrices, vol. 1. Chelsea, New York (1959)
15. Genova, D., Hoogeboom, H.J., Prodanoff, Z.: Extracting reaction systems from function behavior. J. Membrane Comput. **2**(3), 194–206 (2020). https://doi.org/10.1007/s41965-020-00045-z
16. Hadfield, S.: On the representation of Boolean and real functions as Hamiltonians for quantum computing. ACM Trans. Quantum Comput. **2**(4) (2021). https://doi.org/10.1145/3478519
17. Hamming, R.W.: Error detecting and error correcting codes. Bell Syst. Tech. J. **29**(2), 147–160 (1950)
18. Hirvensalo, M.: Studies on Boolean functions related to quantum computing. Citeseer (2003)
19. Hunter, J.D.: Matplotlib: a 2D graphics environment. Comput. Sci. Eng. **9**(3), 90–95 (2007). https://doi.org/10.1109/MCSE.2007.55
20. Manev, K., Bakoev., V.: Algorithms for performing the Zhegalkin transformation. In: Proceedings of the XXVII Spring Conference of the Union of Bulgarian Mathematicians, pp. 229–233. Union of Bulgarian Mathematicians, Pleven (1998)
21. Peres, A.: Separability criterion for density matrices. Phys. Rev. Lett. **77**(8), 1413–1415 (1996)
22. Reed, I.S.: A class of multiple-error-correcting codes and the decoding scheme. Trans. IRE Prof. Group Inf. Theory (PGIT) **PGIT-4**(4), 38–49 (1954)

23. Roth, R.M.: Boolean Functions: Theory, Algorithms, and Applications. Springer (2009)
24. Shannon, C.E.: A mathematical theory of communication. Bell Syst. Tech. J. **27**(3), 379–423 (1948)
25. Suprun, V.P.: The complexity of Boolean functions in the reed-muller polynomials class. Autom. Control. Comput. Sci. **51**(5), 285–293 (2017)
26. The Sage Developers: SageMath, the Sage Mathematics Software System (Version 10.3) (2023). https://www.sagemath.org
27. Vajapeyam, S.: Understanding Shannon's entropy metric for information (2014)
28. Vidal, G., Werner, R.F.: Computable measure of entanglement. Phys. Rev. A **65**(3) (2002). https://doi.org/10.1103/physreva.65.032314
29. Walsh, J.L.: A closed set of orthogonal functions. Am. J. Math. **45**, 5–24 (1923)
30. Wei, T.C., Nemoto, K., Goldbart, P.M., Kwiat, P.G., Munro, W.J., Verstraete, F.: Maximal entanglement versus entropy for mixed quantum states. Phys. Rev. A **67**(2) (2003). https://doi.org/10.1103/physreva.67.022110
31. Wolfram, S.: A New Kind of Science. Wolfram Media (2002). https://www.wolframscience.com
32. Žegalkin, I.I.: Sur le calcul des propositions dans la logique symbolique. Rec. Math. Moscou **34**, 9–28 (1927). http://mi.mathnet.ru/eng/msb7433
33. Yczkowski, K., Horodecki, P., Sanpera, A., Lewenstein, M.: Volume of the set of separable states. Phys. Rev. A **58**(2), 883–892 (1998). https://doi.org/10.1103/physreva.58.883

Author Index

E. Formenti and J. Durand-Lose (Eds.): MCU 2024, LNCS 15270, p. 153, 2025.
https://doi.org/10.1007/978-3-031-81202-6